Praise For
A LIBERTARIAN WALKS INTO A BEAR

"[Hongoltz-Hetling] reconstructs a remarkable, and remarkably strange, episode in recent history.... The resulting narrative is simultaneously hilarious, poignant, and deeply unsettling." —*The New Republic*

"An alarming, eyebrow-raising and often hilarious true life tale of what happens when a fringe political ideology clashes with the real world, in ways which incorporate economics, conservation, zoology, parasitology, environmentalism, various types of psychology and animal behaviour studies, and more." —*BBC Science Focus*

"The bears become the Moby Dick for a town full of Ahabs, careening on their own personal Pequod into oblivion." —Chapo Trap House podcast

"Amazing.... This is a story of how the rubber met the road. And how the rubber found that the road had massive, massive potholes that it was incapable of driving on because of the nature of libertarianism." —Sam Seder, The Majority Report

"This quirky book about bears is timely and now carries an urgent global message.... Hongoltz-Hetling takes the time to render the real people of Grafton on the page." —*LA Review of Books*

"[A]n eminently readable, frequently hilarious book." —*Seven Days Vermont*

"Every once in a while, a book comes along that is so darkly comedic, with such a defined sense of place and filled with characters that range from the fascinating to the bizarre to the earnest, that partway through reading, it hits you: This has got to become a Coen brothers movie.... Hongoltz-Hetling is a master of the turn of phrase. His voice is breezy and critical, with a finely tuned eye aimed at the absurdities as well as at the earnestness of the Free Town Project." —*Star Tribune*

"[A] witty and precisely observed debut.... Hongoltz-Hetling skillfully probes shortcomings and ironies in the libertarian philosophy.... The result is an entertaining and incisive portrait of political ideology run amok."

—*Publishers Weekly*

"An entertaining sendup of idealistic politics and the fatal flaws of overweening self-interest." —*Kirkus*

"Since the beginning, Americans have been fighting about the balance between individual liberty and the common good. Hongoltz-Hetling shows what can happen when one rural New Hampshire town went to the libertarian extreme in this madcap tale that zig-zags between tragedy and farce, with the possibility of being eaten."

—Colin Woodard, *New York Times*-bestselling author of *American Nations and Union*

"*A Libertarian Walks into a Bear* is a finely drawn portrait of one freedom-loving town, and a joyful romp through the dark corners of the American psyche. Matthew Hongoltz-Hetling is a gifted writer with a high-powered radar for the strange details of American life. He skillfully portrays the dreamers and eccentrics who populate Grafton, and the bears lurking just beyond its tree lines. At turns hilarious and alarming, this story had me firmly in its jaws from the opening pages." —Evan Ratliff, author of *The Mastermind*

"Matthew Hongoltz-Hetling's wild and wonderful blend of small-town America and large-scale ideals, imparted with humor and insight reminiscent of Sarah Vowell and Bill Bryson, is an unpredictable and endlessly fascinating feat of immersive reporting, filled with singular characters and doughnut-eating bears."

—Michael Finkel, bestselling author of *The Stranger in the Woods*

A
LIBERTARIAN
WALKS INTO A
BEAR

A LIBERTARIAN WALKS INTO A BEAR

THE UTOPIAN PLOT TO LIBERATE AN AMERICAN TOWN (AND SOME BEARS)

MATTHEW HONGOLTZ-HETLING

PUBLICAFFAIRS

New York

PublicAffairs
Hachette Book Group
1290 Avenue of the Americas, New York, NY 10104
www.publicaffairsbooks.com
@Public_Affairs

Printed in the United States of America

Originally published in hardcover and ebook by PublicAffairs in September 2020.
First Trade Paperback Edition: September 2021

Published by PublicAffairs, an imprint of Perseus Books, LLC, a subsidiary of Hachette Book Group, Inc. The PublicAffairs name and logo is a trademark of the Hachette Book Group.

The Hachette Speakers Bureau provides a wide range of authors for speaking events. To find out more, go to www.hachettespeakersbureau.com or call (866) 376-6591.

The publisher is not responsible for websites (or their content) that are not owned by the publisher.

Print book interior design by Amy Quinn.

The Library of Congress has cataloged the hardcover edition as follows:
Names: Hongoltz-Hetling, Matthew, author.
Title: A Libertarian Walks into a Bear : The Utopian Plot to Liberate an American Town (And Some Bears) / Matthew Hongoltz-Hetling.
Description: First edition. | New York : PublicAffairs, 2020. | Includes bibliographical references.
Identifiers: LCCN 2019055813 | ISBN 9781541788510 (hardcover) | ISBN 9781541788480 (ebook)
Subjects: LCSH: Free Town Project (Grafton, N.H) | Libertarianism—New Hampshire—Grafton. | Decentralization in government—New Hampshire—Grafton. | Human-bear encounters—New Hampshire—Grafton. | Grafton (N.H.)—History. | Grafton (N.H.)—Politics and government.
Classification: LCC F44.G75 H66 2020 | DDC 974.2/3—dc23
LC record available at https://lccn.loc.gov/2019055813

ISBNs: 9781541788510 (hardcover), 9781541788480 (ebook), 9781541788497 (paperback)

LSC-C

Printing 1, 2021

To Kimberly, who has spent the last eighteen years filling
our home with kindness, reason, ethics, and love

CONTENTS

BOOK THREE: BOUNDLESS RUINS

THE FIREFIGHTER AND THE BEAR

> It seems strange that bears, so fond of all sorts of flesh, running
> the risks of guns and fires and poison, should never attack men
> except in defense of their young. How easily and safely a bear
> could pick us up as we lie asleep!
>
> —John Muir, *My First Summer in the Sierra*, 1911

During the summer of 2016, the firefighter became convinced the bear was watching him.

Somewhere up in the tree line, for the whole summer, it must have monitored the old schoolhouse on Slab City Road while the firefighter's tall, lean figure moved about below.

How else could John Babiarz explain the various times he would leave for a quick errand only to find, upon his return, that his ramshackle chicken coop, aging apple tree, and makeshift sheep paddock had been de-chickened, de-branched, and de-sheeped? In broad daylight no less?

Even when the bear situation threatened to get out of hand, Babiarz didn't call wildlife officials. Seeking help from the government was not his style.

I came to know Babiarz while exploring a series of mysteries in Grafton, a flyspeck town buried in the woods of New Hampshire's western fringe. A rural, isolated community of about 560 homogenous households (97 percent of Graftonites are white; 0 percent are black), Grafton is a place people come to in search of freedom.

Grafton has made national news just twice over the past twenty years. In 2004, it received brief attention as the site of one of the most ambitious social experiments in modern American history, the so-called Free Town

Project: freedom-focused libertarians from around the country announced that they would move to Grafton to "liberate" it from the strangling yokes of government. Then, in 2012, Grafton rose to infamy again when it hosted New Hampshire's first modern credible account of a wild bear attacking a person in living memory.

The two events seemed unrelated, tied together only by the shared setting of a brooding New England forest. But in fact, I was to learn, the town's longtime Graftonites, libertarian liberators, and bears of unusual enterprise were connected by far more than the dirt roads wending through its wild hills and valleys.

As I circulated around Grafton with a pen and journalist's notebook, I came to know several residents, among them: Jessica Soule, a Vietnam-era veteran who became an acolyte of the controversial Reverend Sun Myung Moon; Adam Franz, a poker-playing communist who dreamed of founding a survivalist community; Doughnut Lady, a kind and giving grandmother who asked to remain anonymous; John Connell, a Massachusetts factory worker on a mission from God; and, of course, John Babiarz, the firefighter libertarian who opened Grafton's doors to the Free Town Project and then spent the next decade trying to explain it to his nonlibertarian neighbors.

When I visited Babiarz on a Saturday morning in 2017, he invited me into his home, an 1848 one-room schoolhouse that he'd renovated and outfitted with solar panels. Amid the potted plants and political detritus that cluttered the small kitchen, a lawn sign urged me to elect Harry Browne president in 1996.

Babiarz had run for public office himself, several times. He was a politician, and I was a journalist. We'd both learned that smiling while talking can patch over vast political differences, and so there we stood, smiling and nodding at each other while he explained how the libertarian philosophy of unfettered personal and property rights intersects with the issue of bear management. He told me the town's bear problems were just a natural result of an incompetent government.

"If the government won't do its job, the people will," he said, chuckling.

Babiarz had a very distinctive laugh, one that I slowly realized reminded me of Krusty, the clown from *The Simpsons*. It was very disarming; I soon found myself agreeing with him. Dang government!

Babiarz was shot once, not during his tenure with the US Air Force, but in his own front yard. A confused pheasant hunter shot him in the ass.

"Did that hurt? Oh Jesus, the guy is lucky I didn't pull out my gun and return fire," he said, referring to one of the many guns he had cached throughout his property.

More smiling. I was really getting to like Babiarz. Dang pheasant hunter!

Finally, Babiarz got around to the topic of the bear that had been watching him. During the summer of 2016, the two had a disagreement that defied easy compromise: Could the bear eat all of his chickens? Or none of them?

He showed me two chicken coops that held three dozen birds, a mess of colors indicating a mix of breeds including Barred Rock (prolific egg counts, bossy with other breeds), Buff Orpingtons (big eggs, friendly personality), and Ameraucanas (blue eggs, cold-hardy). But it was a rotating cast, because the bear typically ate three or four chickens a pop.

After the bear began coming through the walls of the older coop, the firefighter decided to condense all the birds into the newer, stronger coop. But one chicken, which had survived three or four bear attacks by that time, refused to be corralled.

"It was elusive," he said, laughing.

I laughed too. Dang chicken!

A few days later, Babiarz still hadn't cornered the chicken. But one afternoon, as he crested the slope near a small outbuilding, he saw the bear, about thirty feet away, chasing the bird in tight circles on the grass between the old coop and a tractor.

The chicken, a black Australorp (good layer, leads bears to humans), caught sight of Babiarz and rushed toward him, the bear right behind.

As the chicken literally leapt into the firefighter's arms, the bear stopped, perhaps seeing Babiarz for the first time. Man and bear locked eyes. In the outbuilding next to him, Babiarz knew an AR-15 was leaning up against the wall, between a filing cabinet and a paper shredder. But could he get to it in time?

"Don't you even think of it." He spoke aloud to the bear. "Boy, my gun's right here, and boy, you're gonna—I'm going to drop you."

After a long, tense moment, the bear ambled away, past the firefighter's target shooting range and toward a swamp.

"It had no fear," Babiarz noted. "Which is, which is—which is a problem."

Other Graftonites, many with bear experience, used similar words when telling me about their encounters. The bear was bold. It didn't seem afraid. It watched them, thinking, before moving on, they said. What I eventually learned was that Grafton's first modern bear attack should have been predictable. And in fact, future attacks are more predictable still.

That was not the last Babiarz would see of that particular bear—he called it his Moby Dick.

"Somehow, I've had this adventure with bears for many a decade," he said. "Maybe it's my, quote, evil spirit. I don't know."

Certainly something unusual seemed to be plaguing Grafton, something with the power to pit neighbor against neighbor, freedoms against security, man against beast. But an evil spirit lurking behind Babiarz's smile? That seemed unlikely.

We looked at each other and laughed.

BOOK ONE
VERGE OF WILD

A peasant had a docile bear,
  A bear of manners pleasant,
And all the love she had to spare
  She lavished on the peasant:
    She proved her deep affection plainly
    (The method was a bit ungainly).

. . .

The watchful bear, perceiving that
  The gnat lit on her master,
Resolved to light upon the gnat
  And plunge him in disaster;
    She saw no sense in being lenient
    When stones lay round her, most convenient.

. . .

Of course the bear was greatly grieved,
  But, being just a dumb thing,
She only thought: "I was deceived,
  But still, I did hit something!"
    Which showed this masculine achievement
    Had somewhat soothed her deep bereavement.

—Guy Wetmore Carryl, "The Confiding
Peasant and the Maladroit Bear," 1898

1
A FELINE FEEDING

[Father] ought to remember one special night when he left me by the barn of the field we called "the Mountain field" when I actually saw the nose of the bear between the bushes, only the nose, and it looked a good deal like a pig's, but it made me very unhappy.

—Letter from Willa Cather to Elsie Cather, 1911

If Jessica Soule had known how close the bears were, of course she wouldn't have gone outside that afternoon, no matter how damn hot her living room got. If she had known, the whole cat-eating affair might never have happened.

Soule says that the summer of 1999 was the first time she started thinking of Grafton's bears as unusual. For many in town, it was already shaping up to be one more bad year in the seemingly never-ending string of bad years that nibbled away at the community's fragile bonds.

The first half of the year unfolded in the midst of a severe drought; in the forest, every plant, from the mightiest oak to the tiniest wisp of lichen, felt the lack of moisture and responded by withholding the usual bounty of fruit and foliage. That's when the burden of want fell onto the shoulders of the woodland beasts. Most could slake their thirst from the brackish ponds and small rills left from the once-bubbling brooks, but each day the scarcity of food drove them closer to the brink of desperation.

For Grafton's human residents, wells were depleted and haying operations stood at a standstill; the town's few remaining farmers watched the stunted grass, hoping against all evidence that it would develop into something worth cutting.

But those hopes slowly wilted.

In July, the drought was capped by a heat wave that scorched the parched grass to a sickening brown scrub; in vegetable gardens, tomatoes unlucky enough to be in direct sunlight literally roasted on the vine. The specter of fire—from a poorly extinguished campfire or through the spontaneous combustion of a few kerosene-soaked rags in an old barn—was everywhere.

Few Graftonites have air conditioning, so people tried to beat the heat in other ways. For many, including Soule, that meant sitting outside in the evening, often with a beer in hand, to enjoy the heat's recession, sometimes speeded by a much-appreciated summer breeze.

As the sun sagged into the horizon, she slipped out the front door of her quirky timber-framed home to go sit at her backyard picnic table, her only company the newest members of her family—three small kittens, recently dropped off at her house in the middle of the night by persons unknown, wrestling in the grass near her feet. Wild Meadow Road, the dry dirt lane that ran nearby and was named by the region's first white settlers, kept her house continuously dusted.

The liquid silver of what the native Abenaki would have called Temaskikos, the Grass Cutter Moon, slid silently down tree trunks until it gently limned the ground. Dusk.

At the same time, plumes of microscopic particles of Soule and her kittens rose into the overheated July air. They floated across her lawn, winding through the surrounding bramble and wood like the beckoning scent of a cartoon pie. Finally, some very tiny percentage of those particles were caught in a sharp snorting intake of air that delivered them deep into a pair of bestial nostrils, where they presumably triggered the same physiological response that causes human mouths to water in the presence of aromatic lasagna or a fine ribeye.

But Soule was unaware that she'd been scented. She was serene, allowing the melody of the crickets and the muted light show of the fireflies to off-gas the worries of the day, and relax her mind.

This was the sort of freedom that made living in Grafton special. Here, one could be an individual without facing much judgment from the neighbors, if for no other reason than that the ample distance between houses took the sting out of most criticisms.

Soule's thoughts were interrupted when something rushed toward her back, something so heavy she could feel the vibration of the footsteps in the dry ground beneath her.

Before she could react, the bear was within feet of her. It didn't go for Soule—perhaps, when it got close enough, it lost its nerve. (The sturdy forty-five-year-old had once used a shovel to beat off an attack by a large, vicious weasel.) In 1999, the bears of Grafton were not bold enough to attack a woman of Soule's stature.

Instead, the bear blew right past her and continued on into the forest, the rustling of the dead leaves beneath its feet a counterpoint to the sudden frantic mewlings of two kittens—Jessica's kittens—now in its mouth.

Beyond the tree line, the bear reemerged, a bulky silhouette against the moon. It stopped at a small creek running through the rear of Soule's property. Now there were other shadows—bear cubs, crowding alongside their mother.

Soule said she could only watch, horrified, as the bears finished their prize. She'll never forget the sounds.

Soule scrabbled in the tall grass near the tree line, searching for the third kitten and trying to watch in all directions for the return of the bears, which had disappeared from sight.

"Amber," she stage-whispered. Her calls slowly grew louder, more plaintive, but produced no kitten. Not until morning did she find the bedraggled Amber, huddling beneath the carpet of leaves.

———

THE ATTACK ON Soule's kittens—an extremely rare example of a bear eating a domestic cat—would have been strange in any circumstances. But Soule told me it was only the beginning.

The sow that ate Soule's kittens apparently developed a taste for cats. It taught its two cubs to eat cats, and soon an extended family of bears was predating upon the cats in Soule's neighborhood.

That this was not more widely remarked upon is perhaps not as strange as it seems.

Though the world thinks of Grafton as a single tiny town in the woods, it is actually broken up into even smaller, discrete historical villages that reflect an earlier era. Graftonites think of themselves as living in East Grafton, Grafton Center, Grafton Village, Slab City (audaciously termed a "city" by its residents, who number, literally, in the dozens), or West Grafton. Each little village is a neighborhood unto itself, and the encroaching forest has increasingly isolated the villages from each other.

Soule's village, centered on Wild Meadow Road, is called Bungtown, named for one or more barrel bungs that once popped out during a carriage transport and spilled a remarkable amount of alcohol onto the roadway.

Outside of Bungtown, not many people made the connection between the shrinking number of housecats and bears. But Bungtowners found the bears' taste for cats to be particularly unsettling.

Mightn't eating cats, they wondered, be a kind of gateway drug to eating humans?

People took precautions.

While walking their dogs, they began avoiding the path that ran along the town's rusty old rail lines and other known bear hotspots. Before doing yard work, they might strap on a firearm, just in case. And they began keeping a closer eye on small children, mindful perhaps of April 27, 1905, the day that two-year-old Elwin Braley ran merrily around the corner of his family's Bungtown farmhouse, and briefly out of the sight of his mother. Young Elwin cried out—his mother would later say that it was difficult to tell whether it was with joy or terror—and was never seen again. The mother blamed a panther, or possibly a bear. Many in the community blamed the mother, though no criminal charges were ever filed.

At any rate, the cat-eating bears of 1999 were just a blip in Grafton's ongoing bad year. June's drought and July's heat wave were quickly forgotten in September, when deadly Hurricane Floyd ripped through the region, disrupting power lines, peeling shingles from roofs, and uprooting trees. Over the course of a few days, the town went from parched to inundated. Soon, five-hundred-year-high floodwaters had gouged washouts up to eight feet deep into Grafton's dirt roads and completely isolated some of its residents from the larger world. Grafton's road crew, tiny and ill-resourced, was quickly overwhelmed by the scope of the work that faced them after the floodwaters receded. In a typical example of Grafton's municipal dialogue, someone responded by angrily smashing the windows of the town dump truck.

It was Soule's story of cat-eating bears that first drew my attention to Grafton. I was working as a reporter for the *Valley News*, a regional daily newspaper, and I was immediately captivated by the idea that Grafton's bear population might be exhibiting behavior that lay somewhere on the spectrum of rare to unheard of.

At first, I was skeptical that many cats in Grafton were eaten by bears, or even that one cat in Grafton was eaten by a bear. There was no video evidence. And when cats are swallowed up by the New Hampshire woods, blame is typically assigned to other animals, like coyotes. As one pet recovery expert told me, "The only way you know is if you find those remains."

I began paying attention to notices about Grafton's lost cats, both online and on posters tacked to trees around town.

"Mostly white cat with dark tabby patches, or perhaps some black spots. Her name is Abby . . . We miss her much," read one, while others pleaded for information about Buddha (large, orange, long hair), Bryce (brown/black tiger with white markings), and Brother ("This is the first time he has gone missing and we are devastated").

Something, it seemed, was emerging from the underbrush to snatch up felines when backs were turned. If bears were indeed the culprits, Grafton was in the midst of an invasion.

Or, as I would soon learn, two invasions.

2
A TAXING TRADITION

When first my father settled here,
'Twas then the frontier line:
The panther's scream, filled night with fear
And bears preyed on the swine.

—Abraham Lincoln, "The Bear Hunt," 1847

Even before New England colonists began warring with the British monarchy, they were engaged in long-standing open hostilities with the region's bears, a fact that, in the summer of 1776, came home to a young man named Eleazar Wilcox in a violent and visceral way.

Life had gotten harder for the athletic newlywed, age twenty-five, since the previous fall, when he'd moved from his boyhood home on the Connecticut coast and into New Hampshire's wooded frontier. Here the lack of roads, noted a historian, "necessitated the coarsest fare and the plainest living." Bean porridge, leather clothing, and homemade furniture were the order of the day. "The ground had to be cleared of the dense growth of trees before any crop could be planted and a constant watch kept against the bears and the wolves that by day and by night prowled around the log huts."

Despite his newcomer status, Eleazar knew enough to drop a few musket balls into his pants pocket when leaving the safety of his log cabin. One day in early summer, he headed out to his pasture and first saw the immense bear about seven car lengths away (a measure that would have perplexed Eleazer, as cars had not yet been invented). Scrabbling a bullet out of his pocket, Eleazer fired with pinpoint accuracy—a direct hit to the head.

The bear fell heavily. But as Eleazer ran to the corpse, it rose up in a decidedly uncorpse-like manner and bolted, bleeding, into the woods.

Pursuing the bear would have been foolhardy. The homestead's cleared pastures, long sight lines, and sturdy house functioned as a bright little oasis of safety—just beyond, in bear country, towering black spruce, hemlocks, barren oak, and bitter hickory created a state of permanent gloom. Some areas were dominated by spreading balsam firs, needles so thick they cut visibility to near-zero; other areas were covered in muck or choked with thorny scrub growth, all of which served to hide bears and impair human movement.

On the other hand, the only thing more dangerous than having a bear nosing around your homestead is having a wounded bear nosing around your homestead.

Eleazar sought help from a woods-savvy friend, Joshua Osgood, and the pair entered the damp spring forest, following a trail marked by drying blotches of tacky blood. Miles on, the drops turned more viscous—fresh blood. At this point, to maximize their chances of getting a clear shot, the two men split up, which is why Eleazer was alone when the bear charged. With spectacularly poor timing, his musket misfired harmlessly.

One account says that the bear struck Eleazer in the head and that he fell, then rose to his knees as the bear pressed down on him from above. Another says that the bear swiped the gun (which future generations cherished as a claw-scarred family artifact) from Eleazer's hands and grabbed him, and that Eleazer responded by seizing the bear's tongue and crying for help.

Osgood arrived in time to save Eleazer's life, but he had to be carried back to his wife on a litter, with an injured back and forty-two flesh wounds. Though Eleazer lived, his health never fully returned. It was years before he had any children, and the rest of his life was plagued by what he called his "bear fits."

Eleazer Wilcox was one of many settlers discovering the prominence of bears in the primeval New Hampshire forest, as evidenced by modern maps pockmarked with Bear Hills, Bear Hollows, Bear Ponds, Bear Brooks, and Bear Creeks. Two distinct mountainous areas were named Bear World, while Lake Winnipesaukee's Bear Island earned its name after a group of land surveyors in 1772 used both guns and knives in a successful, though bloody, effort to dispatch four bears.

To the bears, the homesteads brought a welcome addition to the landscape.

"He places himself between two rows of corn," complained one contemporary account, "and with his paws breaks down the stalks of four contiguous hills, bending them toward the center of the space, that the ears may lie near to each other, and then devours them. Passing through a field in this manner, he destroys the corn in great quantities."

In addition to corn, the bears were fond of sweet apples. They were drawn in great numbers to sheep. They devoured barnsful of young swine. At times, it seemed that New England's entire agricultural economy was in danger of disappearing down their bottomless gullets.

Worse, unless they were being actively fired upon, the bears showed little fear of the pale-faced primates in their midst. One Grafton County bear hunter, Jonathan Marston, was treed by a bear and spent the entire night trying to get back down. (A search party eventually ended the standoff.) Bears browsed through barns and peeped into kitchen windows, burly bundles of ursine meat watching ambulatory hominine meat cooking juicy chunks of ovine meat.

Sometimes the people themselves were the meals.

Late one August day in 1784, a Mr. Leach saw a bear seize his eight-year-old son from the pasture and drag him toward the undergrowth. Leach, horrified, attacked with a wooden stake, but it "broke in his hand; and the bear, leaving his prey, turned upon the parent who, in the anguish of his soul, was obliged to retreat and call for help."

After a fretful night, a search party followed a short and grisly trail to the boy's carcass, his throat torn out and one thigh eaten. The bear emerged from the undergrowth and tried to drive the humans away, but they brought it down in a volley of gunfire, burning the corpse as if it were a demon that could otherwise rise again.

———

KEEPING THE BEARS away at night was nearly impossible. Log deadfall traps, baited with pig offal, were labor-intensive to build and only spottily effective. Dogs well trained enough to babysit a patch of corn overnight were likely to be slaughtered by a marauding bear before a gun-toting farmer could arrive as backup. Some farmers guarded herds or crops all night long, but this was dangerous and, as some noted, "too tedious to be constant."

One solution was to "place a loaded gun, and stretch a line, connected with the trigger, across the field, so that the bear in his walk, by pressing against the line, may draw the trigger, and kill himself." Though clever, the brutal downside of such booby traps became quickly obvious.

"People not apprised of the design may," a contemporary wrote, "in passing through a field, kill or wound themselves, and in fact this mode of setting guns has, in some instances, proved fatal."

England's monarchs, separated by an ocean from the colonists, never quite grasped the immediacy of the American bear problem, any more than they understood a host of other gripes. The British Crown's failure to engage in bear management was a natural feature of a nation built on belief in a greater power—for millennia, any state-sanctioned killing of bears would have been acceptable only if it were done in the name of gods or monarchies.

This conceit served the ruling class much better than those ruled, and America's revolutionaries, springboarding off ideas first widely disseminated by philosopher John Locke, called bullshit on the entire enterprise. In arguments that were firmly baked into the US Constitution and the Declaration of Independence, they flipped the script on dictatorships, asserting that the right to rule came not from divine law but from the consent of those governed.

Shortly after embracing the somewhat novel concept of individual rights, America's postrevolutionary leaders took up the bear problem. They soon found themselves, however, in a dilemma of their own devising: how to kill bears in the name of liberty.

Ordering people to kill bears would smack of monarchism. And funding a costly, state-run bear hit squad would require imposing unpopular taxes.

Instead of these options, lawmakers devised a low-cost solution that would preserve the right of the individual to act freely: it put a price on bear heads. At a pen stroke, this bit of capitalist innovation turned every armed homesteader into a potential bounty hunter who could cash in on an adult "bar's head" with both ears on.

And when New Hampshire's freedom-loving individuals were asked to bear arms against bears, Grafton County went to war.

One farmwife attacked a bear in the middle of the night with a hand ax. The notably muscular Joseph Hatch found two mother bears and four cubs eating his corn crop and went after them with a spike, keeping them at bay until his neighbor shot them. Others baited bears by sheathing clumps of cruelly pointed fishhooks in balls of tallow to literally tear their innards apart. Hunters shot bears out of trees, and pairs of trappers slung dead bears onto poles to carry home. Two teens found a bear treed in a tall pine near their home; the family musket lacked a firing mechanism, so they ignited its powder with a metal poker from the fire. The meat, so the story goes, saved the family from starvation that year.

Long after it was no longer practically necessary, killing bears remained popular. Boys grew up eager to shoot a bear as a rite of passage; middle-aged men shot them as an assertion of manliness; old men prowled the woods with guns at the ready to show that, for now at least, they still had the ineffable "it" that could otherwise be expressed only by dropping one's trousers, ruler at the ready.

Richard "Dick" French boasted of killing more bears than anyone else in Grafton County. And Jonathan Marston—after spending a night treed by an angry bear—went on to claim that he'd "killed more ursuline brutes" than anyone else in America. There are no records of either man's kill total, but they must have been staggering, given the number of bear kills attributed to men who made no such claim of a remarkable body count.

After a devout Grafton County Methodist named Benjamin Locke was driven from his homestead by bears, his uncle, Tom Locke, killed sixteen in a single season. Elsewhere in the county, a Scotsman caught bears in a massive steel-toothed trap that his grandfather brought from Scotland in 1727. He counted forty-nine kills, including a 450-pounder.

And just as bear-killing fueled one's manhood, lack of such prowess did the opposite. In neighboring Vermont in 1815, Governor Jonas Galusha, seeking reelection, proudly announced that he would hunt a particularly notorious bear known as "Old Slipperyskin" with a hitherto-unknown hunting method. Galusha slathered himself with female bear scent and strode off into the woods, only to return to his entourage at a full sprint, the bear behind him. (He lost the gubernatorial campaign.)

In 1783, American colonists exported 10,500 bearskins to England, and by 1803 that number had risen to more than 25,000, with each skin fetching about 40 shillings. As bear populations dwindled, the landscape lost its mystical power over the spirit of the townspeople. The region's forbidding forests were terraformed into an unconscious re-creation of the open African savanna on which humans evolved.

Groups began to make militia-like incursions into the deepest bear strongholds—in Andover, amid angst over sheep loss, a posse containing "as many men as could be induced to join the battle" stormed the rocky and ravine-laden terrain of Ragged Mountain for two years running. "During this final hunt, so much noise was made by shouting and the firing of guns that the surviving animals, of which several were seen, were probably frightened away," they noted.

It took years. It took decades. Untold thousands of animals were slaughtered, bear by bear by bear; untold millions of trees were felled, trunk by trunk by trunk. Untold billions of dollars in natural resources were liquidated, pelt by plank by perch. When it was over, the settlers raised their grandchildren in a new world, built from the bones of a wilderness that—seemingly—had been vanquished.

INTO THIS INTENSE cauldron of deprivation and bear-battling came Grafton's first settlers. Military captains Joseph Hoyt and Aaron Barney brought one hundred apple trees, their families, and a few dozen other optimists, hoping to carve new lives from the bear-infested Connecticut River Valley.

Their raggle-taggle group included Eli Haskins, already a Revolutionary War veteran at the ripe old age of sixteen; Captain Hoyt's brother Jonathan, a shoemaker (whose head was destined to be crushed by the wheel of an ox-drawn wagon); several farmers with monosyllabic names like Smith, Dean, Cole, and Gove; and Barney's son, Jabez Barney, who would go on to marry a young woman that a county history delicately referred to as "Miss Barney" (they were cousins).

During those first critical years, Hoyt, Barney, and many of the other able-bodied men were called away to serve in militias under George Washington, general of the newly formed Continental Congress. This left the women to care for the children and the infirm while, "in the night, the woods would ring with the howling and fighting of wolves and other furious animals," noted a local historian.

The settlers hated bears with the sizzling, white-hot hatred that comes from living in constant fear. But there was something they hated even more—taxes.

Grafton's founders had not braved the throat of this godforsaken wilderness to pay taxes. In fact, they demonstrated very little appetite for law of any kind.

Their first order of business was to completely ignore centuries of traditional Abenaki law by purchasing land from founding father John Hancock and other speculators. Hancock had bought the land from King George III. King George had gotten it from God.

Once the Abenaki were safely cut out of the picture, Grafton's second order of business became overthrowing King George, who God had also, it turns out, imbued with the divine right to impose onerous taxes and policies. For example, Britain ordered New Hampshire's foresters to reserve the colony's towering white pines for use as naval ship masts. This decree sparked the Pine Tree Riots, in which Grafton-area townspeople disarmed a royalist sheriff and his deputies, beat them with tree switches, and sent them home on horses that, in an unfortunate example of misplaced anger, had been shaved and de-eared.

Grafton's settlers, very much on board with the anti-tax, anti-law sentiment, named their community after the Duke of Grafton, a notoriously lusty British nobleman who'd earned the honor by suggesting that the Crown impose fewer taxes on the American colonists.

As the Revolutionary War began to tilt in favor of Washington's forces, Grafton's proud anti-tax revolutionaries got stunningly bad news—the Continental Congress, like the British before them, intended to levy taxes on Grafton.

Faced with a new tax bill for the murky benefit of "protection," many Graftonites felt like they had merely swapped one unwelcome master for another. And so, safely beyond the reach of both Abenaki and royal law, Grafton's third order of business quickly became the avoidance of US taxes. It's a pursuit that continues today.

Just a year after the Declaration of Independence, Grafton produced the earliest surviving record of its disquiet with taxes—a May 1777 petition in which town leaders tried to convince the ruling New Hampshire Council that they should be exempt.

Even accounting for a certain looseness in spelling common to the period, the petition was glorious in its semi-literacy. It got off on the wrong foot by mistaking the state in which they lived as "New Hamsheir" and went rapidly downhill from there, referring to state officers as, variously, "your honours," "your Honners," and "your Onners."

"Wee take this opertunyty to inform your onners that you demand more of us than Wee are Able to perform," they wrote. They concluded their call for tax abeyance with more pride than word spacings: "sonomore."

The petition, signed by nineteen Grafton residents, including the Barneys, was delivered by horseback to the New Hampshire Council, but drew no reply.

Two years later, the town sent another, even more strenuously worded (and semi-literate) petition seeking tax relief. This one was written by Jabez

Barney, whose marriage to his cousin had apparently not disqualified him from taking a leadership role as Grafton's town clerk.

"If we Should bee obliged to Pay the tax thats Proposined on us and that we Expect to follow it would Reduce the Most of us to be a Specttickle of Pitty to All human Cretures a Great Part of hour People Came in to this Wilderness in Such dificult times that it has all most Redused Them to Nothing," he wrote.

Though the letters were worded as requests, those who oversaw the state coffers could hardly fail to notice that, as due dates came and went, Grafton's tax bills remained unsettled.

Grafton's petitions were in fact part of a simple, two-step plan.

Step 1: Ask not to pay taxes.

Step 2: Just don't pay them.

The foot-dragging on the tax-paying caused much hand-wringing among the government-running. The New Hampshire Council was facing its own financial pressures and couldn't even afford to pay its modest staff. The council's first president, Harvard graduate Mesech Weare, seemed flummoxed at the thought of these country rubes engaging in blatant tax evasion.

In an angsty (though grammatically commendable) letter, President Weare complained that "the County of Grafton, except two or three towns, have not paid any taxes for several years, have no courts of law or any proper regulations. . . . I can hardly persuade myself that they are carrying on a negotiation."

The Hoyts and Barneys may have lacked a Harvard degree, but they understood that simply withholding payment wouldn't stave off Weare's tax collectors forever. And so they did what any community of reasonable people would do.

They voted to secede from the country.

The opportunity for such grand scofflawery came in January 1781, when Vermont leaders invited more than a dozen border towns, including Grafton, to a formal convention. Though it had contributed men to fight the British, Vermont was technically an independent republic and had no formal standing among the thirteen US colonies.

At the convention, Vermont suggested that its borders could be expanded to encompass Grafton and its neighbors, thereby relieving them of their duties to the United States. The town representatives promptly voted down the seemingly ludicrous proposal and prepared to saddle their horses for the journey back home.

That was when the door opened to admit a late arrival—Colonel Ethan Allen. A fiery farmer who'd been clapped in irons in solitary confinement during nearly three years as a British prisoner of war, Allen well understood the Graftonites' desire for freedom.

He hinted to them about "the advantage to joining Vermont, by which they would evade a large burden of Taxes."

Well, the delegates asked (we can imagine their gruffness and skepticism), what about the taxes in Vermont?

Vermont's citizenry, Allen smugly replied, paid no taxes of any sort. The republic's coffers were financed by selling land and chattel houses seized from the Tories.

Though this gravy train would clearly run out, the notion of leaving New Hampshire was no longer laughable. In fact, Grafton was smitten. The convention attendees hastily reversed their initial decision and voted to instead bring the secession proposal back to their towns. Once Grafton voters heard about the tax-free nature of the republic just across the river, they affirmed the decision, electing Russell Mason to the Vermont Assembly.

Back at the New Hampshire Council, President Weare, nerves already frayed by Grafton's tax intransigence, received a flabbergasting report: Vermont brigadier general Peter Olcott was raising a brigade of ten thousand fighting men in the Grafton area to help defend Vermont's right to sit out the remainder of the Revolutionary War—or even ally with Britain.

Faced with the specter of being beaten by bumpkins, Weare called upon George Washington, then at the height of his power and influence, for help. An unamused Washington, who was still battling the British, vowed that, if Vermont persisted, "he would turn his back on the common enemy and lead his whole force against that State and destroy it entirely."

Sadly, for the Graftonites, all was not as it seemed. Though Allen had dangled a tax-free republic before them, his actual goal was Vermont statehood. A Vermont claim on established New Hampshire territory gave him a bargaining chip against efforts by New Hampshire to annex Vermont out of existence. In this extended diplomatic maneuvering between New Hampshire, Vermont, Great Britain, and the Continental Congress, Grafton was merely a pawn.

For months, negotiations dragged on as Graftonites tried to get used to living in Grafton County, New Hampshire, at the same time they lived in Grafton County, Vermont.

Confusingly, the two states each appointed their own slate of county sheriffs to the disputed territory. Throughout the summer and into the fall, the two criminal justice systems simply coexisted in an uneasy truce, with each sheriff enforcing his state's court orders. The truce fell apart in November 1781, when Isaac Griswold, a deputy sheriff enforcing Vermont's laws, arrested Enoch Hale, a sheriff enforcing New Hampshire's laws.

That caused a flurry of escalations, and the Grafton region began to mobilize against New Hampshire. Told that there were six hundred fighting men ready to defend the area against him, President Weare ordered the New Hampshire militia to muster one thousand soldiers for a civil war.

Bloodshed was ultimately avoided at the negotiating table when Vermont, having extracted promises for statehood, backed down.

Now bereft of allies, Grafton had no hope of standing against the US militia forces, and so it grudgingly accepted the authority of the state of New Hampshire. But forevermore, in Grafton, the United States government, like the British before them, was simply an occupying force to be resisted.

In the meantime, there were those tax bills.

Russell Mason, relieved of his lofty position as Vermont General Assemblyman, was appointed as Grafton's new "town Clark" (as he spelled it). In 1783, Mason wrote a new petition to New Hampshire taxing authorities.

"As wee Look on your onners to be the gard Deens of our Rights: our Eiys are on you for Releas in this time of Distress: And Releaf we Pray your onners to grant us," wrote Mason.

Such a lack of money "was Never Experienced by the Free People our Taxes are Large & Not Money in the Town to Discharge one Twentieth Part of the Tax & it Seems at Such an innormous Rate."

Knowing they had to offer some begrudged token of their fealty to the United States, Grafton made a new proposal. Rather than cash, they announced, they intended to pay the taxes in grain.

If any reply came from the Weare administration, it has been lost to history.

3

THE LOGICAL LIBERTARIAN

Sir,
I beg leave to return you my thanks for the Bow and arrows
you were so kind as to send me, as also for the two Grisly bears
which I have since recieved & now have here in good health.

—Thomas Jefferson, 1807 letter on grizzlies that briefly lived on the
White House lawn (and were subsequently given by Jefferson to a
man who, after failing to domesticate them, shot them dead)

When John Babiarz grew up as the son of Polish immigrants in the 1960s and '70s in Southington, Connecticut (English is his second language), his household was haunted by the ghosts of monolithic governments run amok.

"My father and my mother, during World War II, suffered government oppression," he said. "My father was taken by Communists to Siberia, my mother to a Nazi work camp."

Babiarz, raised to be wary of government overreach, grew up on guard for signs that America too was sliding into authoritarianism. After he left his childhood home, he did a stint as a radio communications analyst in the Air Force, but only stayed for four years. He discovered in himself an aptitude for the then-nascent field of computer programming—a logic-based universe in which the right answers were ordained by constellations of bright green letters glowing against a black abstraction. He joined a Sacramento-based computer user group that included some of computer coding's biggest names, before coding went mainstream.

"If I stayed there, I would have probably been one of these Silicon Valley wonders," he said.

Instead, he took a job designing software and hardware for a company called Data Products, before moving on to his own computer consulting firm, primarily for factory automation projects. In 1987, four days after his thirty-first birthday (and a little before lunchtime), Babiarz was on the first day of a new consulting gig in the sprawling Aetna headquarters, which faces off with the St. Joseph's Cathedral across Farmington Avenue in downtown Hartford, Connecticut.

The ever-confident Babiarz sidled up next to an attractive woman.

"Well," he said, "I don't see anybody jumping out of windows."

"I guess not," she answered. Her name was Rosalie. She'd been tasked with getting him oriented at his cubicle. She also had to take him to lunch.

Babiarz said he thought maybe he knew why no one was leaping to their deaths.

"The windows don't open!" he pointed out. The punch line drew a brief chuckle. Not much, but it was a start.

The joke about the dearth of Aetna suicides would have been bizarre on any other day, but this was Monday, October 19—also known as Black Monday. The stock market was in its biggest panic in more than fifty years, and he was consulting for Aetna's investments division, the company's biggest moneymaker.

"People were running around screaming, 'The market's falling!'" Babiarz would later recall.

As they watched the rapid decline, stock investors—known as hyper-rational computing machines that run on haute cuisine and fine wines—should have remembered to place a much higher weight on the stock market's long-term track record of growth than the hysterics of the day. Instead, they suddenly found their white starched shirts soaked with the acrid smell of fear. People—smart people, people who'd been studying the stock market for decades—were acting irrationally.

It may seem strange that Babiarz, who had significant investments on the line, was able to remain calm while expert investors crumbled. But, coding aside, Babiarz belonged to a group of people who outdo even traders in their fidelity to logic: libertarians.

Libertarians have a vision for America that includes lots of personal freedom, very little government, and a pure marketplace that will sort out societal problems like climate change, education inequality, and rising health care costs.

Rather than religious values or a belief in a moral obligation to help the vulnerable, libertarians believe in rationalism. A 2012 research analysis of the personality differences between Republicans, Democrats, and libertarians found that libertarians place the highest value on using logic and cognitive skills to solve questions of policy.

Formed in 1971, the Libertarian Party became a magnet for hundreds of thousands of Americans like Babiarz, who appreciated logic and distrusted authoritarian governments.

But in 1988, when the party's standard-bearer—former US representative Ron Paul—garnered just 0.5 percent of the vote in his bid for president, the fundamental problem facing the logicians became apparent. How could they bring their superior thinking skills out of the fringes and into the political mainstream? They needed to show their emotional, less clearheaded fellow Americans how great a libertarian-led society would be.

The problem was still hanging over the heads of the party in 1992, which is when Babiarz and Rosalie (also a libertarian) got married and decided that Connecticut's high income tax was cause to flee the state.

———

AFTER A STINT in Vermont, the Babiarzes quickly realized that New Hampshire was a better bet for those who wanted to "Live Free or Die"—a state motto so beloved that, in the 1970s, when a Jehovah's Witness covered up the words "or Die" on his license plate because they offended his religious sensibilities, the state jailed him.

Despite priding themselves on their logic, libertarians harbor a passion for individual rights that borders on fanaticism. Babiarz took New Hampshire's motto both seriously and literally.

"To me 'or Die' means that as an individual you have a commitment to . . . fight any force that will prevent you from doing so until the day you die," he wrote. "Death is not the worst of evils; subjugation may be. A quick death is kind compared to years of cruelty, deprivation, and slavery entangled within a system that robs the human spirit."

In 1993, while John and Rosalie were out for a rambling country drive, they found themselves on a remote dirt road that ran through Grafton's barely populated neighborhood of Slab City. It was almost as if they had driven through a time warp and into New England's revolutionary days, when freedom outweighed fealty and trees outnumbered taxes.

A FOR SALE sign marked a particularly scenic spot with a spectacular view of Smith Mountain in the background, a brook and cultivated fields in the foreground, and a small brick schoolhouse perched in the middle of it all.

Soon they were on the phone with June Burrington, the no-nonsense matriarch of an old Grafton family. After raising her children in Slab City, June had abandoned the schoolhouse for a high-lying farm property off Tunnel Road, on the other side of Grafton.

That November the Burrington and Babiarz families signed sale paperwork for the schoolhouse, and John and Rosalie spent six months carting up all of their worldly possessions in the back of a small pickup truck.

Here in Grafton, they could finally live free. They equipped the schoolhouse with an array of solar panels, planted vegetables, and experimented with agriculture—bees and pigs, a greenhouse, chickens and turkeys and sheep. Joining the fire department as a volunteer was a good outlet for Babiarz's boyish enthusiasm; when emergencies hit, he threw himself into the role like a scripted action hero. His profession became more personal, and more whimsical. He called his new small computer company Intergalactic Software and followed that up with Endor Communications (named for the Ewoks' home planet in the Star Wars franchise), which he ran out of an old outbuilding on the schoolhouse property and used to provide Grafton with its first internet services.

As John and Rosalie settled into their new life together in Grafton, the springtime snow and mud along the town's travel corridors was increasingly riddled with piles of scat and huge paw prints, while garbage cans were being raided in the night. Soon after Jessica Soule's kittens were snatched by bears, John and Rosalie began having bear problems of their own.

"I promised her," he told me once, while she sat by his side, "never a dull moment."

"And I've been begging for them," Rosalie deadpanned back.

The bears knocked apart their wooden beehives, raiding the sweet honey within. They weren't alarmed, but decided to take the safe step of erecting a high-voltage electric fence to protect their latest homesteading experiment—a handsome black ram and a ewe. The ram, John said, was "rambunctious," always looking for an opportunity to butt him, though it was unclear whether in anger or for sport.

The ram didn't last long. One day, after returning from a call at the fire station, Babiarz found that the animal had been violently torn apart.

"The bear just eviscerated him," he would later say. "This place is so . . ." he stopped. It was clear that Grafton's distance from central authority could be as challenging as it was charming. His bear woes were heightened because Grafton was caught between settler-era wilderness surroundings and an obligation to follow modern-day rules about wild animals. Under libertarian ideals, John Babiarz could have followed the example set by Eleazer Wilcox more than two hundred years ago—exercise his freedom to pursue the bear that killed his ram. But under the state's wildlife management laws, he could only shoot bears that were actively threatening his property, a description open to interpretation. Though Babiarz has never killed a bear illegally, it's pretty clear that he disagrees with the law.

"I feel on my property, I have the right to defend and protect my property," he says. "If I see a problem bear, I will deal with it. We can argue about it in court later on."

When he wasn't swatting bears off of his honey hives, Babiarz was steeping himself in state politics and quickly climbing the ranks of the small New Hampshire state Libertarian Party. In 2000, he announced his first bid for governor of New Hampshire, driven by a successful petition drive by libertarians who collected thousands of signatures to get him on the ballot. Babiarz appeared on C-Span for an October 2000 debate with Democratic governor Jeanne Shaheen and two other candidates. His first appearance on the national stage was generally uncomfortable. He stared and sounded stilted, stumbling over rehearsed lines.

But there were bright spots. He articulated the Libertarian Party's basic principles to an audience that was probably unfamiliar with them. The government's real function, he said, was to protect individual property rights, and he expressed the libertarians' moral opposition to the income tax, the sales tax, and the property tax.

His best moment against his more polished opponents came when he looked at the camera and said, "Government is not the solution. It's the problem."

Although Babiarz garnered only a little over 1 percent of the vote, he ran again in 2002. That time he built on the political contacts he already had in place and netted about 3 percent of the vote—six times higher than Paul's presidential bid, and better than almost any libertarian gubernatorial candidate, in any state, to date. In the ongoing effort to mainstream libertarian politics in New Hampshire, Babiarz sensed that he was on the cusp of something huge, if he could only continue to build his political base.

Somehow, he needed more libertarians.

4

A QUARTET OF COLONISTS

I might as well have struggled with a bear, or reasoned with a lunatic. The only resource left me was to run to a lattice and warn his intended victim of the fate which awaited him.

—Emily Brontë, *Wuthering Heights*, 1870

In February 2004, a van lurched from one tiny, frozen New Hampshire town to the next. Inside, four men fortified by tobacco, alcohol, and firearms held court, every conversation tinged by an undercurrent of understanding that the Republican Party lacked the balls to get serious about freedom.

Like Babiarz, the travelers were libertarians. One of the pernicious obstacles to the growth of the party has been its commitment to following logic chains into whatever dark place they lead, regardless of social mores. That's why, in one true sense, the philosophy is deeply ingrained with America's founding principles but, in an equally true sense, still engenders earnest debates over whether consensual cannibalism should be legal.

Though the road-trip roster varied over the course of the three-day journey, a core four was there for the whole ride.

Tim Condon, a well-spoken if bombastic fifty-five-year-old lawyer (like computer coders, lawyers thrive on logic-based language), had been a political activist for thirty years. After serving in Vietnam as a US Marine, he returned home and found inspiration in the writing of conservative politician Barry Goldwater (who would later become an important bridge between Republicans and Libertarians).

Condon flew up to New Hampshire from his home state of Florida, as did Larry Pendarvis, the oldest of the group at sixty-one. Pendarvis was traveling under the pseudonym "Zack Bass," possibly to prevent anyone from linking him with his time working an office job for a health unit within Florida's Department of Health and Rehabilitative Services. That job had been abruptly terminated when coworkers, suspicious of his secretive computer habits, found digital files that led to a conviction for 129 counts of child pornography. Pendarvis was sometimes described as a split personality—reserved in person, but a vituperative troll online. During his child pornography trial, the prosecutor showed the judge and defense counsel a list of words written on a large notepad that described Pendarvis with words like "shy" and "introvert." Once the defense counsel had indicated it had no objection to the list being shown to the jury, the prosecutor surreptitiously used a pen to alter the word "introvert" so that the jury read it as "pervert." When Pendarvis's lawyer complained about the deception, the conviction was reversed. Pendarvis walked free and according to news articles happily began building a new enterprise—a Philippine-centric mail-order bride business. (Pendarvis himself had been married seven or eight times at that point, depending on whether one counted a brief period of polygamy as one marriage or two.)

After their plane landed in New Hampshire, Condon and Pendarvis met up with Bob Hull, a thin-lipped, well-to-do, thirty-eight-year-old New Jersey businessman known for both his quiet demeanor and his disco-era fashion sense.

The dream team was rounded out by the van's bushy-bearded owner, Tony Lekas. Soft-spoken and intellectual, the forty-eight-year-old was the only New Hampshire resident, having moved there from Chicago in 1979. He was a software engineer by profession, but he was increasingly consumed by the prospect of becoming a firearms instructor.

Many libertarians feel a deep kinship with America's early days, which they view as a utopian golden age when government was small and people lived freely. The connection with that halcyon era felt particularly strong as they drove along, swapping stories of freedom. Just like the founding fathers, they tended to keep firearms within easy reach and were acutely aware of personal rights. And just like the founding fathers, they intended to father a new founding.

These four dreamers had struck upon a plan to answer the decades-old problem of mainstreaming libertarian ideas and had now come to New Hampshire to lay tracks for the boldest social experiment in modern American history: the Free Town Project.

If all went as planned, hundreds of Free Towners would concentrate their voting power to effect a political makeover, transforming a small American town from a stodgy and unattractive thicket of burdensome regulations into an "anything goes" frontier where, according to a website created by Pendarvis, citizens should assert certain inalienable rights, such as the right to have more than two junk cars on private property, the right to gamble, the right to engage in school truancy, the right to traffic drugs, and the right to have incestual intercourse.

Oh, and also, Pendarvis sought to assert the right to traffic organs, the right to hold duels, and the God-given, underappreciated right to organize so-called bum fights, in which people who are homeless or otherwise indigent are paid small amounts of money to engage in fisticuffs. Logic is a strange thing.

The creation of America's first Free Town was so ambitious in scope that it seemed doomed from the start, and indeed, almost every such population-level social experiment in history has failed spectacularly. Most efforts at planned communities involve artificially populating an uninhabited place, like a stretch of desert or an island—as in 1972, when a Nevada millionaire and his libertarian friends declared independent ownership of an island off the coast of New Zealand (a claim that was promptly quashed by the New Zealand military).

The building of utopias is limited by the rarity of visionaries with deep pockets. Building a new community from scratch requires millions or billions of dollars to create an infrastructure and overcome the challenges preventing people from living there in the first place. Henry Ford, whose assembly line kick-started the automobile revolution, learned this the hard way when his planned Amazonian utopia, Fordlandia, succumbed in the 1930s to the threats of rainforest blight, disease, cultural clashes, and an unhelpful Brazilian government.

The four libertarians who came to New Hampshire had thinner wallets than Ford and other would-be utopians, but they had a new angle they believed would help them move the Free Town Project out of the realm of marijuana-hazed reveries and into reality.

Instead of building from scratch, they would harness the power and infrastructure of an existing town—just as a rabies parasite can co-opt the brain of a much larger organism and force it to work against its own interests, the libertarians planned to apply just a bit of pressure in such a way that an entire town could be steered toward liberty.

That the perfect town would lie somewhere in "Live Free or Die" New Hampshire, the first of the thirteen colonies to declare statehood, seemed almost a foregone conclusion. In a country known for fussy states with streaks of independence, New Hampshire is among the fussiest and the streakiest. It's one of only five states with no sales tax, one of two states that limit the governor to two-year terms, and the only state in New England that still allows the death penalty. (No one has been executed since 1939, but they like to keep their options open.)

But which town? They drove about, canvassing communities, searching for the perfect place. The town of Roxbury was appealing, but since there wasn't much land for sale, colonization would be difficult there. Lempster, with a stagecoach hotel on the market, seemed like a promising launching pad for incoming revolutionaries. But when they went to check it out, someone told them that the town was about to adopt zoning regulations—building codes designed to keep structures habitable and safe from fire. That was an absolute deal-breaker.

"Zoning might be used as a statist weapon by existing local political powers to block any large-scale immigration . . . into the town," Condon wrote in a blog post about the trip. "In addition, the existence of zoning suggests a 'busybody-friendly atmosphere' among the current populace. We wanted no part of any such place."

In all, they considered and rejected twenty towns—too cold, not enough land, too many regulations, and so on.

Then they got to Grafton, forty-six square miles of rugged bear country in the southernmost reaches of Grafton County. Here, over the course of the last five years, Soule and her Bungtown neighbors had watched as the signs of bears—scat, tracks, and manifest appearances—increased, but as the colonists drove in on Route 4, the only paved road that led into Grafton, they saw no bears. Nor did they see much in the way of commerce—in fact, there were no coffee shops, no restaurants, no retail businesses of any kind, save a tired traditional general store, which was fronted by a sagging wooden porch overlooking a single gas pump.

Clearly, this was a place where the "busybody-friendly" civic pride Condon abhorred was on the wane. In fact, outside of the general store, Grafton seemed to have just a few notable community features—in Grafton Center, there was the historic Grafton Center Church (which dated back to 1798) and a flagging roadside attraction in the Ruggles Mine, a former commercial mica excavation. The only visible municipal assets were the modest Grafton

Public Library and the fire station, which also served as the town's de facto ambulance garage and communal meeting space.

The fire station was where Lekas finally turned his van off Route 4 and pulled into a parking lot. The libertarians disembarked, stretching legs and cracking backs. They knew little about the town. The town, in turn, was equally ignorant about them. Though the would-be colonists were walking into a public building to talk about a matter that would have been of major public interest, the meeting itself was decidedly private. No one knew they were there—other than John and Rosalie Babiarz.

The colonists entered the building and walked down a short hallway, marked by a couple of doorways leading into the offices of department heads, fire chief among them. The hallway opened into a cavernous bay where a plastic table and folding chairs had been set up alongside the emergency vehicles. Joining the Babiarzes at the table, they sat down on the folding chairs as snow from the parking lot melted off their shoes into small puddles on the concrete floor.

Right away, Grafton sounded promising. John Babiarz told them that native Graftonites were "unsupportive of bureaucracy" and "hostile toward zoning" and other busybody regulations.

That was good. They also got the sense that Grafton was a sandbox in which they could play, with little state or federal supervision. No longer tethered by rail lines and commerce to the broader world, Grafton had become a tiny fragment of civilization hidden away among the trees. And because Grafton had far more land than people, plenty of plots were available for would-be homesteaders.

Together, the colonists and their hosts strategized a naked power grab of the town government. Grafton had fewer than eight hundred registered voters, most of whom didn't show up on election days. They figured that just a couple of dozen new voters could join an existing base of like-minded people to tip the scales in favor of a new order.

Might it be possible, Condon asked, to defund the local public school district?

There's already talk about that, said Rosalie, who was a payroll clerk with the local regional school district.

At one point, their conversation was interrupted when Merle Kenyon, the chief of the Grafton Police Department (and its only full-time employee), walked through. The always-folksy Kenyon stopped to make small talk for a few minutes before moving on.

After Chief Kenyon left, the colonists concluded that he didn't seem the sort to harass and arrest people for victimless crimes. Besides, "the police chief is an elected position in Grafton," Condon wrote later, "so if power were abused, he could be voted out of office."

Condon and the others asked their hosts if they had "any hesitation about a bunch of wild libertarians invading your quiet town? . . . Should we choose Grafton as the Free Town?"

"Absolutely," said Rosalie.

It's not clear whether, at this point, the Babiarzes fully understood that the libertarians were operating under vampire rules—the invitation to enter, once offered, could not be rescinded.

John smiled.

"Sure!" he said. "Why not?"

A bevy of libertarian neighbors could only help his mission to build New Hampshire's Libertarian Party infrastructure—perhaps even help him become the nation's first Libertarian governor. And anyway, logically speaking, the Free Towners and Grafton's longtime residents all hated taxes.

What could possibly go wrong?

5
A ROUSING RESPONSE

"Why, you self-sufficient bear," said the hermit, "not a day passes but I am justified in my purpose by the conversations I hold here; not a day passes but I am shown, by everything I hear and see here, how right and strong I am in holding my purpose."

—Charles Dickens, "Tom Tiddler's Ground," 1861

"One person!" called the moderator, desperate to keep order before the palpable ugliness in the room spiraled completely out of her control.

Usually a sleepy civics exercise, the New England town meeting is perhaps the purest form of direct democracy left in the United States, dating back to the earliest days of the American colonies. When some pressing business arises, the town's elected officials muster all the pomp, dignity, and ceremony within their means and invite the entire community to a single large room. Those who care to show up act as both voter and legislator, with full power to propose legally binding action and suggest amendments to actions proposed by their neighbors.

Each town meeting is an opportunity for a small community to demonstrate that, given the reins of power, it can rise above the failings of Washington politicians.

It is also an opportunity to flop spectacularly.

"One person!" repeated the moderator. "Raise your hand!" Outside, an implicit threat in the form of a coffin was propped up against the building, a hearse parked alongside.

It was June 19, 2004, just four months after Grafton was chosen as the site of the Free Town Project, and it was already shaping up to be an unmitigated disaster.

Things had started off in February with the thrill of big, secret plans.

After talking with the Babiarzes in early 2004, Hull, Condon, and the other Free Town founders were excited. This was a chance to create a model libertarian community that could showcase its successes, teaching the entire nation that oppression by government was not the only way.

Bob Hull quietly bought up multiple tracts of land, including the old Hoyt Farm and, in mid-May, 237 acres along Route 4. He planned to allow libertarians to live on the land either permanently or temporarily, depending on the terms of private agreements negotiated with each individual. He called the access road to one such tract Liberty Lane.

They also began working to convince a critical mass of libertarians to move to this backwoods area without hairdressers, movie theaters, pizza parlors, tennis courts, concerts, cell-phone service, or jobs, to take just a few examples from the endless list of things that Grafton lacked. Condon and Pendarvis created websites that outlined the project in glowing terms, explaining that coming to the Free Town was a chance to be part of a historic moment in libertarian political history. They also circulated the phone number of a libertarian-friendly realtor and announced that they were easing the transition for incoming Free Towners by connecting them with temporary housing, greeting them with welcome parties, and doing what they could to match them up with local employers.

Within the narrow limits of internet "freedom forums," it suddenly seemed to libertarians around the world that everyone who was deeply committed to freedom was living in New Hampshire, moving to New Hampshire, or considering a move to New Hampshire.

The Free Towners linked their messaging to liberty's revolutionary salad days, when New England's Americans founded their own communities, each one vibrant with the promise of a future shaped by its residents.

But of course, they were not really breaking ground on some hitherto undiscovered frontier. In much the same way Englishmen had once crashed through the bramble of what they thought was a New World, they were actually inserting themselves into a long-established community of natives who regarded them not as benign colonists, or liberators, but as invaders.

Though, of course, most people in New Hampshire—most people everywhere—had no opinion on the libertarians. They didn't even know they were coming.

In the spring of 2004, as the first few cars of Free Towners rolled down Route 4, no one, save the Babiarzes and a few other sympathetic supporters, knew what was about to happen.

The project remained under the radar until a local author named Lisa Shaw noticed the plan, which was spelled out in detail online, and sounded the alarm. In a mailing she sent out to every address in town, she described the project in unfavorable terms. (It "was really quite nasty," Condon would later write.)

Once Grafton townspeople began to zero in on that narrow band of cyberspace devoted to the plans—public-facing discussion forums and websites—there were no more secrets. Stories about the Free Town Project broke in the local press, then went regional and eventually national.

During a television interview, a Grafton resident accused the Free Towners of "trying to cram freedom down our throats." The libertarians circulated the quote widely, scoffing at the illogical notion that freedom could ever be seen as a negative. Though the accusation might have been seen as an early sign of trouble, most Free Towners still assumed that the tax-phobic Graftonites would treat them as liberators and political brothers. Condon was among the many organizers who expected that "the people of Grafton would welcome us with open arms."

But the arms attached to many people of Grafton remained stubbornly closed. Grafton's minority of liberals and pro-government folks were predictably aghast, but there was also an unexpected twist in local attitudes: many small-government conservatives, the Free Towners' presumed political allies, also seemed angry.

One big problem was the Pendarvis website—when he called for Free Towners to overwhelm the "Authoritarians and Statists," his strident tone was a rallying cry for devoted libertarians, and when it came to building bridges in the community . . . let's just say it wasn't helpful. Speaking for the project, Pendarvis explicitly said that Free Towners would overwhelm the "Authoritarians and Statists." In libertarian circles, calling someone a "statist"—one who prefers a large and active government—is a real insult, one that ranks right up there with "racist" in its ability to provoke heated defenses. Pendarvis also vowed to force Grafton to withdraw from the school district and to legalize organ trafficking, cannibalism, and duels, among other things.

"All of a sudden people saw what he was saying," said Babiarz. Like many Free Towners, Babiarz implied that it was grossly unfair for people to judge the Free Town Project by the views expressed on the Free Town Project website. "People picked up on that and used that as a form of xenophobia."

Hoping to smooth feathers and win new converts, Condon and a handful of other Free Towners agreed to explain the project during an informational town meeting.

On Saturday, June 19, the first sign that Grafton's town meeting process might be headed for trouble came when the venue—an abandoned schoolhouse that had been repurposed as the town hall—proved to be too small. It filled, then it overfilled, and by the designated starting time of 1:00 p.m., with people outside complaining loudly that they were being denied their right to participate, it nearly burst apart.

When the meeting was transferred to the fire station, a fleet of pickup trucks tooled the mile and three-quarters down the road to the new location, where folding chairs were arranged in messy rows. As they filed in, the hundreds of attendees had ample opportunity to see the hearse and coffin, which was decked out with a sign indicating that the Free Town Project could "RIP."

That was the mood people were in.

Shortly after the moderator opened the meeting, Libertarian Mike Lorrey, big, beefy, and balding, stood in front of the crowd. They had nothing to fear from the members of the Free Town Project, he told them.

"These are the kind of people that you would be proud to have as neighbors, I gotta tell ya," said Lorrey. But rather than placate the crowd, his words just touched off a wave of derisive laughter that rolled across the sea of angry faces.

A man stood up and told Lorrey that he himself had moved to Grafton without trying to bring along a voting bloc. The man's voice was raised, but that was unremarkable; everybody's voice, it seemed, was raised.

"What is it you're trying to do?" he shouted.

Though the logicians were armed with buckets of well-reasoned arguments (and probably guns), they quickly realized that the meeting wasn't really primed for teaching moments.

John Babiarz sat in the crowd with his fellow Graftonites, rising to field a share of the angry questions. Rosalie sat beside him, quiet.

"I never knew till that point how Hitler could get people all riled up to support him in war," John would later say. He called it a mob mentality. "It was interesting, because it was all emotion-based. Logic and reason was out the door."

The couple felt growing unease as their neighbors tore them apart.

"It's hard to look back on it now," said Rosalie.

"There were people there we've known for about ten years," John said. "All of a sudden I'm the devil? Wow."

Despite all the warning signs, the Free Towners were caught unprepared—the scorching attacks by a roomful of busybodies were the complete opposite of what they expected from the Grafton they'd been briefed on. Before the meeting, John Babiarz had told them that Graftonites "tend to stay to themselves. . . . Everybody goes their own way." Even Shaw, their putative opponent, called it "a town of hermits."

But the Graftonites in front of them were, emphatically, not hermits. They seemed eager to fund the town library and fire station with their tax dollars and to support community endeavors like the general store and the stately old Grafton Center Church.

Condon, using his best lawyerly voice, sought to reassure the public that no organized effort was afoot to take such measures as privatization of the roads (under which each person would spend the money or labor to take care of the stretch of road that ran past their home).

"We want freedom-loving people to come together and move here, and then it's up to them," he said. He was met with jeers and catcalls.

"Don't judge us all by Zach Bass," said Lorrey, using Pendarvis's pseudonym. (Meanwhile, that same day, "Bass" told a New Hampshire Public Radio reporter that the public school system should be dismantled because it was "not right to force someone to pay to educate someone else's child.")

After three torturous hours of angry speeches, the meeting finally sputtered to a halt.

The townspeople of Grafton had spoken, with a more or less unified voice, and delivered an unmistakable message: we don't want you here.

That was it then. The libertarians had misjudged Grafton. The Free Town Project was dead on arrival.

Except it totally wasn't.

AFTERWARD, THE LIBERTARIANS got together to talk about what had happened.

The Free Towners had been picturing a placid exchange of ideas in which they would explain the virtues of government-free living to the local Graftonites. By that measure, the meeting was a total bust.

"One of them said, 'I wish we hadn't gone. I wish we had not agreed to meet with them. . . . We just contributed more fodder,'" said Rosalie Babiarz.

Though some defended Pendarvis as a truth-teller, many of the disheartened libertarians blamed him for ratcheting up the rhetoric around the most inflammatory topics, like bum fighting. The state's Libertarian Party, which considered itself a different entity than the Free Town Project, sent Pendarvis a strongly worded email accusing him of poisoning the well in Grafton.

"The people of Grafton are armed, dangerous, and extremely pissed at you," wrote John Barnes of the state party. He instructed Pendarvis to stay away from New Hampshire. "We will certainly not protect you."

Though Pendarvis never renounced his libertarian ideals, he promptly gave up his designs on New Hampshire and disappeared from public view.

Pendarvis's quick fade contrasted sharply with the reaction of Tim Condon, whose sometimes combative style was also questioned. (Some libertarians blamed him for publishing the blog post that first brought unwanted attention to the project.) Condon added fuel to the fire when a local newspaper reporter heard him tell other libertarians that the town meeting attendees were "a vicious crowd of xenophobes and rednecks," after which Condon told the reporter he was just kidding.

After the meeting, a forum posting attributed to Condon's user account struck an even more confrontational tone.

"The only reason I didn't tell [a vocal opponent of the project] in a mannerly way to 'go fuck yourself, piss ant,' is because we were working hard on being calm and mannerly to everyone," Condon wrote.

Babiarz said the true extremists at the meeting were the statists, who merely used Pendarvis as an opportunity to mischaracterize the libertarians as the extreme ones.

"There's a faction that likes to, quote, build up government more, and they saw this as a way of painting libertarians as anarchists or whatever, and destroying them," he said.

With emotions running so high, some suggested that the project should be shifted to another community—somewhere else in New Hampshire, or perhaps out west, where an open-armed welcome was still a live possibility. But the more they talked about it, the more it seemed like the community voice they had heard during the town meeting wasn't as unified as it had seemed.

Maybe what they had witnessed, they reasoned, was a unified *faction* of Grafton. Condon said that it was obvious who turned out for the meeting. The Democrats. Even a town of hermits has its statists, they mused.

As they talked, the libertarians grew to believe, with rising hope, that the vitriol wasn't necessarily representative of the majority of Grafton residents.

After all, though a sizable number of people had shown up to yell at them, it was only logical to conclude that even more people hadn't shown up. There were hundreds of Graftonites living in the woods who, through their absence, were offering either tacit support or at least neutrality.

The silent sylvan majority.

The hermits.

Though they had very little evidence to support the notion, they thought that, if the Free Town Project moved forward, these were the people who would help them undermine the local governmental structures.

Grafton could still be liberated, they concluded. It could still become America's first Free Town.

In this, as it turned out, the logicians were completely correct.

6

THE CONVERTED CARETAKER

The Puritan hated bear-baiting, not because it gave pain to the
bear, but because it gave pleasure to the spectators.

—Thomas Macaulay, *The History of England*, vol. 1, 1848

In searching for parallels to the Free Town Project, many Graftonites
thought, naturally, of one summer in the early 1990s when people noticed
an unusual amount of traffic heading to the remote upper reaches of Wild
Meadow Road. Neighbors reported that cars and campers with out-of-state
plates were overflowing the dooryard of an old farmhouse, disgorging dozens
of people who were smiling and calling out greetings to one another. Some of
them were Asian. It seemed like a cult.

When the suspicious Graftonites checked the property records in the
municipal offices, they found that the farmhouse had been purchased by the
Unification Church, a national organization that became famous in the 1970s
for holding mass wedding ceremonies performed by its charismatic leader, the
Reverend Sun Myung Moon.

Many locals were displeased with the church's presence in town. Following the lead of national media outlets that were publishing unflattering
portraits of the Unification Church, dark rumors began to circulate about
what they called "the Moonie House." Strangers began selling flowers along
Route 4. It seemed more like a cult than ever.

When I asked Jessica Soule, whose kittens were bear-snatched from her
residence down Wild Meadow Road, about the time the Moonies founded a
community in Grafton, she laughed.

"Well," she said. "I guess I was the head Moonie."

SOULE'S PATH TOWARD the Unification Church—and Grafton—began on a Friday morning in the summer of 1974, when she awoke and tried to make sense of the sensory inputs all around—the hard ground beneath her twenty-year-old body, the low leafy branches near her face, the dull ache of an empty stomach, the distant, but not too distant, sound of brisk footsteps on pavement.

When the fog of sleep cleared, she crawled out of a gap in the shrubbery that grew around the Ohio statehouse in Columbus and stood, bare feet beneath denim jeans, wondering how she was going to get through another day of homelessness.

How could you let this happen to me? she asked God. She'd been on the street for four days. Or was it five? But he didn't answer.

Over the next several hours, Soule sat on benches and wandered aimlessly, reflecting on how far she'd come since her childhood in a Massachusetts church community. Her family was headed by her well-to-do lawyer father, and she'd once had dreams of becoming a doctor. Those dreams didn't last. When she was fourteen, her parents divorced, and she wound up living with her cousins.

At eighteen, she thought her life was taking a positive turn. She joined the US Navy and fell in love with another recruit at a naval base in Philadelphia. But within two years, a series of unexplained seizures caused her to be discharged; she married the man, but what she thought was his minor alcohol problem turned out to be a major drug problem. After a bitter fight, she fled their apartment. She'd been sleeping beside the statehouse ever since.

As she sat on the bench, despondent, she watched the trolleys rolling past and the people walking by, businessmen and sideburned factory workers on lunch breaks, tourists gazing up at the tall buildings, and parents headed to the park to get in a bout of summer exercise for their pets and schoolchildren. Everyone had a destination. Everyone had a purpose.

Soule came to a decision. From a likely-looking place on the sidewalk, she stood facing traffic. When a bus came by, she waited until the last possible moment and then rushed out onto the street in front of it.

"Those Ohio bus drivers are good," she later said. She hadn't timed it quite right, and the bus didn't even make contact. "He slammed on the brakes and jumped out."

"I know what you were doing," the driver said, herding her onto the bus. She feigned innocence, but he sat her down between two women and took her back to the bus station. There, she told him that the suicide attempt had been a passing, crazy thought, and she walked away. But she was already planning to find another, better spot, one where the bus would be going faster.

On the way out of the bus station, a pair of young women stopped her and handed her a flyer. She was about to blow by, but her ear was caught by their accents; one was from France, the other from Germany.

"Will you come to a spaghetti dinner tonight?" they asked in rough but passable English.

It was the right question. Soule couldn't remember the last time she'd eaten. Soon the young women were driving her to Ohio State University and leading her into a conference room crackling with youthful energy. Before the food was served, everyone's attention was directed to a podium at the front of the room.

"This Japanese guy got up and said God is both masculine and feminine," Soule said. It put her in mind of her jeans, which were a minor act of rebellion against the church communities she'd grown up in.

After the dinner, they asked her to stay for the weekend, to listen to other talks. On Friday evening, Soule was ambivalent about the message. By Sunday evening, she wanted nothing more than to dedicate her life to the church.

"I like it here," she realized. "The people are kind of good. Some people might be naive or a little over the top, but this was a niche I fit into."

The weekend conference was being run by the Unification Church, which then had about five thousand followers, many of them young people disaffected by the social upheaval of the '70s.

Soule moved into a former fraternity house off the university campus, along with about a hundred other new church members. The men lived on one floor, and the women on the other. They bought her clothes and gave her food, but the important thing to Soule was her spiritual education.

"The teachings, they were the world to me," she said.

She tried to reconcile with her husband, but he couldn't abide by the church's strict stance on sobriety. When he faltered, Soule found it much easier to turn her back on him than on her new peers.

Though it didn't yet have a large national presence, the Unification Church was already beginning to draw criticism for its unusual practices and its political beliefs—Moon was using his wealth and influence to mainstream his hard-line anticommunist messages into the media. On top of a faith-tinged business empire, he would eventually become a billionaire and attract a religious following of seven million.

In September, Soule hopped a bus with other churchgoers headed to New York, where Moon himself was scheduled to speak. After hearing so much about his towering presence, she discovered that he was much shorter than she had expected. Still, something about him captivated her.

"He stopped his speech, and he looked at me and smiled, probably because my big eyes were bugging out," she said. "He stopped and looked at me and smiled and did the little Asian head nod."

It was electric.

"The girls on either side of me, we were all in the same group, they elbowed me and said 'He looked at you! He looked at you!'"

Afterward, a senior member of the church invited Soule to join Moon and other church leaders in his hotel room. The invitation was the first of many, and Moon became Soule's mentor, encouraging her to rebuild her relationship with her parents and to pursue a college degree. At his invitation, she and hundreds of other church members moved into a theological seminary in Barrytown, New York, where she had frequent contact with Moon's children.

When the church's national profile rose, she watched as the press asked repeatedly whether the members were tortured or subjected to brainwashing. Government agents approached her and asked her questions about what really went on in the church's inner circle. To Soule, the questions were silly. Nothing was going on but spiritual teachings.

"People say he's a monster. But no, he wasn't. He was the nicest man I ever knew in my life," she said. "He turned me around so much."

In 1975, after Soule had been at Barrytown for a little over a year, Moon told his young wards that it was time for them to carry the church's teachings out into the world. He sent many to serve as missionaries in other countries, but others, like Soule, were told to find their own path, in their own way.

She started by founding the Family Unity Network, a nonprofit in Minneapolis, and when that shut down, she turned to social work in Wareham, Massachusetts. She stayed there for years, sometimes talking to Moon on the phone or visiting when he came to speak in Boston.

When Moon was put on trial for tax evasion in 1982, he drew the support of mainstream religious figures and civil libertarians. When he was sentenced to be jailed, Soule prepared to chain herself to the prison fencing in protest, but her friends in the church talked her out of it. About a year later, Moon was released and resumed his position.

As the Moon family continued to build its business empire, one of the sons, Kook Jin Moon, proved to have aptitude as an executive. In 1993, he founded a small arms company, Kahr Arms, that sited its main production facility in Worcester, Massachusetts. He went on to take a leading role in the family's other business interests, including military hardware for the South Korean army and ginseng.

"He was a great believer in the Second Amendment," said Soule.

Reverend Moon had a bleak outlook on the midterm prospects of the governmental institutions that upheld law and order. He saw a society on the brink of collapse. The guns, he told Soule, would help the church members to defend themselves during the imminent chaos.

IN THE SUMMER of 1994, a church administrator telephoned Soule, who was then thirty-nine and living in Lynn, Massachusetts. He told her about the church's summer camp and retreat in rural New Hampshire and said that the hostility from the native Graftonites was getting to be a problem. Every time the church sent someone up to host a retreat, they would find that the vacant building had been vandalized—windows broken, items gone missing, sometimes wanton destruction.

Soule quickly agreed to move to New Hampshire to serve as the caretaker for the property. Her mission was to provide a year-round presence and help demonstrate to her Grafton neighbors that the Moonies were decent people.

When she arrived, she explored the old Bungtown farmhouse. Small bedrooms, large woodstoves, and a more modern addition that they used as a lecture room. The remoteness of Grafton, awash in deer and wild turkeys, was exhilarating. She took daily drives and came to love the feel of the breeze in her hair. The church, like so many others, had identified Grafton as a place where dreams could be pursued, uninhibited by the forces that had persecuted Reverend Moon.

"It was out in the middle of nowhere," she said. "I figured, there's no street signs, so the government couldn't find me."

When summer camp or a retreat was happening, the house would fill with children from the city, with the overflow set up in tents and campers on the eighteen-acre property. In between sessions, the church office in Boston would sometimes call her and tell her to set up some bedrooms for church members who needed temporary lodgings.

It didn't take long for Soule to experience the conflict between the church and the locals. She was asked whether the people at the Moonie House engaged in orgies.

"Do you know what abstinence is?" Soule would shoot back. "That's what we go through to get married in the church."

And those were the good interactions. One neighbor gave her the finger every time he drove by and someone used his vehicle to knock the church's mailbox down in the night. After it happened twice, she remounted the mailbox on a concrete post. "The next time he did it, he broke his truck," she said. "And he got arrested."

Soule got a gun license and bought a pistol. Privately she dismissed the locals as inbred, but publicly she helped coordinate church events that were open to the public and gave out gifts of food to Graftonites in need. For years some residents talked about the day the church gave out free lobsters.

Tensions with the town ratcheted up over the issue of whether the Moonie House was a tax-exempt church or a taxable residence for Soule. Eventually the Unification Church, which was by then a well-established religious organization, prevailed, and relations began to ease once again.

After two years in Grafton, Soule won a court case against the Department of Veterans Affairs, which had initially denied her claim for benefits. When she received a large lump sum to make up for years of nonpayment, she used the money to buy a house of her own, located just a few miles down the road. A couple of years later, the church closed the camp down, but Soule didn't leave town. She'd fallen in love with Grafton's reforesting hills and the endless possibilities of the lonely dirt roads.

She had little inkling that her kittens would soon be eaten by bears. And even if she had, she would have even less inkling—like, zero inkling—that the freak incident would prove to be just the beginning of her bear problems.

7
THE BLACKNESS OF THE BEAR

He observed in Vienna a bear deliberately making with his paw a current in some water, which was close to the bars of his cage, so as to draw a piece of floating bread within his reach. These actions . . . can hardly be attributed to instinct or inherited habit, as they would be of little use to an animal in a state of nature. Now, what is the difference between such actions, when performed by an uncultivated man, and by one of the higher animals?

—Charles Darwin, *The Descent of Man*, 1871

At the same time the Free Towners set themselves to shaping the community to their liking, the town's bears were working to create their own utopia.

At first, the bears went unseen in the nighttime, like mischievous elves descending from the woods. But instead of mending shoes or spinning straw into gold, they cracked compost bins, tore open beehives, and licked small traces of beef tallow from backyard grills, only to disappear with the first hint of the rising sun. Bungtowners watched uneasily as a series of raids in a century-old barn reduced a feral colony of hardy barn cats from a population of twenty to zero.

People also began reporting other incidents that didn't quite gibe with how a bear ought to behave. One night in Bungtown, a Vietnam veteran named Dave Thurber, feeling uneasy, tweaked his living room curtain and saw a bear lumbering across his front yard, leaving deep claw marks in the snow.

Right off the bat, this was a bit unnatural. During a New England winter, a bear—or to be more precise, a normal bear—is in the middle of a season-long slumber. For five or more months, the bear lies in a den, its heart rate lowered to a somnambulant eight beats per minute; it does not eat, drink, defecate, or urinate until the warmth of spring signals the promise of new vegetation to eat.

But this bear was far from unconscious. It walked to a tall metal post where Thurber's calorie-laden bird feeder perched out of reach. Making short work of the post, the bear easily brought the payload of seeds earthward, then cracked open the feeder's plastic hull.

As the bear began to eat, a car bumped up the rutted dirt road, high beams sliding across the lawn like prison searchlights scanning a jail yard for escaping convicts. And indeed, Thurber saw that the bear acted like a convict, deftly avoiding the light streams by flattening itself just beyond their reach, in the shadowed lee of a large snowbank. As soon as the lights swept on, the bear reclaimed the bird feeder, delicately licked up the remaining seeds, and walked toward the nearest neighbor—perhaps the cat barn—to see what might be on offer there.

Thurber's experience with the bear was surprising, because the bear wasn't simply seeking cover when humans approached. Rather, it seemed to be specifically avoiding the light.

Which suggested that the bear knew human passersby could only see where the light struck.

Which further suggested that the bear had the mental capacity to understand the physical properties of his surroundings, *as they would appear to a human*, and act accordingly—and under our common human understanding of animal intelligence, that would make this particular animal some sort of bear genius.

In a sense, evolution grants every living thing a brilliant talent for squeezing life from its surroundings—the more extreme the habitat, the greater the savant. Frogs, for example: The Panamanian Golden Frog, which cannot make itself heard above the roaring waterfalls of Panama, attracts mates through the use of semaphore. New England's Eastern Gray Tree Frog, on the other hand, can survive being frozen nearly solid; all winter its organs sit like tiny hunks of beef jerky in an icy slurry of body fluids.

But these sorts of biological precocity are the domain of specialists. Against this backdrop, some living things exhibit an even greater level of genius, having evolved the gray matter needed to unlock a wide array of habitats. Humans are one of these problem-solving species. Bears are another.

Bears have so many physical gifts that it's hard to imagine why they would need to problem-solve at all. Their large, padded feet carry them over swampland like rugged boots; each boot terminates in five blunt, pocketknife-sized claws that can tear open stumps and burrows or climb trees to access beechnuts on the branch. With their enormous strength (they can bend a car door in half) and size (hunters have killed quarter-ton black bears in New Hampshire; the national weight record is 886 pounds), they can prey opportunistically on a wide variety of smaller creatures, including young deer and moose. Outside of human hunters, the only things that eat bears are larger bears (though researchers are at a loss to fully understand the reasons behind black bear cannibalism).

Bears have sharper eyesight than people (with night vision to boot), ears that are twice as sensitive, and noses capable of scenting a carcass twenty miles distant (seven times better than a bloodhound).

If escaping a bear's notice is unlikely, so is escaping the bear itself. Humans can dive into water to flee cougars, climb trees to evade raging rhinoceri, and outrun alligators. But the average black bear swims speedily and climbs quickly. It could spot Usain Bolt 25 meters in his world-record-setting 100-meter dash and still pounce on the world's fastest man well before the finish line.

To be clear, bear attacks are very rare. From a statistical standpoint, you're more likely to suffocate in a giant vat of corn than be injured by a bear.

But modern attacks do happen, with seriously not-good outcomes.

Cynthia Dusel-Bacon, by all accounts a rugged thirty-one-year-old geologist, was conducting a land survey in the Alaskan bush in 1977 when she saw an aggressive black bear beelining toward her. Dusel-Bacon waved her arms and shouted, right up until the moment the bear knocked her down, after which she decided to play dead so the bear wouldn't see her as a threat. That was a consequential error in judgment, experts said afterward, because the 170-pound bear likely never saw her as a threat. It was just hungry. When she stopped resisting, it dragged her into the trees and began to eat her alive. Even as some parts of her body disappeared down the throat of the bear, other parts of her body, quite heroically, accessed a communication device and alerted a partner in the area as to her emergency. Other geologists arrived in a helicopter and scared the bear off in time to save her life. The never-say-die Dusel-Bacon went on to post instructional YouTube videos in which she demonstrates how to chop carrots, wash dishes, and get dressed with two prosthetic arms.

For the residents of Grafton, whose homes were being probed with frightening regularity by a resurgent bear population, ursine intelligence levels were a key factor in a question most people never have to ask: how close am I to a bear right now?

After all, it's one thing to be appropriately respectful of a creature's brute force. It's quite another to live alongside one sly enough to case your home with the cool calculation of a professional burglar.

Graftonites weren't the first ones to concern themselves with bear IQs. Those who suspected high-level thinking in Grafton's bears had a rogue scientist champion—Ben Kilham, one of the foremost bear experts in the world.

Kilham (featured as the "bear whisperer" in a panda bear documentary narrated by actress Kristen Bell) employs many of the controversial methods employed, famously, by the primatologist Jane Goodall. He names the bears he studies, attributes emotional motivations to their behavior, and probably wouldn't have to work too hard to get a nod from Guinness as the world record–holder for enduring the highest number of nonfatal bear bites.

When Kilham is not living in the woods alongside wild bears, he sleeps in his human home, which is not twenty-five miles from Grafton.

Many Graftonites, including John Babiarz, referred me to Kilham, and so I called to find out whether bears are indeed smart enough to avoid the light of a passing car, surveil farmsteads, snatch cats, and do many of the other things reported in Grafton that struck me as improbable.

Kilham (who also happens to be a former gun designer) answered a few of my questions and then said that, if I really wanted to learn more about bear psychology, I should buy a book that gets into the nuances. He recommended one in particular, titled *In the Company of Bears*, available in paperback from Amazon for $24.49. The book was written by Ben Kilham.

Kilham has seen more of the inner workings of bear life than anyone. In the book, his vivid description of their intricate society suggests that bears are even smarter than sign language–savvy apes.

Kilham credits bears with self-awareness, the ability to count to twelve (primates can only manage a three-count), and cooperation to enforce a bear justice system. He says they can remember the distant past, mull over the likelihood of events in the distant future, and communicate and empathize with one another. One resource-strapped female bear can even, he says, engage in the incredibly complex negotiation of asking another, better-off female to adopt her cub.

After reading Kilham's books and other research, I was thoroughly convinced that bears are smart enough to employ high-level reasoning in their efforts to plunder calories from humans. But brains alone didn't explain some of the behaviors I was hearing about from Graftonites like Tom Ploszaj.

Soon after moving to town in 2008, Ploszaj (it's pronounced rarely) decided to hike a trail from Hardy Hill Road to the Pinnacle, a high peak that overlooks the valley in which Grafton is situated. Ploszaj (really, it's pronounced "PLO-zhay") knew of a crumbled concrete platform at the top and the remains of a few historical homestead foundations along the way. Grafton is like that—those who know where to look can find artifacts of a bygone era hidden in the woods, like shipwrecks submerged in an arboreal ocean. There are cemeteries in various states of senescence, stone walls that echo farms long since abandoned, schools shuttered, mills decommissioned, and mines whose hollowed bones of stone stud the mountains—all demonstrating the abject failure of three centuries of attempts to subjugate wild nature.

Ploszaj says he's not a libertarian—he has no faith in any political party—but he frequents their events and shares a lot of their beliefs about freedom. When Ploszaj came to Grafton during the Free Town Project, Babiarz set him up with a temporary living space and a volunteer post at the fire department.

"John was the one who opened up to me and said, 'We need you here,'" Ploszaj said. "I never did fire before. He was so inviting to me. He introduced me to friends."

Partway through his hike to the Pinnacle, Ploszaj sat on the ground to consult a compass and topographic map. He thought he was alone, until the silence was broken by a humanlike snort. If not for that sound, he never would have seen the bear standing less than fifty feet away, its black fur and lighter brown nose blending into the treescape.

Ploszaj froze. The bear watched him intently, seemingly to gauge his reaction to the snort, and then, after long, tense moments, he ambled away. Ploszaj went the opposite direction.

Ploszaj had just experienced what I was beginning to think of as "the assessment." It was described to me many times: rather than bolting, an apparently unafraid bear would stare and consider its options before sauntering away.

It was only a matter of time before a bear would opt not to so saunter.

8

THE SCRAPPY SURVIVALIST

Bear have become so troublesome to us that I do not think it prudent to send one man alone on an errand of any kind, particularly where he has to pass through the brush. . . . I have made the men sleep with their arms by them as usual for fear of accidents.

—Captain Meriwether Lewis, journal entry, 1805

Freedom.
Freedom!

To the obedience-averse libertarians, the clarion call was—ironically—irresistible, a liberation-tinted tractor beam that drew them deep into Grafton's wilds.

Those who moved to Grafton under the banner of the Free Town Project between 2004 and 2009 were free radicals, unbonded to existing living situations, because they had either too much money or not enough.

In those first few years, optimism flowed like wine. Every extremist view associated with the Free Town Project had been safely heaped upon the lecherous shoulders of the ousted Pendarvis, leaving everyone else clean and sin-free.

A few months after the shouty town meeting, the project got a boost when no less a personage than New Hampshire governor Craig Benson came to a $25-a-head barbecue at the home of John Babiarz and shook hands all around, hugging some of the libertarians in attendance, clinging to them like a statist liberal to a tree. Benson, who had appointed Babiarz to a cost-cutting task force, made Free Towners swoon by expressly saying he would welcome an influx of libertarians, not just into Grafton but into the entire state. The red carpet gave them hope that their ideas, currently on the fringe of the political landscape, could indeed be mainstreamed.

No one knows exactly how many libertarians moved to Grafton for the Free Town Project. Census records show that the town's population swelled by more than two hundred between 2000 and 2010, but there could have been fewer libertarian colonists than that, or there could have been more.

The Free Town Project took on a distinctly masculine feel. Although the movement included some families, they were mostly individuals, and mostly men. The United States, New Hampshire, and Grafton County all have majority-female populations, but by 2009 the town of Grafton had 608 men and 488 women, giving it one of the highest male-to-female ratios in the state. And because many of Grafton's women, as longtime residents, skewed older, the gender imbalance was even more pronounced among the young. The town was home to only 39 women in their twenties, as compared to 105 men. Many of the men went by colorful nicknames or simple surnames, like Redman, Chan, the Mad Russian, and the copiously bearded Richard Angell, a libertarian anti-circumcision activist whose favored moniker was, at one time, "Dick Angel." The Free Towners made at least one serious miscalculation: they assumed that branding Grafton as the ultimate Free Town would draw only libertarians.

They weren't counting on people like Adam Franz.

I meet Adam when I pull onto the shoulder of a winding dirt road and walk a downward-sloping driveway toward a dingy-walled camper. The camper, though theoretically capable of travel, exudes a dejected air that suggests it lies on a deathbed of forest humus. Soon the door opens to reveal the red-whiskered Franz, disheveled and looking like he is in need of some combination of caffeine, pot, and alcohol to take the roughness out of his voice. He's got a revolver in his hand.

After a couple of minutes of introductory comments, he launches into a story about bringing a .357 Magnum to his favorite gun shop to consult with the owner about possibly trading it in for something larger—a Taurus Judge .410.

The difference in caliber refers to the diameter of the projectile—the .357 was part of a Prohibition-era generation of bullets designed to penetrate the car doors of bootlegging gangsters, while the wider .410 (which slots comfortably into a shotgun) gained fame among firearm enthusiasts as the bullet of choice of Floridian judges, who wanted to be able to gun down raging criminals in their courtrooms.

But when Franz asked the gun shop owner for advice, he wasn't thinking of gangsters or courtrooms.

"I said, 'What's your thoughts dealing with bears?'"

The gun shop owner—also Franz's friend—redirected the question. Either revolver was capable of launching its payload straight through a bear's shaggy hide and internal organs, he said. It came down to what type of bear-shooting situation Franz might be planning for.

"It's kind of six-of-one-half-a-dozen-of-the-other," he told Franz, "because number one, the .357 is going to give you much longer range."

The Judge, on the other hand, might provide more certainty if the bear was as close as, say, a carjacker.

"If they get close up, you're going to do a lot more damage a lot faster with that."

The redirect left Adam free to choose whichever one he wanted.

"You know what?" he responded. "I'm only interested if they get close up. I'm not trying to fucking shoot them from fifty feet away."

The Judge is what he now holds, and the chamber is currently loaded with large .410s staggered with even larger .45 long colt bullets (the ammunition of choice in modern-day cowboy action shooting competitions, in which outlaw-shaped targets are shot by contestants decked out in Old West–themed kerchiefs, boots, and cowboy hats. The participants are mostly grown men.) The bullets are so large that Adam's revolver can only hold five at a time.

"Yeah," Adam says, "that's my bear gun."

I like his smart confidence and restless, friendly energy as he riffs on a wide range of topics. He drops his credentials, none of which fully explain how he makes a living now. He's studied comparative economics, designed computer programs, been ordained as a minister. In his early twenties, around 2001, he played poker, first in Philadelphia barrooms and Atlantic City, then in a poker room near his childhood home in Seabrook, New Hampshire. There, he got into an argument with a heavily tattooed rock 'n' roller.

After Adam got lucky in a hand, the musician unloaded on him. "What a fucking donkey," he said. "Playing the top pair with the ten kicker. Fuckin' kid don't even know how to spell poker."

Adam was incensed.

"Fuckin' crybaby bitch," he says. "And I almost punched him in the face. The only reason I didn't was that there was a cop right there."

The poker boom ended; Adam went through a messy marriage, and in a few different professional directions, none of which were enduring.

That's when he got a vision: he would found a planned community of survivalists, people who could live off the land and fend for themselves.

"I personally, as a big fan of Native American studies, a little Native American blood in me and everything else, I'd like to get to that level," he says. "I'd like to get to what I say is 'fully off grid,' or 'no grid,' which is no gunpowder, no electricity, and no gasoline or petroleum products. It would be bow-hunting. Basically anything that we can't make or build here ourselves, we don't need."

It was a vision of perfect self-sufficiency. It was a vision of freedom.

He chose—naturally—Grafton, where the Free Town Project had been announced and where there was a police force of somewhere between one and two people at any given time.

"We've got nobody coming around and really messing with you," he says. "This is the place where you can do what you want to do. Be what you want to be. And don't worry about it." Adam's commitment to survivalism flows naturally from his other beliefs, one of which he shares with leaders of the Unification Church—that society will soon crumble, not just in Grafton, but everywhere. Adam estimates that, for the general population, panic will set in four days after the grocery stores run out of food.

The underground bunker crowd, Franz confides, is kind of wacky.

"Number one, what are you going to do when the food runs out? When the bullets run out? That's not a long-term plan."

Much better, he says, is to internalize humankind's earliest skills of hunting and gathering—a complete return to ferality.

Adam is emphatically not a libertarian. And though he uses political labels all the time, he's uncomfortable with being boxed in by any label himself. Don't call him a liberal. American liberals are "too far—way too far—to the right for me."

Since he first conceived of his planned community, he's been called an atheist, a survivalist, a communist, an anarchist, and an anarcho-communist. His overarching political belief is that capitalism is bullshit.

"Government isn't ruining capitalism. Capitalism is ruining government. I think that's kind of obvious," he says. "If you take capitalism out of government you get simple public representation. If you take government out of capitalism, you get slavery."

Even though this puts him in diametric opposition to the Free Town libertarians, they are unified by a common cause. Grafton's emphasis on free-dom creates a space, Adam says, that lets the extreme left and the extreme

right collaborate on the dismantling of societal norms, with minimal interference from authorities.

"When it comes to tearing down this system, I'm right beside you the
whole way," he says. When the lights go out, he predicts that surviving capi-
talists will swiftly cannibalize themselves, and it doesn't seem like he's using
the term figuratively.

"And when you're done, when the last man's standing on top of a pile
of bloody bones, he can come over and we can work shit out," Adam says.
"What's the endgame of capitalism, if not a big fat white man sitting on top
of a pile of bloody bones with no one around him, crying because nobody's
around to make him a sandwich?"

Despite their differences over the free market, Adam and the libertarians
do agree on some issues, including vigorous defense of the right to bear arms.
This is, in fact, a point of agreement for a broad swath of New Hampshirites,
even those who do not regularly don vintage cowboy chaps to dispatch fictional bad guys with nonfictional guns.

Contrary to New England's lefty reputation, guns hold a special place in
New Hampshire, where a long-standing hunting tradition has coexisted with
a commensurate level of appreciation for guns in the politest of societies.

In 2012, in a change that cannot be positively associated with New
Hampshire's libertarians, the state attained the highest per-capita rate of
machine-gun ownership in the nation. Federal data indicated the presence
in the state of nearly ten thousand registered weapons, which meant that if
you were in a fully packed three-hundred-seat New Hampshire movie theater
watching the latest *Death Wish* revival, there were, statistically speaking, two
registered machine-gun owners sitting beside you in the darkness, drinking
it all in and getting—if Bruce Willis did his job well—really into the idea of
being pushed to a point where the only noble option was to open fire.

In Grafton, in the years after the Free Town Project launched, the cul-
turally accepted practice of carrying hunting rifles in trucks began to be sup-
planted by the more highly visible, and in some ways discomfiting, practice
of openly carrying revolvers and other nonhunting firearms while walking
about town on daily errands.

Free Towners began to show up "with a gun under each arm," as one resident told me, at the general store and at the town transfer station (where residents bring their trash, because town taxes do not fund a municipal pickup
service). At Grafton's church-based town meetings, the once-civil tone of
discourse became strained, as citizens debated amendments and motions

under the double scrutiny of Free Towners openly displaying 9 millimeter handguns and armed officers from the Grafton County sheriff's department, which decided it had better send someone, just in case.

Franz believes that people who openly carry their guns undercut the very rights they're trying to protect. It makes him furious (though, to be fair, so do a lot of other things).

"These assholes," he rants, "these idiots who walk around open-carry, when there's no reason to be open-carrying. You're making people uncomfortable. You're making them anti-gun. You're making them vote against guns. You're costing us our fucking gun rights. You're not being responsible. You think you're a fucking cowboy who likes to walk around with a gun on his hip because it makes you feel like you've got a big dick. No. No. Put that under your fucking jacket. If you really feel you need one, put it under your fucking jacket like a normal human being. Respect other people's sensibilities."

Graftonites in particular would suffer if they were to lose their gun rights, says Adam, because they need their guns even more than most people. This is because guns are about the only advantage Grafton's humans hold over Grafton's bears. That's why he's so angry with the people who openly display their guns.

"I live with fuckin' bears. I need my gun," he says. "You know what I'm saying. Just in case, I need my fucking gun. And if I lose my gun rights, I'm not going after the fucking liberals, I'm going after the gun nuts who provoke the liberals into doing it in the first fucking place."

Adam admits a moment later that people might see him with his Judge hanging from his waist—but only when they drive by his remotely located camper.

"Ever since we started having more bear issues, I always have my gun on me. When I'm at my property, it's open-carry, you know what I mean? So I'm either carrying in my shoulder holster or my side holster. So I probably get seen with a gun more often than most people."

In fact, he concedes, with no evident shame, people might sometimes get an eyeful of his Judge in other parts of town.

"And there have been once or twice that I forget to take it off when I go to the store," he adds. "And my friend Donny too, sometimes forgets to take it off."

After inviting me to hold his gun—and I am genuinely touched by the weight of his trust in my palm—Adam takes it back, then pauses, wanting to communicate something else before he puts it away.

"And uh," he says, smiling beatifically, "I love that fuckin' thing."

Each day Grafton seemed to grow fuller. More full of bears. More full of libertarians. More full of guns. And more full of people who loved bears, libertarianism, guns, or some combination of the three—and who were increasingly prepared to fight for what they loved.

Oh and doughnuts. The doughnuts were on the rise too.

9

THE ANIMAL ADMIRERS

He thought he saw a Coach-and-Four
That stood beside his bed:
He looked again, and found it was
A Bear without a Head. "Poor thing," he said, "poor silly thing!
It's waiting to be fed!"

—Lewis Carroll, *Sylvie and Bruno*, 1889

One morning in the summer of 2004, right around the same time the Free Town Project got rolling, Doughnut Lady fed the animals their usual early morning fare of grain, dog food, sugar water, cat food, and, naturally, a box of doughnuts (purchased from the local Market Basket). Then she and her husband went to see a man about a cow.

After moving to Grafton in search of freedom, the couple had carved out a large, landscaped yard with a vegetable patch and apple trees. They bought two cows, which Doughnut Lady named Buttercup and Princess. When Princess died, Buttercup was bereft.

The following day, Doughnut Lady found Buttercup alone, crying.

Buttercup was also crying the next day.

And the next. And the one after that.

As the days passed into weeks, it seemed that Buttercup's grief would never end. Doughnut Lady was distraught.

Nearly a month after Princess died, Doughnut Lady was reading the local newspaper when she came across an article that got her thinking. The article was about a man across the Connecticut River—in Corinth, Vermont—who was having trouble caring for a cow.

The details were sparse, but it appeared that the man, Chris Weathers-bee, had allowed one of his steers to die of starvation. The animal's brother, Monty, was not doing well.

The thought of the starving steer galvanized Doughnut Lady into action. She called Weathersbee, and soon their voices were intermingling on the phone line—hers kindly, his gruff with suspicion.

"I'd like to take your steer," said Doughnut Lady.

Weathersbee did not embrace the idea as quickly as she might have hoped.

"I don't know about you," he said. After the newspaper article, he was being hammered in the court of public opinion and was unsure of where she stood.

Doughnut Lady knew what to say.

"I have a cow that's lonely."

There was a brief silence, as spirits considered the possibility of kindredness.

"I might lease him to you," allowed Weathersbee. They arranged for her to come see Monty, and he hung up the phone. To transport the cow across state lines, Doughnut Lady needed a certificate from a veterinarian, but none would agree to meet her at Weathersbee's farm. When she and her husband headed to his property, they didn't know what to expect.

Weathersbee, then in his sixties, was the British-born son of Mary Lee Settle, an actress–turned–respected historical novelist. She had purchased the property in Corinth; when Weathersbee moved there in 1997, it had just three goats on it.

He began to think of the twenty-nine-acre farm as a goat sanctuary, one that would run in accordance with his Buddhist beliefs. He started taking in stray Nubians and Cashmeres; because he thought it inhumane to isolate, castrate, or slaughter his bleating wards, they were free to breed with one an-other, a freedom of which the goats took full advantage.

Within four years, in 2001, the property was home to 252 goats, and Weathersbee—by then widely known in the community as Goat Man—was devoting most of his days to their care.

By the time Doughnut Lady and her husband pulled into the messy, muddy driveway of the once-proud farmhouse, Weathersbee had been com-pletely overwhelmed by his charges. No one answered their calls of greeting or their knocks on the door.

And so, like a modern-day Goldilocks of a certain age, Doughnut Lady cautiously eased herself inside, onto footing that was strangely, organically, uneven.

They saw no one. Well, no people.

The previous winter, Goat Man had become concerned about the ability of his flock's newborn goats to survive an unusually intense cold snap. So he moved the babies into the house. Ditto their nursing mothers. Ditto the oldest goats. Ditto the sick and the frail. In all, his extended goat slumber party included seventy goats, all allowed to stay inside the house until the cold snap passed.

But, as Doughnut Lady saw, and as other visitors would also eventually describe the scene, when the cold snap passed, Goat Man never evicted them.

Just inside the front door, goats milled aimlessly around the house, into and out of the kitchen, in small circles in the living room, up and down the stairs. Chickens foraged on the kitchen counter. In the living room, a goat stood on a wing chair overlooking a sleeping bag on the floor, where Goat Man reportedly slept while restless goats stepped onto and off of him all night.

Doughnut Lady saw that the uneven footing was from the layers of hay and goat shit that Goat Man had allowed to accumulate on the floor in such thickness that one's head nearly bumped the ceiling. She and her husband backed out of the kitchen and entered the barn, still looking for their mysterious host, whose absence was becoming a bit unsettling.

If the house looked like a horror movie trailer, the barn was the full feature. It was as if some elder Cthulu god had been handed a wooden, barn-sized bowl of sacrificial chevre and cast it down, disgusted at the enormous mass of shit and dead goats mixed in with the living.

When she later described the number of goat corpses she'd seen, Doughnut Lady was characteristically diplomatic.

"He was trying, you know," she said kindly. "He had a problem."

When Goat Man eventually materialized, Doughnut Lady convinced him to surrender Monty to her. She drove the emaciated cow to a veterinarian and then headed home.

It was, perhaps, one of the last truly happy resolutions for an animal on Goat Man's farm. Animal rights activists, neighbors, state officials—none of them had Doughnut Lady's knack for getting Goat Man to part with his wards peacefully. Authorities suggested that, if he didn't care for the animals better, they might be seized.

"I said, 'I will resist you by every means at my disposal,'" Goat Man told *Goat World* magazine. "If the sheriff comes, you'll have to shoot me."

The final straw came a couple of weeks before Christmas of 2004, when someone—possibly an irate neighbor—shot one of the goats in the face and left the body in Goat Man's front yard.

Just days later, Goat Man, who was still facing enforcement actions on animal cruelty charges, loaded up the seats of his small car with as many goats as it would carry and fled. He apparently landed in Ohio and began the whole goaty cycle over, because the following year he fled that state in similar circumstances, leaving the authorities behind him to discover 220 live goats and 80 dead goats.

Police, following a trail of dead goats that spanned four states, finally caught up with Goat Man in West Virginia. When he was arrested, he had sixteen goats in his possession (including one in the freezer). Stripped goatless, he soon disappeared from the public eye.

Without any knowledge of the dark days that awaited Goat Man, Doughnut Lady and her husband drove home, reflecting on a man who had seemed somewhat out of synch with reality.

Anyway, Doughnut Lady was anticipating the happy moment when she could introduce Monty to her bereaved Buttercup. She sure hoped Monty would get along with her bears.

Hmmm.

Her bears.

———

IT'S HARD TO imagine what it would have been like for Monty the cow, that moment when he stepped off the trailer to behold Doughnut Lady's woodland home for the first time. His past had been dominated by the darkness of Goat Man's chaotic, shit-strewn farmstead, where his brother had literally starved to death.

Now he stood on a bright hillside, birdsong washing over a long, sloping pasture where every detail spoke of care, and love, and order. A beautiful house towered over meticulously kept flowerbeds and fruiting apple trees. The tufted meadow was lush and neat, and Doughnut Lady's tone was warm and soothing.

Feeders overflowing with sunflower seeds were aswarm with chirping chickadees and juncos, while deer and wild turkeys regularly ventured out of the woods to nibble at fallen apples or landscaped greens.

Instead of legions of bleating, half-starved goats, Monty's companions would now be a few amiable dogs and cats—and there was the lovely Buttercup, fat with grain and sweet clover, utterly content to chew her cud while shading herself from the summer heat.

One might expect that after being delivered from goat hell into this bovine paradise, Monty would kick up his heels and frolic on the soft grass beneath his hooves. Instead, he lay down, touched his big horns to the ground, and rolled his eyes back in his head.

It was hard to say what ailed him. Had his rough living sickened him to the point where he just couldn't keep steady on his feet? Was it a kind of bovine Stockholm syndrome, making him pine for Goat Man? Or was he, perhaps, distraught that the idyllic surroundings were saturated by a heavy, invisible pall of bear scent?

Doughnut Lady didn't know. But the depths of his despair were clear.

"He wanted to die," she said.

Knowing that the life of a downed cow is always in peril, Doughnut Lady pleaded with him to take to his feet. But Monty wouldn't listen.

So she went and fetched a handcart, then wedged the edge beneath the cow as if he were a refrigerator to be moved. But still, Monty wouldn't listen.

Finally, Doughnut Lady called a friend with livestock experience for help. Could it be bloat, the man asked?

Doughnut Lady didn't know.

When her friend arrived, he approached Monty with a knife in his hand, wondering again whether it was bloat. If it was bloat, he said, he could cut into Monty's side to relieve the gas pressure. Confronted with both cart and knife, Monty finally listened. Making the wise decision (the one that left his hide intact), he rose on unsteady legs.

"He was beautiful," Doughnut Lady said. She didn't even mind that he quarreled with Buttercup to the extent that she had to keep them separated. The important thing was that he would live.

Monty wasn't the only one who felt apprehensive about Doughnut Lady's carefully cultivated property. Dianne Burrington (as the daughter of June Burrington, she had grown up in the schoolhouse that was purchased by the Babiarzes) expressed a similar sentiment.

Burrington was as leery of the property as Monty. The problem was the bears.

In Grafton, some residents work hard to discourage bears from entering their property by getting fierce dogs and putting up electric fences. Burrington, who kept up her mother's sheep farming tradition, used a tractor to bury her dead animals deep in the ground. When the ground froze and she could no longer dig such graves, she drove the carcasses up an old county road to dump them around the back side of a rugged outcropping known as Aaron's Ledge, where the bears were thick as trees.

Burrington told me that, when she drove by Doughnut Lady's home one day, she looked down the sloping pasture to the rear of the house.

"All I could see was brown. I said, 'Jesus!'" Burrington tried, and failed, to count the animals she saw milling around. "I don't know how many bear there was, but there was a lot of bear down there."

The reaction wouldn't have surprised Doughnut Lady. She understood that most people are afraid of bears. She used to be afraid of bears too.

10

FANNING FREEDOM

Socially, Ahab was inaccessible. Though nominally included in the census of Christendom, he was still an alien to it. He lived in the world, as the last of the Grisly Bears lived in settled Missouri. And as when Spring and Summer had departed, that wild Logan of the woods, burying himself in the hollow of a tree, lived out the winter there, sucking his own paws; so, in his inclement, howling old age, Ahab's soul, shut up in the caved trunk of his body, there fed upon the sullen paws of its gloom!

—Herman Melville, *Moby Dick*, 1851

The libertarian assault on Grafton's mores was only loosely coordinated; every day, it seemed, some random Free Towner was pulling on another thread in the fabric of Grafton's traditional way of life and enthusiastically giving it a tug, seeking to warp the weft.

When they encountered resistance from locals, the libertarians chalked it up to ignorance: soon, they said, everyone would realize that life was better when the government left its citizens alone. But their educational efforts were spurned by a stubborn rearguard of civic-minded residents who seemed to feel that the Free Towners themselves were the main obstacle to left-aloneness.

Years later Babiarz acknowledged the disconnect while explaining that libertarians, though logic-heavy, tended to have poor communication skills.

"The libertarian movement is more cerebral, if you will," he said. "They lack the ability to deal with people at the human level."

And indeed, the same psychological study that found libertarians to be more logical than Democrats or Republicans also found that they are less socially connected and loving. "Libertarians have a lower degree of the broad social connection that typifies liberals as well as a lower degree of the tight social connections that typify conservatives," wrote the authors, speculating that natural loners might be attracted to a political ideology that celebrates freedom. So the libertarians were perhaps not the best equipped to carry a message of freedom to the people of Grafton, but they tried. Oh, how they tried.

They began building a culture from the ground up, always seeking to infuse their fervency with a sense of fun—they drove cars with vanity plates like LES GOV; nicknamed themselves "Porcupines" (peaceable animals, but dangerous ones to attack); and they held an annual apple festival where parents cheered as kids dipped homemade United Nations flags into a bonfire. They uploaded videos of themselves confronting town officials and police officers over real or imagined slights. One elderly Graftonite posted the ultimate do-it-yourself dentistry video: while friends laughed raucously, he used a pair of pliers to wrench out one of his teeth (or, put another way, half of his teeth).

Though the libertarians asserted such rights at every turn, it was difficult to say whether, in aggregate, significant progress was being made toward creating America's first Free Town.

At Grafton's annual town meetings, the libertarians floated all sorts of new ideas, hoping to find common ground with longtime residents. They were stymied in their efforts to withdraw Grafton from the regional school district, explicitly condemn *The Communist Manifesto*, and eliminate funding for the Grafton Public Library. They were successful, however, in getting a measure passed to cut 30 percent from the town's $1 million budget, as well as another to deny funding to the county senior citizens' council. They failed to muster enough votes to abolish the town planning board but did manage to stock it with libertarians, who effectively shut it down.

In one notable town meeting skirmish, resident Rich Blair grew upset with the libertarians' formal proposal to declare Grafton a "United Nations Free Zone." Rather than simply voting against the idea, Blair submitted an amendment that replaced "United Nations" everywhere it appeared in the proposal with the name of a certain cartoon character. Thus, residents eventually voted on whether to protect the town citizenry "from taxation without representation, by forbidding the implementation within the town limits of any tax, levy, fee, assessment, surcharge, or any other financial imposition by Sponge Bob Square Pants."

Not all of the Free Towners stuck with the movement—"founding fa-ther" stalwarts like Hull maintained their prominence, but others, like Larry "Zack Bass" Pendarvis, took their slash-and-burn rhetoric elsewhere. Pendar-vis advocated loudly for the rights of women, though he never seemed to get beyond a very narrow zone of empowerment that largely concerned itself with the right to go without bras and underwear and the right to sell sex. After being ousted from the Free Town Project, Pendarvis used eBay to sell a Floridian island that he had acquired under questionable circumstances. He used the proceeds to advocate for a similar liberty enclave in Loving County, Texas (where he was roundly rebuffed). As it became evident that the cloud of self-defeating chaos enveloping Pendarvis was persistent, some libertarians speculated that he was actually a federal agent provocateur working to infil-trate and bring down extremist groups.

Meanwhile, Mike Lorrey's participation in the Free Town Project took a backseat to a new venture—buying and selling real estate in the virtual reality "Second Life," where, he claimed, he parlayed a $200 investment up to $250,000 in annual real-dollar revenues. But when Lorrey clashed with Lin-den Labs, the company that owns the Second Life platform, his account was eventually suspended and all of his "virtual real estate" was seized.

But even as Lorrey and Pendarvis faded into the Free Town's background, new faces emerged to carry the banner of liberty ever forward.

For example, Free Towner Bill Walker, known in internet freedom fo-rums by the user name "topgunner," was driving his Mazda pickup truck down the streets of Manchester early one morning in October 2008 when a policeman pulled him over for a loud muffler. During the stop, the officer discovered that Walker had two loaded pistols and numerous magazines of ammo in his waistband and was also wearing body armor. His passenger, Sharon "Ivy" Ankrom, who owned the truck, was also carrying a firearm (for which she had a permit). The pair offered no public explanation for the firepower and body armor, other than to assert that it was legal under the US Constitution.

Ankrom argued her traffic violations all the way to the state Supreme Court, in part on the legal theory that state requirements for a driver's license unconstitutionally restricted her right to travel. She lost.

Ankrom was not the only Graftonite pushing Free Town ideals in the courtrooms. In 2006, Babiarz sued the town of Grafton for a procedural issue related to libertarian efforts to get elected to the planning board. He lost.

Tom Ploszaj, the firefighter who met a bear while hiking toward the Pinnacle, joined Free Towner Jeremy Olson and a couple of other co-plaintiffs in suing the town of Grafton for obstructing their proposals, among them: that the police chief be ordered not to enforce marijuana laws, that the licensing of dogs be abolished, and that town officials be instructed not to cooperate with the National Security Agency on anything. They lost.

After Babiarz lost his suit against the town, he and Hull sued Grafton County to stop a 2.3 percent wage increase for the high sheriff and three other county employees. They lost. Then they appealed to the New Hampshire Supreme Court. Where they lost. The changes affecting Grafton were not limited to the highly visible public sphere of town meetings and courtrooms. While driving along Grafton back roads one day, I learned that the most dramatic structural changes were hidden behind the forest's endless scrim of dangling leaves.

THE ENCAMPMENT IS invisible from the road, even in the early spring, when the tree limbs are bare and layers of compressed snow dominate the muddy slope of land below. Only when I eased my car up that slope with the help of a rocky, corrugated dirt driveway could I see the hidden world of campers, Airstream trailers, and broken-down recreational vehicles that served as homes for the people—mostly men, all seemingly armed—who lived there. An excavator covered by a bit of snow sat like a forgotten sandbox toy among displaced heaps of muddy earth. At one point, the property owner had planned to build a proper house here, but he reportedly gave that up in favor of building a gun shop (which also never happened).

I was there to meet Ploszaj, who emerged from one of the trailers with a friend of his, a ponytailed folk singer named John Redman. They were scruffy.

"You look at me, I have that bum look," Ploszaj said at one point. "This is the way I dress."

The guy who owned the trailer where they lived was still sleeping, so we talked in my car, Ploszaj in the passenger seat and Redman behind me. As we spoke, I faced the camp, which looked nothing like either a proper house or a gun shop, and tried to imagine what living there would be like. I'd been told that, in addition to the camp, the woods in this region provided cover to modern-day bootleggers, who were growing marijuana and cooking meth with relative temerity, knowing that the citizenry would react negatively to aggressive enforcement by the town's sole full-time police officer. I saw no sign of a drug trade here, and certainly not involving Ploszaj, who was serious and earnest in helping me understand the dynamics of Grafton politics.

Redman, a Burning Man aficionado, mostly tried to keep from getting bored. He kept inserting himself into the conversation with outrageous assertions, at one point slapping a gun clip holding .45 bullets down on my car console, with little preamble or pretense.

"I got a crow story for you," said Redman in a throaty drawl. "The day before yesterday, I saw one flying right past here. Upside down! Having a ball. It was cawing and it was flying upside down. Just for the fun of flying. . . . I've seen hundreds of thousands of birds. I never saw one flying upside down so joyfully before."

Ploszaj and Redman were used to nighttime visits from bears looking for beehives and garbage.

"There were three of them out here, bashing our garbage cans around," said Redman. "I got out my great big restaurant-sized container of cayenne pepper. I use an awful lot of spices when I cook. I got it from the restaurant supply store. Fifteen dollars. Dashed it all around the inside of the dadgum garbage can. And that was it."

Ploszaj, trying to keep it real, corrected him. It wasn't the garbage cans, he said—it was a tub of empty tin cans.

"No, they weren't empty," said Redman.

"The recycled tin cans," said Ploszaj, patiently.

"No," said Redman, exasperated. "That was the *raccoon* doing that. I *shot* the raccoon. But the bears were over there by the excavator, smashing away. . . . It happened three times."

"Then we got the better cans," said Ploszaj.

"And then we deployed the cayenne pepper," said Redman.

Ploszaj faced me, in a vain effort to cut Redman out of the conversation.

"And the better cans," he said.

Redman said that he caught a bear rummaging through the garbage cans recently and took the (to my mind unnecessarily) brave measure of walking toward it and stomping his feet until the bear fled.

"That was our fault," Ploszaj explained. "Because we got lax with the garbage cans."

When the interview was done, I reversed my car back down the muddy driveway and headed out onto the highway, windows wide open (to dissipate that bum smell). I thought about how the camp, steeped as it was in an atmosphere of individuality and transience, contrasted sharply with the more stable, family-oriented homes that dominated the landscape of neighboring towns.

When I asked other Graftonites about the unusual living situation I'd seen, I learned that it was not the only such camp in America's first Free Town. As libertarians across the country pulled up stakes and headed to Grafton, the first pressing need they faced was often housing. Some had the means to purchase homes, but many, lacking such resources, turned to the chain of such camps emerging in the wilderness. They built homes out of yurts and RVs, trailers and tents, geodesic domes and shipping containers. Some chose, like the European colonists who came 225 years before them, to live alone in isolated structures buried in the weald like witches' cottages; others, like Redman and Ploszaj, clustered in lots that functioned as permanent campgrounds, with rotating casts of residents.

The complete lack of zoning regulations, code enforcement, or building codes eliminated any burdens associated with demonstrating that their new homes were habitable and free of fire hazards, and so these ad-hoc solutions functioned as a sort of ultimate free market, where men floated freely between the camps in pursuit of what they valued most at the moment—a heated camper, a solitary yurt, better roommates—cross-pollinating friendships and political ideas along the way.

Of course, all this activity was of intense interest to a certain segment of the town's longtime residents: the bears. From their perspective, a checkerboard of smorgasbords was suddenly springing up in their woodland territories, each camp burgeoning with calories. Through trial and error, the problem-solving bears quickly learned that their new neighbors were loath to call state wildlife authorities to report bear incursions. Each pocket of Free Towners, they deduced, preferred to resolve the problem in their own creative and constitutionally protected way.

And not all of the camps got the better cans.

11

THE PRINCIPLED PASTOR

The morning was bright and propitious. Before their depar-
ture, mass had been said in the chapel, and the protection of
St. Ignatius invoked against all contingent evils, but especially
against bears, which, like the fiery dragons of old, seemed to
cherish unconquerable hostility to the Holy Church.

—Bret Harte, *The Legend of Monte Del Diablo*, 1863

In 2010, John Connell, age fifty, stood in the summer heat outside the
town's greatest historical treasure: the Grafton Center Church. The beams
alone—massive timbers hewn from old-growth American chestnuts that
have all but disappeared from the Grafton-area landscape—were worth a
fortune, but no one would dream of selling them. Over the course of a century, prayerful Graftonites had hallowed the wood—swelling it with baptis-
mal holy water, inundating it with the molten-golden notes of matrimony,
burnishing it with anointing oil, and bowing it down with the somber weight
of a thousand caskets.

If people driving through Grafton on Route 4 notice the town at all, it
is because of this surviving nod to cozy Yankee traditionalism, a structure
whose two-stage belfry tower and gabled roof overlook a graveled parking lot
and a quaint, grassy green.

As Connell watched, a car pulled into the parking lot and one of the
town's selectmen emerged, calling out a friendly greeting. Connell wasn't surprised. Nearly everyone in town was talking about him, it seemed. Because of
what he'd done.

Just weeks earlier, Connell, a libertarian, was one of the countless people impressed by the church's stately presence. But instead of just casually

oohing and aahing, he'd gone that extra mile. John Connell, a factory worker from Massachusetts unknown to almost everyone in town, had purchased the Grafton Center Church.

And now, this selectman was here. Under the veneer of welcoming Connell to the community, he was feeling Connell out about the church's future. They engaged in a bare minimum of small talk before the selectman got to the point.

"What are you going to do when we send you a tax bill?" he asked Connell.

"Hmm," Connell would later say, recounting the conversation. When he speaks, each word is water-stamped with the Boston-area blue-collar accent that imbues the friendliest of phrases with a don't-fuck-with-me undertone.

"Interesting way to treat someone who's trying to save the church building," he recalled, wryly emphasizing the word "interesting," lest anyone mistake his meaning.

But on that day he answered the selectman's question with one of his own.

"You don't tax churches, do you?" Connell asked. "And he looked at me like, *Oh boy, I guess because this guy's a freedom guy, that he's buying it just to avoid taxes.*"

That town leaders had concerns about Connell's intentions contained a great irony in that, had they been a bit more open-pocketed, the historic meeting place would have never been vulnerable to a purchase for a pittance by an outsider.

The reason for its predicament dates back to the unique circumstances of the church's construction in 1796, when Grafton voters—always eager for an avoid-tax-quick scheme—declined to finance the construction of a town meetinghouse. Instead, they agreed to buy a few pews in the planned church, which not only helped the congregation build its church but also gave the town partial ownership of the structure.

For well over a century, the church was shared by taxpayers and tithepayers alike, the parishioners' ongoing litany of litanies alternating with the business of formal town meetings within its hallowed walls. As the center of both religious and civic life in the village, the building became known among the secular as the Center Meetinghouse.

The decades ticked by. Through the years, as the property passed through the hands of different congregations, the precise terms of the town's legal ownership of the building became murky. When the building was in need of repairs, Grafton taxpayers were reminded that they enjoyed using the space much more than they enjoyed paying for the space. In 1856, to resolve questions of responsibility for repair costs and avoid unnecessary commingling of church and state, the town and congregation agreed to split the building into two parts—like a sitcom scene in which disputed room ownership is delineated with a strip of masking tape. But over time even that level of financial responsibility seemed too much for town taxpayers. In 1963, they renounced all claims to ownership of the Grafton Center Church, preferring to describe the relationship as a leasing arrangement.

With the town relegated to mere tenant status, the building fell wholly under the control of a dwindling population of faithful churchgoers. In the years after the Free Town Project was announced, the Grafton Center Congregational Church, which had owned the property for decades, called it quits and moved elsewhere (to the Danbury town line, under a new name).

The church leadership, which no longer needed the building, offered to sell it to the town.

For many, hopping on the chance to buy and control the fate of the property (which Grafton historian Ken Cushing called "the soul of the town") was a no-brainer. But spending tax funds on a suspiciously sentimental concept like protecting "the character" of the town was opposed by a burgeoning population of libertarians. The Free Towners joined ranks with the reluctant taxpayers among Grafton's longtime residents to form a large, vocal majority of those who expressed a position on the church's disposition. In the end, the town rejected the offer.

Remarkably, the church leadership responded to the rejection with an even more generous offer. They asked if the town wanted the property for free.

Even more remarkably, the town said no.

It came down, once again, to money. Because there were no zoning requirements in Grafton, the town had never formally inspected the building, so questions about the maintenance costs remained unanswered. The property could stand for another hundred years, or it might be on the verge of succumbing to fire, flood, or roof collapse. Without spending money on a formal assessment, there was no real way to tell. Rumors that the church was structurally unsound circulated through town, said Deb Clough, the town librarian.

"That led the selectmen to say, 'It's another money pit,'" said Clough.

And so the church put the now-vacant building on the open market.

Just a few weeks later, in an instance of what some might call proof of divine providence and what others might call proof of the chaotic and coincidental nature of the universe (and still others might call the entirely predictable outcome of offering to sell a property with inestimable historic value for dirt cheap), the building caught the eye of John Connell.

Connell was born in Salem, Massachusetts, in 1960. For nearly three decades, beginning when he graduated from high school in 1978, he worked twelve-hour shifts at Stahl Chemical, a leather treatment factory situated between a tavern and an auto body shop in Peabody. In the mid-2000s, there was a reactor fire at the factory. Connell later said that he stayed in the building beyond the point of safety to help get the fire under control.

"I suffered exposure to some very nasty stuff," he would recall. "With numerous strange symptoms, I was very, very, very worried about my health. I was thinking I might die."

For a few years, Connell kept pushing himself to show up for his factory shift, but "he was often tired and kind of sick," reported an online radio station in a feature on Connell, a lifelong music lover. (The station showcased music produced by and for local libertarians as part of the larger effort to build a more freedom-friendly culture.) Connell wasn't interested in curing his ailments through conventional medicine, which he referred to as "the medical-industrial path," and he also declined to sue the company. That wasn't his style.

"I had been paid for my work," he said. "I had taken risks." Connell may have been unsure about his health when he left the factory, but he knew for certain that he wanted to get away from the stultifying grind of Peabody. During visits to the "Live Free or Die" state, he had found fertile ground to express his more artistic and spiritual tendencies, and so he moved into temporary digs in the town of Salem, New Hampshire. After embarking on a path of enlightenment, Connell found that working on his emotional health helped him to cope with his physical health. He forgave those who had harmed him. He began to meditate. He found God (though he would later say that God found him).

After undergoing a spiritual reawakening, he said, "my good health returned. I had not felt better since I was a teenager."

The rejuvenated Connell wasn't sure what came next. He had a unique blend of passions—libertarian politics, the arts, and his Christian faith. He sensed that he was in a position to do something important, but he wasn't sure what.

The picture began to come into focus for him a little more clearly when, during an extended stay with libertarian friends in Grafton, he saw the church's For Sale sign. As he admired the architectural flourishes of its cornices and returns, he was suddenly seized with the idea that he should purchase it. He would later describe it as a voice, a something, speaking to him. *Just do it, dude*, the voice said to him. *Because if you don't, where's the rest of your life? Are you going to look back and say, "Maybe I should have done that"?*

Without involving any lawyers or banks, Connell made a cash offer of $57,500. That represented most of his 401(k), and he had no idea what he was going to do with the building if the sale went through. The voice inside him was reassuring. *Don't be afraid*, it said to him.

But Connell wasn't afraid. Mostly he was feeling calmness and joy.

Connell's offer was accepted. By the time the paperwork had been processed and Connell was approached by the selectman that summer day, he had the rough outlines of his calling in mind.

The former Grafton Center Church, he announced, would remain a church, with regular services taking place behind its handcrafted wooden doors. The property would also serve as a showcase for his artistic and spiritual expression. Though he had no formal training, he, John Connell, would live inside the church as its sexton and pastor. And, he vowed, he would not pay taxes.

No matter what.

━━━

A century before Connell ever laid eyes on the Grafton Center Church, a man named Louis stood in Grafton, shouting from atop the world.

It was 1904. Beneath him sprawled a green and brown patchwork defined by tiny stone walls. Clumps of white fuzzy dots grazed unconcernedly, while toy horses dragged gumdrop-sized wagons between matchbox homes. The forest that had once threatened the settlers was gone; in its place, a pastoral valley hummed with cultivation, industrialization, education, and proselytization.

"I will stand upon my watch and set me upon my tower," Louis thundered, with all the gravitas he could muster.

Louis was more properly known as Louis Banks, and more properly yet known as the Reverend Louis Albert Banks, Doctor of Divinity, a celebrated

Methodist who, at age forty-seven, had already churned through a series of life adventures that included entering college at age eleven, being shot in Seattle while fighting on behalf of the Chinese during the anti-Chinese riots, chastising saloon-keepers and sweatshop owners for their respective roles in oppressing the poor, and running a distant third in the 1893 race for governor of Massachusetts.

When Banks came to Grafton, he found a prosperous community that was reaping the twin benefits of bear extirpation and capitalism. The town appealed to Banks for some of the same reasons that it appealed to Connell—there was room to operate here. Banks made it clear in his many books that he held freedom as a sacred principle. In one dedication, he credited his parents, "who instilled into my mind and heart . . . their own love for liberty and hatred of oppression."

The people of Grafton, equally liberty-loving, had left the dark settlement days behind them. Bear numbers had crashed (they thought forever), while human numbers had exploded. Between 1786 and 1800, Grafton's population doubled from 354 to 682. By 1860, it had nearly doubled again, to 1,259, and there were now 190 working farms of various sizes and agricultural pursuits laid out beneath Banks, many using freight trains on the newly built Northern Rail to ship tons of wool, potatoes, firewood, maple sugar, and dairy products to market at a tidy profit.

During this heyday, Grafton boasted of three post offices, eleven schoolhouses, a creamery, fourteen mines, and fifteen mills churning out processed forms of everything from grain to clothing. (The largest, a sawmill, could produce more than a million feet of lumber per year.) A rich deposit of clay beneath Slab City was used to build a half-dozen thirty-foot-long charcoal kilns, which transformed forest, earth, and clean air into bricks and smog.

When he decided to move to Grafton, Banks could have considered buying any of several attractive properties. Bungtown featured the two-hundred-acre Martin farm (named for wheelwright Nelson Martin and his wife, a noted cheesemaker), which included a beautiful traditional farmhouse, a solid post-and-beam barn, two hundred sugar maples, and a hodgepodge of quaint outbuildings including sheds and a workshop. Bungtown was also where the Kimball family had built the finest barn in town, one so solid and grandiose that it was referred to as the "Great Barn."

Another attractive property was just down the road from the Great Barn and the Martin Farm, at the corner of Grafton Turnpike at Route 4—a bustling general store run by Guy Haskins, who lived above the store when he wasn't selling penny candies, ceiling-hung hams, chocolates, soda crackers, ice cream, grain, and gasoline.

As he eyed the real estate on offer, Banks appreciated the appeal of farmhouses and general stores, but he was after something a bit more epic. After seeing an ad in a newspaper in 1900, he bought a massive two-thousand-acre plot in northwestern Grafton with a magnificent farmhouse, three barns, and one of the town's great natural resources—a granite outcropping known as the Pinnacle (the same spot that would eventually be a hiking destination for Tom Ploszaj).

From the north, the Pinnacle topped a 150-foot sheer cliff, but the south was accessible from a much more gradual ascent, with a winding path wide enough for a four-horse carriage. It is clear that Banks, who sometimes sermonized about the efforts of man to take flight as a means to get physically closer to God, saw the lofty environs as a spiritual boon—but one that could be improved upon.

For a person with a vision, even a daunting one, implementation was often simply a matter of means and ways, and Banks had the means to get his way. He soon convinced a company of men to cart construction equipment up to his recently acquired mountaintop. In early 1902, they erected the scaffolding of a steel tower. It was magnificent—stretching forty feet above the highest point of the Pinnacle, with a runged ladder going up the side. At the top perched a small, round platform built of wood, ten feet in diameter, like a plated offering to God himself.

On July 6, 1902, a large crowd responded to an invitation to witness Banks's inaugural high-flying sermon. A long train of horses and ambulators scaled the southern approach. Every man's Sunday best was topped by a brimmed hat; every woman and child wore crisp whites; a blind woman, Belinda Stevens, sat in a cart that bumped up slowly behind a pair of steady-footed oxen.

When Reverend Banks gripped the iron rungs of the ladder, the eyes of a crowd of five hundred onlookers were riveted on him as he went up, and up, and up. The stakes were (like Banks) quite high. He wanted to retain them as parishioners, and he knew that many of the potential new congregants currently craning their necks had come only for the spectacle. Banks was counting on his rhetorical skills to hold their interest beyond death-defying stunts and keep them coming back for revelations of God's glory.

He had chosen, appropriately, the theme of "the Vision from the Tower" and was quoting verse.

"I . . . will watch to see what he will say unto me, and what I shall answer when I am reproved," he shouted to the sea of upturned faces.

As Banks preached, he must have been ebullient. Never had a sermon been watched with such intensity. Every movement he made, every flutter of the flag announcing a slight gust of wind, drew the crowd deeper into God's word.

After he concluded his sermon, an exhilarated Banks made the long, step-by-step journey back down to the earth below. It's not clear how many hands he pumped and smiles he received before he had his own minor revelation. While watching the man forty feet above them, very few people had been able to hear much of what he had actually said. It was later reported that the acoustics of the peak carried his words to neighboring properties much better than to those who stood at the tower's base.

Though the settler days were long gone, Grafton was clinging to those notions of personal freedom that would, one hundred years later, prove so appealing to a new generation of libertarians. They'd built a town with few taxes and little state involvement, where a man was free to build an epic, towering pulpit that, once scaled, rendered one nearly inaudible.

12

A BATTLE WITH BEARS

I knew his times and his seasons, as he knew mine, that fed
By night in the ripened maizefield and robbed my house of bread.
I knew his strength and cunning, as he knew mine, that crept
At dawn to the crowded goat-pens and plundered while I slept.

—Rudyard Kipling, "The Truce of the Bear," 1898

A frantic bleating woke Dianne Burrington from a dead sleep. The sheep farmer reacted instinctively, throwing back her covers and reaching for iron.

Burrington didn't know if the marauder was man, beast, or supernatural being, but she didn't really care. Even sleepy and barefoot, she was not a shit-taker. She was a shit-kicker.

She grabbed the rifle leaning up against the wall in a corner of the kitchen, just in case. And she grabbed the pistol out of the kitchen drawer too. Just in case.

Then she burst out of her front door, a frumpy bulwark of civilization in a wilding world.

Despite the best efforts of civic-minded people like Burrington, in the decades since Louis Banks preached from the Pinnacle, Grafton had gradually slipped down an entropic slope. In the early days, the hands on the clock of enlightenment busily swept away Grafton's wolves and bears and trees in favor of houses and farms and sheep. But when its capitalistic motor was stilled, that clock began rusting away, a slow fade of civilization punctuated by fire and flood. Between 1935 and 2002, the county lost 92 percent of its farmland, and fields reverted to impenetrable thickets of bramble, then tangles of young trees. Roads once supported by tax dollars became blackberry patches favored by foraging bears. The most heavily farmed region in the state became the most heavily forested. And even as camps have arisen in the woods in the first decades of this century, census data show that a third of Grafton's permanent housing units stand vacant. The wilderness's encroachment is presaged by advance troops of mice building nests in homes and under the hoods of cars. Left unchallenged, the vermin unpave the way for further intrusions by larger animals, water, wind, and vegetation. The state now considers Grafton a single, near-continuous block of bear habitat.

Though they played an unwitting role in making the Free Town possible when they sold a home to the Babiarzes, Burrington's parents spent their whole lives in civic service. For forty years, June Bassett drove Grafton's children to school (at first in an ancient bus owned by the police chief) and balanced municipal accounts as town treasurer; meanwhile, John plowed and maintained as many roads as he could under the title of town road agent (a post that would eventually be held by his son). In 1961, the Bassetts, then in their twenties, spent $7,000 to buy a 450-acre plot of reforested land in Slab City that included a derelict schoolhouse. At the time, the property was covered with scrub trees and overgrowth; only granite steps and cellar holes marked the sites of buildings that had either burned in the fires caused by the charcoal kiln explosion or crumbled into ruin. The Bassetts reclaimed the land for cows and sheep and modernized the schoolhouse with a septic system and other improvements to make it habitable. When Dianne, who grew up in the schoolhouse, got married, she and her husband dug up some cull bricks from the old kiln operation and used them to build a hearth fireplace.

In 1993, after selling the schoolhouse and some of its newly cultivated land to the Babiarzes, Dianne and her mother transferred their energy to their new home—it was built on a high, mountainous pasture overlooking Grafton Center, a tiny sheep-studded island of grass holding the line against an inexorable sylvan tide.

As Burrington hurried down her porch steps, front door banging in her wake, she felt the wide range of uncertainty about what, exactly, had emerged from the dark woods to threaten her sheep. That was the norm in Grafton, where a strange alchemical brew of perception and reality has transformed the surrounding wood into a unique and alien landscape populated by creatures both toothsome and mythic.

In most places, the further back in history one goes, the murkier and more mysterious a forest's denizens become, and indeed, Grafton's earliest European settlers suffocated beneath a dangerously heavy mythos of demons, devils, witches, and vampires. But the new wood has acquired its own modern myths, which have set their hooks deep into the psyche of Grafton's collective mind-set.

One reason is that some weird creatures really do live in the woods there. In 1890, a wealthy and eccentric land speculator named Austin Corbin built a visionary game preserve just twenty miles from Grafton. Corbin Park was surrounded by thirty miles of heavily stockaded fence designed to prevent the escape of imported species, which included bighorn sheep, Russian wild boar, elk, and what became the largest herd of bison in the world.

But with *Jurassic Park*–like flair, the Great New England Hurricane of 1938 breached Corbin Park's stockade fence. Hundreds of animals escaped into the timberland, and some established breeding populations. Even today there are documented reports of wooly, tusked boars that can weigh up to 700 pounds. (For reference, that's twice the size of most full-grown black bears, but only half the size of the region's behemoth moose, which very occasionally trample people to death.) The hurricane's 186-mile-per-hour wind gusts also resculpted the landscape by flattening homes and uprooting trees; in the storm's wake, acres of windsnap and blowdown formed dense, near-impenetrable tangles of dead wood. Six years later, in 1944, New Hampshire's first coyote was documented in Grafton County. They are much bigger and hardier than coyotes in other parts of the country—genetic tests have revealed that they are actually 30 percent wolf—and they sometimes form packs to skulk after dog-walkers along Grafton's forest paths.

Amid all these potential threats, Burrington defends her pastureland with her guns, her booming voice, and a high-voltage electric fence running all around the perimeter. The bears sometimes pace the fence, looking for a weakness, while the coy-wolves prefer to lie in wait, hoping an unwary sheep will stray close enough for the burly canids to set their teeth and rip a steaming piece of mutton through to the other side. Burrington has shot and killed these hybrids in the past, but there is no hunting them to extinction because they respond to low population densities by having more frequent, and larger, litters to fill the void. It seemed that no amount of hunting would stop the town's emerging ferality, and the Free Town era had only accelerated the pace of change.

In addition to the formidable creatures for which there is ample scientific evidence, undocumented megafauna, several people in Grafton believe, roam the woods. A man told me that more than once he'd seen dragonflies as big as hawks. In this area known by cryptozoologists as a Bigfoot environ (and one only fifty miles from the most famous UFO abduction account in American history, reported by Betty and Barney Hill in 1961), another man said he'd seen footprints of a bird with feet much larger than a human hand. Many in Grafton swear to the presence of mountain lions, a species whose existence is not formally recognized in the state.

So there was really no telling what Burrington would encounter when she ran out onto the wet ground, "half-assed dressed," the hem of her night-gown flapping between a coat she'd grabbed and her bare feet.

The porch of the house leads directly onto the tufted pasture, which is swept with a high, howling wind that rarely stills. Burrington sprinted up the rise and toward the far side of the barn, where an odd, honking bray cut through the bleating.

What the hell is he doing? she thought to herself.

She recognized the honking as coming from her llama, Hurricane. When he was stressed about a potential danger, the llama tended to respond with a soulful hum. He resorted to this braying sound, a penetrating cry full of aggression and fury, only during a crisis.

As Burrington rounded the corner, the faint light of the dawning sun revealed what looked like a slaughter in progress. A bear, perhaps emboldened by successful raids on Grafton's nearby human camps, had slipped between Burrington's electric fence wires like a pro wrestler entering the ring. Lured by the smell of mutton-on-the-hoof, it paid the electric sting no more mind than it would give a bee protecting a honeypot, and now it was trying to latch onto an individual among the general commotion of darting sheep.

Burrington charged into the yard. Most of the sheep had stampeded into the shelter of the barn, but some combination of sheep and bear had rammed into the fence with such force that it had been ripped off the post, severing it from the power source. A ewe, panicked and struggling, was completely tangled up in the netting.

Christ, Burrington thought. *Now she's going to get strangled.*

She turned her back to the bear, trying to juggle the pair of firearms while pulling scissors from her coat pocket. Two expert snips freed the ewe, which looked miraculously uninjured.

Burrington rose and faced the bear, a rifle in one hand, a pistol in the other, her eyes filled with the hard glint of a farmer who hadn't had her coffee yet. But the bear, its plans for a quick and quiet lamb-napping long since dashed, was already fleeing toward the cover of the dark forest. As it turns out, Hurricane the llama wasn't finished yet. Raised among sheep, Hurricane was a sheep lover. His best friends were sheep. The llama thought that he himself was a five-foot-nine, four-hundred-pound monster of a sheep. And because he was the biggest, toughest animal on the ranch, he played deputy to Burrington's sheriff. For years he had patrolled the fence line, scanned the woods for danger, waited with the little ones out in the rain, and moonlighted evening stragglers, walking tight to make sure they got into the barn at night.

When the bear fled, Hurricane flashed past Burrington and out onto the pasture.

"Hurricane!" Burrington bellowed. "No!"

But Hurricane, gone full-blown vigilante, was now a streak of light chasing a streak of darkness down the slope, long neck stretched out before him like a galloping camel.

Stupid llama, thought Burrington, and she started running herself, a pathetically distant third in the race. Looking ahead at the path the bear was cutting, she suddenly realized that there was another crisis looming.

What's he going to do when he gets to the fence?

The fine fence she built to keep bears out was about to keep one in. Hurricane was now so close to the bear, actually nipping at its rounded ass, that the bear, once it reached the barrier, would have little option but to turn and defend itself by killing the llama.

With two firearms in her hands, Burrington wished fervently for a third.

I probably should have brought something bigger with me, a cannon or something, she thought. *Now do I go back to the house and get the thirty aught six, or do I stay here?* She couldn't get a clean shot off anyhow, so she kept running, cocking her pistol in case the bear finished with Hurricane and then came for her.

The bear, apparently having forgotten about the fence, barreled into the six high-tension wires at a full sprint and caromed off at an angle, spinning sideways, the llama still right behind.

Now out of options, the desperate bear turned and launched itself at Hurricane with deadly intent. The fight was an absolute bloodbath, so brief that Burrington could only watch, helplessly.

"That's when," she would later say, "I got to see everything I had read about llamas."

Hurricane exploded at the bear, a spinning, category 5 blur of lashing hooves and biting teeth. The llama's blows mostly landed on the bear's throat, chest, and head. Meanwhile, the bear snarled and snapped ineffectively, seemingly unable to lay a claw on Hurricane.

Bruised and bleeding, the bear mustered a last bit of strength, if not dignity. It pushed through a gap in the fence and into the willows, headed toward a huge bog with thick brush where it was unlikely to be pursued. Hurricane, nearly unscathed, paced the fence line, snorting and braying and stomping his feet.

Burrington went back inside to find her boots.

BOOK TWO

RUGGED GROWTH

Grass-blades push up between the cobblestones
And catch the sun on their flat sides
Shooting it back,
Gold and emerald,
Into the eyes of passers-by.

And over the cobblestones,
Square-footed and heavy,
Dances the trained bear.
The cobbles cut his feet,
And he has a ring in his nose
Which hurts him;
But still he dances,
For the keeper pricks him with a sharp stick,
Under his fur.

Now the crowd gapes and chuckles,
And boys and young women shuffle their feet in time to the
    dancing bear.
They see him wobbling
Against a dust of emerald and gold,
And they are greatly delighted.

The legs of the bear shake with fatigue
And his back aches,
And the shining grass-blades dazzle and confuse him.
But still he dances,
Because of the little, pointed stick.

—Amy Lowell, "The Travelling Bear," 1915

1
UNLOCKING UTOPIA

He wished to know whether it were possible that a constant outward application of bears'-grease by the young gentlemen about town had imperceptibly infused into those unhappy persons something of the nature and quality of the bear. He shuddered as he threw out the remark; but if this theory, on inquiry, should prove to be well founded, it would at once explain a great deal of unpleasant eccentricity of behaviour, which, without some such discovery, was wholly unaccountable.

—Charles Dickens, "Full Report of the Second Meeting of the Mudfog Association for the Advancement of Everything," 1837

The ultimate goal of the Free Towners is described in Ayn Rand's novel *Atlas Shrugged*, in which a hidden valley of industrialists form Galt's Gulch, a rogue society ruled by a pure free market. Their capitalist utopia stands in stark contrast to mainstream America, where parasitic governmental interference causes interdependent businesses—railroad lines, copper mines, and steel mills—to fail for want of basic materials, dragging those outside the valley toward a lawless dark age.

For Grafton's Free Towners, Rand's vision of a market-driven society was what kept them privatizing and deregulating everything they could. For seven long years, they joined thrift-minded allies in issuing vociferous challenges to every rule and tax dollar in sight; one by one, expenditures were flayed from the municipal budget, bits of services peeled away like so much flesh.

They permanently extinguished most of the town's streetlights to save on electricity bills and discontinued long stretches of dirt road to save on highway materials and equipment. The town rejected funding for frills like community Christmas lights and Fourth of July fireworks. And though the planning board survived, Free Towners and other like-minded residents gutted its $2,000 budget, first cutting it to $500, then to a token $50. Contrary to the libertarians' expectations, however, real life in the Free Town seemed to be almost the reverse of Rand's fictional vision—by 2011, while the rest of America was chugging along unperturbed, the holes in Grafton's public services gaped stubbornly, creating a spreading malaise.

Despite several promising efforts, a robust Randian private sector failed to emerge to replace public services. A theoretical private fire department run by Bob Hull never seemed to actually stop fires. A freedom-themed farmers' market sputtered along for a while, then faded. A proposed public-service militia never got off the ground.

Meanwhile, the constant bloodletting was turning the once-vibrant town government into a symbol of societal decay. On the town's few miles of paved roads, untended blacktop cracks first blossomed into fissures, then bloomed into grassy potholes. After voters rejected a funding request for $40,000 to purchase asphalt and other supplies, embattled town officials warned that Grafton was in serious danger of losing the roads altogether. The town was also put on notice by the state that two small bridges were in danger of collapse, due to neglect.

Grafton's municipal offices declined from a state of mere shabbiness to downright decrepitude. As the town clerk and a few other staffers processed paperwork and fielded citizen complaints, they stood beneath exposed electrical wires hanging from the ceiling like copper-headed mistletoe. With no money to replace the hot water system when it failed, staff were forced to wash their hands in icy water. And when the building's envelope was breached, nature took full advantage: rainwater poured through major roof leaks and seeped into the side walls, while a biological torrent of ants and termites entered a thousand unseen cracks, crawling over walls, floors, ceilings, desks and, if they did not move frequently enough, people. Tracey Colburn, the town's administrative assistant (seemingly one of the few people in town who did not own a firearm and who did not care for politics), resigned.

As libertarians continued to worry away services, what emerged from the fray was not an idealized culture of personal responsibility, but a ragged assortment of those ad-hoc camps in the woods, some of which began to generate complaints about seeping sewage and other unsanitary living conditions. Other indicators also seemed to be moving in the wrong direction. Recycling rates dropped from 60 percent to 40 percent. The number of annual sex offender registrations reported by police increased steadily, from eight in 2006 to twenty-two in 2010—one in sixty residents. In 2006, Chief Kenyon joined state authorities in arresting three Grafton men connected with a meth production lab in the town, and in 2011, Grafton was home to its first murder in living memory. After a man was accused of being a "freeloader" by two roommates in a temporary shared living situation, he killed them both, using a 9 millimeter handgun and a .45 to shoot one of them sixteen times. In 2013, police shot and killed another Grafton man in the wake of an armed robbery. In all, the number of police calls went up by more than two hundred per year.

In many small New England communities, the growing sense of lawlessness might have triggered an increased police presence, but Grafton's police department was suffering the same fiscal anemia that was affecting everything else. Because of funding constraints, the department's lone twelve-year-old cruiser was frequently in the shop for repairs; as the police chief (whose request for a salary increase was defeated by voters in 2010) noted in his annual report, the need for repairs "created a lot of down time throughout the year."

All of these public services—roads, bridges, town offices, lighting, police mobility, and more—were sacrificed as casualties in the all-important battle to keep property taxes low.

So how low are Grafton's taxes?

Municipal property tax rates in New Hampshire (which, remember, has no state income tax or sales tax) vary wildly. For example, the city of Claremont, a former mill town, had a 2010 rate of $11.94 per $1,000 of home value, among the highest in the state, and it spends that money on a robust offering of parks, infrastructure, economic planning, and public safety resources for its residents.

Like Claremont, Grafton is legally required by the state to provide emergency services, road plowing and upkeep, environmentally responsible waste disposal, insurance and legal services, the licensing of dogs, the maintenance of bridges, the keeping of publicly accessible town records, and other services deemed essential.

Small, rural towns tend to carry out these mandates on a shoestring budget, but some towns' shoestrings are more frayed than others. For example, Grafton and its northern neighbor, Canaan, have similar household income stats but meet their obligations very differently. While almost all public officials in Canaan would describe themselves as fiscally conservative, Grafton has shown a savantlike talent for weaseling out of public costs.

It's always been that way. Even in the late 1700s, when Grafton and Canaan were neighboring settlements with just a few hundred residents each, Canaan spent public dollars to feed its militia members during military training exercises, while Grafton voted against doing the same. Back then, those sorts of decisions kept Grafton's tax rate at two pounds per thousand pounds of valuation (British currency), while Canaan residents were taxed more heavily, at two pounds, three shillings.

Both communities taxed residents with the same fiscal goal in mind of growing their populations. If a community attracts and retains people, it spreads the tax burden over more taxpayers and creates a virtuous cycle of economic growth and prosperity, but the difference between the two towns was that, where Canaan tried to attract people by emphasizing tax-funded services, Grafton emphasized lower taxes.

Inherently statist, the Canaan approach is based on the idea that elected officials are better qualified to spend taxpayer money than the taxpayers themselves. The Grafton approach, on the other hand, is individualistic: people with the freedom to spend their own money make better, more rational decisions than the government.

For two hundred years, the towns carried these differences through the quick boom and then the slow decline of the New England agricultural economy. During the boom years and up through the Civil War, both Grafton and Canaan were buoyed by the capitalistic forces that prevailed in an age of prosperity, with Grafton's population swelling to 1,259 in 1850 and Canaan's going a bit higher, to 1,682.

Following the American Civil War, New England's agricultural economy migrated west, and both communities lost population. Canaan responded by investing in its future, building the sort of public infrastructure it believed would appeal to new residents.

Grafton took a different approach. In 1881, when good times created a surplus in the town treasury, they voted at a town meeting to give everyone a tax-free year. And in 1909, not long after it first declined to fund a fire department, Grafton stymied a plan to build a $150 police station, leaving a chain of police chiefs no choice but to work, conduct interviews, and store criminal records in their own homes for the next eighty-two years.

Grafton's population in 2010 was 1,340, just a hair more than in 1850. But over that same time period Canaan's population ballooned to 3,909, despite its higher taxes.

It was possible to think that Canaan had the better tax plan. But maybe, as the Free Towners likely believed, it was exactly the opposite: maybe Grafton's taxes were still too high. So Grafton doubled down on its anti-tax war. In 2001, the municipal budget included $520,000 in local tax money (a figure that doesn't account for other revenue sources, like state grants). By 2011, the municipal budget contained just $491,000 in taxes. Factoring in inflation, the town had reduced its buying power by 25 percent, even though the population increased by 18 percent over the same time period. Not every service was being cut. Indeed, certain expense categories were expanding. Before the Free Town Project began, the town's legal expenses were usually less than $1,000 per year—they totaled $275 in 2004. But after the Free Town Project began, a more litigious mind-set emerged in Grafton and the town's legal bills began to mount, reaching $9,400 in 2011.

Grafton is also legally required to provide public assistance to income-qualified residents who apply. Before the beginning of the Free Town Project, providing public assistance tended to cost the town less than $10,000. But by 2010 that expense had more than quadrupled, to more than $40,000.

Grafton and Canaan have drifted so far apart that no one would guess they started as virtually identical settlements. After 150 years of community building, Canaan had an elementary school, churches, restaurants, banks, a gift shop, two bakeries, pet boarding facilities, a metalsmithing shop, meeting halls, convenience stores, farms, an arts community, a veterinary clinic, and dozens of small businesses, each of which added something to the town's identity and sense of community.

Grafton, by contrast, had a single, struggling general store, one tourist attraction in the Ruggles Mine, a suite of chronically underfunded municipal services, and a church celebrating the singular ideas of John Connell.

But Grafton had low taxes. Or, to be more accurate, taxes that were low in theory. I assumed that, after all those years of resistance, Grafton's tax rate would be a fraction of Canaan's, but I learned that the difference is actually quite modest. Because it has managed to maintain larger populations over the decades, Canaan can spend much more on public goods, while keeping tax rates in check. In 2010, the tax rate in Grafton was $4.49 per $1,000 of valuation, as compared to $6.20 in Canaan. That means the owner of a $150,000 home would get an annual municipal tax bill of $673.50 in Grafton, and $930 in Canaan.

In other words, Grafton taxpayers have traded away all of the advantages enjoyed by Canaan residents to keep about 70 cents a day in their pockets.

Did Canaan's relative success really say something about taxes, or was that a coincidence? After all, high taxes can drive people out of a community, which is why many regularly vote against tax-hiking public frills like libraries, street lighting, well-maintained roads, swimming pools, tennis courts, agricultural fairs, museums, playgrounds, and gardens.

In 2019, a group of Baylor University researchers decided to check in on people who favored low taxes over these sorts of "frills." They looked at thirty years of data on public spending on optional public services and compared them to self-reported levels of happiness. Their findings suggest that Canaan's success is no fluke, but in fact an entirely predictable outcome: states with well-funded public services have happier residents than those that don't. This happiness gap held up among all sectors of society—rich and poor, well-educated and poorly educated, married and single, old and young, healthy and sick.

The researchers said that the data bore out the commonsense observation that, "when states invest in public goods . . . they often can have the effect of bringing people together in a common space and enhancing the likelihood of social interaction and engagement." Over time, they wrote, "these subtle interactions can help to strengthen social ties among citizens and, in doing so, promote greater well-being."

But there is one caveat. Public spending is *associated* with happiness, but it might not actually *cause* happiness, said the study authors. It's also plausible that happy people of all income levels are simply more willing to spend tax money.

If that's true, it would suggest that Grafton's miserly approach to public spending didn't necessarily cause unhappiness among its residents. Rather, the low tax rate may have been a predictable outcome for a town that had, over the years, become a haven for miserable people.

2
A HISTORY OF HEAT

The Great Sun Buddha in this corner of the Infinite Void gave
a Discourse to all the assembled elements and energies. . . .

"In some future time, there will be a continent called
America. . . . The human race in that era will get into troubles
all over its head, and practically wreck everything in spite of its
own strong intelligent Buddha-nature.

". . . In that future American Era I shall enter a new form;
to cure the world of loveless knowledge that seeks with blind
hunger: and mindless rage eating food that will not fill it."

And he showed himself in his true form of SMOKEY THE
BEAR.

—Gary Snyder, "Smokey the Bear Sutra," 1969

As the Free Town movement gained strength, so too did the enduring belief that too much tax money was going to the fire department. When
fires are spread out over miles and decades, they do seem like only mildly dis-
tressing rarities. But the individual's perspective masks the devastating consequences of fires, not only for direct victims, but for the community as a whole.

Take, for example, the night in 1938 when Mary and Bill Watson were
snuggling in a pocket of warmth, sound asleep and defying the cold winter
air that frosted the panes of their bedroom windows. All across Grafton, the
same minor miracle of warmth was happening, home by home by home, the
bright energy of humanity contriving comfort in the midst of bitter winds
and snow. The Watsons were about to learn, in the worst possible way, what
it meant to live in a community without adequate municipal services.

Their house was part of a modest complex of connected buildings that
included a barn and an auto repair garage. They purchased it in 1927, when

they moved to Grafton from Massachusetts with their children to make a new start.

The garage proved a wise investment. By now, even the most ardent horse-and-buggy enthusiasts had grudgingly admitted that the internal combustion engine was not a fad, and garages were mushrooming up everywhere to take advantage of the virtual explosion of cars on roadways.

American optimism was muted in Grafton, which had dealt in its own strange way with financially backbreaking taxes and anatomically backbreaking bears; still, the Watsons prospered, servicing the cars of farmers and teachers, mill workers and tourists, hoteliers and railroad workers and shopkeepers.

At about 2:00 a.m. on that winter night, something other than the cold reached deep into the Watsons' REM sleep, slowly dragging their consciousnesses up through increasingly shallow layers of haze. It was a smell. Black and sour. One of them came awake and realized what was happening.

The back of the barn was on fire.

The Watsons were incredibly lucky to catch the fire in its early stages. They had time to rouse their children out of bed and raise an alarm before the flames spread to the garage and the house.

It would only have taken a few minutes for a fire truck to drive from the center of Grafton to the Watsons' garage, but that was of little value to the Watsons, in part because, in 1938, Grafton had no fire truck, and also, and mostly, because Grafton had no fire department.

This was not simply a sign of the times. By 1938, the fire department in Hampton, New Hampshire, had been operating for more than a century. Canaan equipped its first firefighting squad with hooks, ladders, and hoses in 1890; Enfield, Grafton's western neighbor, followed suit in 1892.

But Grafton voters had refused to spend the money on firefighting, leaving other communities to literally carry Grafton's water.

As the Watsons fretted, a truck from Canaan's volunteer fire department sped down Route 4 to arrive, mercifully, before the fire could spread to the house. Meanwhile, the Watsons' neighbors were, in their best neighborly manner, carrying furniture and other valuables out of the house and into the field, should the worst happen.

Canaan's firefighters had to contend with not only the distance but also Grafton's infrastructural shortcomings, which included a total lack of fire hydrants. (This deficit was addressed by the federally funded Civilian Conservation Corps, which built a series of strategically located firefighting retention ponds, but Grafton neglected their maintenance until natural sediments filled them in, rendering them worthless.) The Canaan firefighters used their equipment to chop a hole in the ice of the Smith River, which ran along Route 4. Then they tapped the water beneath with their sole pump.

With the garage and house as yet unscorched, the Watsons watched while Canaan's crew knocked the flames back in the barn. But just when the blaze appeared to be under control, the pump got stuck in the mud, interrupting the flow of water.

As the firefighters worked desperately to unstick the pump, the fire rekindled itself. The Watsons could only pace as a reinvigorated inferno consumed the rest of the barn, then the garage, and then, heartbreakingly, their home. By morning, the business and homestead were reduced to a lone chimney, a pile of blackened stone sticking out against the desolate snow-covered landscape.

"A gruesome sight," wrote a Watson descendant, adding that, by the morning's light, they could also see for the first time that someone, in a decidedly non-neighborly manner, had stolen many of their salvaged household possessions from the field.

It was a bad year for both neighborliness and fires. The burning of the Watson buildings was part of a rash of seven unexplained conflagrations that year, sparking rumors that there were, in addition to thieves, arsonists among the more upright citizens.

More so than in cities that sprawl over cement plateaus, towns like Grafton and the forces of nature are in constant tension. On one side, men and women build fences, dig water trenches, and chop grass and trees, leveling their environment to create stability and space. On the other side, nature nibbles away at the edges, slowly but relentlessly rotting wood and cracking foundations with a variety of agents. In Grafton, agents included the sediment that reclaimed the retention ponds, the interloping bears that tore down chicken coops, and, most destructive of all, the fires that incinerated everything in their path.

Unchecked structure fires were vaporizing piece after piece of Grafton's social fabric, helping push the town away from the enlightenment preached by Banks from his Pinnacle and toward a new age of barbarism.

One of Slab City's massive charcoal kilns exploded on a Monday morning in 1888; the resulting blaze destroyed several homes and the local charcoal industry, forever. A few years later, Grafton's biggest sawmill, capable of making one million board feet of lumber per year, burned down to its stone foundation. A 1904 brush fire consumed the Reverend Louis Albert Banks's house and three barns. (Banks survived the fire and intermittently continued to deliver semi-audible sermons from the Pinnacle.) Two years later, on a Sunday morning in spring, a defective chimney caused the Grafton Center train station, along with several homes (though not, thankfully, the Grafton Center Church), to burn to the ground.

In 1918, Lucy Rollins, a thirty-one-year-old mother of eight, accidentally threw a can of gasoline on the woodstove, setting ablaze the house, the barn, a nearby mill, her nightgown, and, tragically, herself. She lingered in pain for a couple of days before dying.

There would be other casualties too—a building that housed the mill workers of the town's largest employer, the United Mica Mine Company, burned; so did the barn of Captain Hoyt's descendant, Augustus Hoyt. A schoolhouse was permanently shuttered after being set on fire by an arsonist. The Kimball family's Great Barn in Bungtown burned down, as did Bungtown's general store in a blaze that melted the penny candies and ice cream and roasted all those lovely ceiling-hung hams to a level of doneness that wouldn't have tempted even the least discriminating bear.

And on, and on, and on.

In 1939, just months after the Watsons lost their home and garage, Grafton's selectboard finally—finally!—decided to take action. During a town meeting, the selectmen asked voters to approve five installment payments of $400 per year (roughly $4,200 in 2019 dollars) to finance a fire truck, fire pump, hose, and accessories.

Voters said no.

Six months later, at about 10:00 p.m. on an August night, Bungtown suffered another loss. A short circuit in a hay-loaded truck parked in the barn of Martin Farm reduced every stick of lumber on the property to ash. (It's possible that, had the Watson garage still been standing, routine truck maintenance would have averted this catastrophe.)

For ten more years, voters fiddled while homes burned.

Though Grafton had nothing in place to address structure fires, the state supported a fire warden program that tried to prevent forest fires by issuing burn permits and educating the public about safe storage of flammable materials.

In 1942, a few years after the Watson garage fire, a man named Les Seamans added the title of deputy fire warden to the list of odd jobs—hunter, trapper, potato digger, woodcutter, tanner, mill worker, fence-builder, and setter-upper of bowling alley pins—with which he supported himself and his family. Seamans had a stake in the town's future. He was raising three young children with his wife Marion, who served as a school board representative, town librarian, and postmaster. His brother was the police chief. These were the people who were trying to keep Grafton glued together.

As a fire deputy, Seamans could see the impact that fire was having, not just on unlucky families like the Watsons but on Grafton itself. Between 1943 and 1948 alone, fires were reported at the homes of Julia Custeau, Olif Harris, the Tuttle family, Frank Dean, Philip Paight, the Gray family, Weston Rollins, the Sulloway family, Laura Sweet, the Tyrrell family, the Sulloway family (again), George Barney, Lester Barney (it was a particularly bad year for the Barneys), and in the chimney of the house of train railman C. B. Lovering—and that's not counting forest fires, such as the one that raged at Banks's Pinnacle, or another along the Boston and Maine Railroad.

With the wind of capitalism flagging, the burned properties were not always being rebuilt. Between 1940 and 1950, roughly 20 percent of Grafton's homes disappeared, many lost to fire. Wherever homes were abandoned, nature crept in. On thousands of acres of untended farm pastures, trees sprung toward the sky, eventually shading the land in a semipermanent, bear-friendly gloom.

But when Seamans began advocating for a fire department, he ran up against a 170-year tradition of tax resistance from those who would rather see their neighbors' homes literally go up in smoke than vote for a tax hike. Seamans and a core group of supporters participated in an intense round of horse-trading that finally, in 1949, yielded a deal. The town would spend $1,200 in tax money to buy a pump and some other pieces of firefighting equipment—but little else. Seamans and the others would have to fight the fires for free, buy their own fire truck, build their own fire station, and donate the land to site it on.

Seamans and the volunteers eventually did all this, raising money through charity suppers and talent shows. They built a ramshackle fire station, bought a secondhand Ford truck, and stuck a five-hundred-gallon water tank on it.

Though its entire seventy-year history has been plagued by a lack of funds, the Grafton Volunteer Fire Department was able to slow the pace of the fires, and of the town's declining population. Around 1970, amid the ashes of the old community, a new Grafton began to slowly emerge. What had once been a town of clustered villages and sweeping pastures now featured cloistered homes tucked into the woods. This new Grafton offered lots of privacy, and low taxes.

In the early 1990s (another bad year for members of the Barney family, who lost a farmhouse and attached horse barn to fire), voters rejected, for three consecutive years, proposals to pay for a modern fire station before finally approving $25,000 in 1993. As part of that deal, the volunteer emergency responders were required to "donate" $15,000 to the project. The station was the last major capital program approved by town voters, and it would become the place where things happen in Grafton—not only for emergency responders, but for the entire town, which uses it as an official meeting space.

Though it now operated from a reasonably modern building, Grafton's fire department never received funding on par with neighboring towns. In 2019, Enfield spent $220,000 on its fire department and ambulance services. Canaan spent $261,000. Grafton spent $29,000. But the volunteerism that once allowed Grafton to fight fires on the cheap has been waning. These days, when a fire truck first arrives at a fire scene, it is often empty of firefighters, save for its single volunteer driver.

The driver is also the new fire chief—who, after recruiting some libertarian firefighter volunteers to the department, had earned the post on an 8–2 vote in 2007.

His name is John Babiarz.

After a lifetime of pushing against statist taxes and regulations, Babiarz was now responsible for keeping Grafton's people and property safe from fire. He took the role seriously, working to build and modernize the department.

Babiarz doesn't support some safety regulations—like, say, seat belt laws—but he sees fire safety differently, because reckless fire practices threaten innocent victims. And as Grafton's fire-laden history has shown, an out-of-control blaze can be devastating to life and property.

Almost every firefighter is keenly aware of the tragedy of death by fire, and Babiarz is particularly attuned to its dangers: fire was sometimes wielded as a weapon by the authoritarian governments that oppressed his parents. Before they escaped to America, his father ran afoul of Soviet Communists, who would be accused of burning enemies of the state alive; his mother survived a work camp run by the Nazis, who burned to death an unknown number of Jewish people in their genocidal campaign.

"I think being burned," Babiarz said, "is one of the most horrible ways to die."

3
THE PASTOR PURPLIFIES

This very bell sent forth its first-born accents from the tower
of a log-built chapel, westward of Lake Champlain, and near
the mighty stream of the St. Lawrence. It was called Our Lady's Chapel of the Forest. The peal went forth as if to redeem
and consecrate the heathen wilderness. The wolf growled at
the sound, as he prowled stealthily through the underbrush;
the grim bear turned his back, and stalked sullenly away; the
startled doe leaped up, and led her fawn into a deeper solitude.

—Nathaniel Hawthorne, A Bell's Biography, 1837

After decades of factory toil, John Connell found that, in the Grafton
Center Church he'd purchased, he could finally live free.

Though he no longer had to punch a time card, he wanted to make the
most of his time. And so the newly declared pastor, sexton, and resident of
the newly formed Peaceful Assembly Church rolled up his sleeves, spent some
of his dwindling cash reserves on a healthy amount of paint and other sup-
plies, and got to work.

In a way, that work mirrored the 1904 labors of the Reverend Louis
Banks, who, in a bid to be closer to God, had topped Grafton's Pinnacle with
a bold reimagining of the pulpit. Though Connell was not as well resourced
as Banks had been, he followed suit by boldly reimagining the church exterior, displaying a sense of flair that slackened the jaws of the area's traditional
churchgoers.

"All I could imagine," a white-sweatered woman would later recall during
a public meeting, "was God looking down and saying, 'You've dressed my
church as a whore.'"

She was referring, in part, to the basketball court–sized rectangle of purple Connell painted on the blacktopped ground alongside the church, centered around a cartoonish white dove staring back up at the heavens.

Purple was Connell's signature color. A rich royal hue soon appeared in blotches on the church's quaint white picket fence; it coated the door frames and most (though not all) of the church's thirty window frames. Connell also purpled the church corners, the trim of the overhangs, and the architectural tiers that supported the beautiful old steeple.

Though purple was his favorite, Connell liked other colors too. The white dove in the purple patch was soon joined by a bright red heart rimmed in yellow on a bold green background. A kaleidoscope of ever-changing chalk art further enlivened the view from Route 4, as did the picket fence, which (in addition to the purple) also hinted at Connell's softer side with Easter-pastel tones of pink, yellow, and blue.

Connell followed up by populating the churchyard with a hodgepodge of sculptures made from found materials. A thick-framed mirror and a thigh-high metal lion sat on a small stack of wooden pallets beneath a pyramid of hollow aluminum poles; wooden obelisks painted white memorialized those who had died at the hands of "government abuse"; slabs of rocks and concrete were piled and decorated with sacred Zen Buddhist enso symbols; there were assorted wind chimes, a man-sized crucifix, a repurposed traffic sign, a dozen banner-bearing flagpoles of varied height, and homemade benches where one could sit and contemplate the cacophonous glory all around.

The overall effect was that the once-stately property now looked as if someone had sourced the inventory for a yard sale by throwing random roadside attractions into a blender—a little of Illinois's green Gemini Giant here, a bit of the Blue Whale of Catoosa, Oklahoma, there, all topped off with a healthy dash of the graffitied cars that make up the Cadillac Ranch in Amarillo, Texas.

Surrounded by the Free Town's forested mountains, breathing its clean air, and living with few restrictions on his daily activities, Connell's exuberant personality really shone. He wanted to advance the cause of freedom in a new way, one that might succeed where more traditional political agitating had failed.

"If we could win on intellectual arguments alone, we would have won a long time ago," he'd once told a group of libertarians. "We need to reach people's hearts."

And so Connell cast himself as a happy warrior, a peaceful rebel who came to Grafton to teach others about the synergy of freedom and devotional enlightenment. He preached spirituality to those inside the libertarian movement, and politics to those outside it.

On Sundays, Connell held lightly attended church services inside the building, where the ancient wooden pews—which once provided the view to thousands of flower-festooned funerals, weddings, and harvest suppers—were now complemented by a hodgepodge of mismatched couches and chairs lining the walls. Untrained as a preacher but animated by a preacher's enthusiasm for evangelism, Connell held forth on a variety of subjects around town. For example, people who carted their garbage to the town transfer station might find "Brother John" holding a sign and advising them as to the disadvantages of proposed changes to the jury system.

Some people felt harangued by Connell, or even intimidated. On the spectrum of human communication, his personal speaking style often hovered within the narrow range between somewhat shouty and very shouty. But in the state's libertarian community, he was a well-loved fixture.

"He was passionate about—sometimes I think too passionate about—his spirituality," said John Babiarz. "You think he's angry at you, but it isn't— that's just the way his voice worked. He would seem mad, but he really wasn't. He had issues to overcome, but he was a kind soul."

And if speechifying was ineffective at converting public opinion, Connell, a lifelong lover of music, was always looking for an opportunity to unsling his guitar and belt out a song. He wrote folksy anthems to commemorate his love of New Hampshire, his disdain for Congress, his admiration for incarcerated libertarians, and, above all, freedom.

"They're searching Grandma at the airport and our children in the schools; they've got cameras and roadblocks on the street," he would sing lustily. "They've got their no-knock warrants, and they're kicking in your doors; it sure looks like a po-lice state to me."

Connell wasn't the type to simply bemoan problems. The chorus of the song (which he titled "Country Went Insane") also advocated a solution—disobedience.

"But we're on the road to freedom, and we're trying something new; now, noncooperation is the key. You can keep on trying all the things you tried before. Or when you're ready, you can come with me."

To Connell, these lyrics were not idle abstractions.

When he wasn't preaching, painting, or politicking, he pursued a personal path of passive noncooperation. He sometimes fasted to protest government actions, and in 2005, after Hurricane Katrina, he joined other libertarian activists to burn FEMA flags. He also publicly demonstrated on behalf of the Browns, a New Hampshire couple who wound up attracting supporters to an armed standoff against police in 2007 over nonpayment of taxes. Once, when Connell got a speeding ticket, he showed up at his court date in sweatpants and carrying no money because, he said, he was prepared to go to jail, but not to pay a fine. (The state agreed to drop the charges, so long as he drew no infractions over the following six months.)

And now Connell had carried that same spirit of resistance to Grafton. Soon after buying the church, he filled out the town's formal application for property tax exemption, based on his churchness. At issue was an annual tax bill of roughly $3,000.

Though Connell was simply staking out his own place in Grafton's carefully nurtured tax-avoidant landscape, news of his request for a religious exemption spread like a shock wave throughout the community. People were intensely interested, because dodging municipal property taxes comes with a certain irony: it's a zero-sum game. Anytime one person successfully avoids paying taxes, others in town must pay more to make up the difference. The system incentivizes people to champion their own reasons for not paying taxes, while attacking the reasons presented by neighbors.

To take just one example, in 2011 the state recommended that all towns consider granting tax exemptions for blind residents. Grafton officials told voters that adopting the exemption would have a negligible impact on the town's tax rolls, because Grafton was home to only one blind person, who lived on a fixed income and paid very little in taxes anyway. Libertarians didn't directly object to that resident getting a tax break—a position too blatantly heartless—but they regretfully opposed the measure anyway on the grounds that, when word got out, scores of blind millionaires might flock to Grafton to take advantage of the loophole. (The measure narrowly passed over these objections, and over the following eight years Grafton's population of blind millionaires remained relatively static, at zero.)

In Connell's case, despite the Sunday services and the addition of a small food pantry for those in need (located just outside his bedroom in the church), most people in town didn't consider the Peaceful Assembly Church a legitimate religious organization—partly because it wasn't affiliated with a nationally recognized church, partly because Connell had no degree in reli-gious education, and mostly because it seemed more political than spiritual, given Connell's personal brand of activism.

Though his messaging was consistent on the themes of peace, love, and forgiveness, those ideas were spawned from a strange brew of influences from outside mainstream Christian dogma. He lined the walls of the stairs that led to the second-floor sanctuary with copies of Henry David Thoreau's essay on civil disobedience and an autobiography of Mahatma Gandhi. He put up posters, including a reproduction of Michelangelo's *Creation of Adam*, and a solicitation for donations to a libertarian "school choice" education fund.

Though most felt that a tax exemption for Connell would be against their own financial interests, a healthy minority of more creative thinkers agreed, in a suspicious display of Christian generosity, that John Connell was a church. In fact, they argued, there could be other, hitherto-undiscovered churches hidden among Grafton's sprawling groves of hallowed hemlocks, white birches, maples, and white ash.

Town officials quickly realized that if they approved Connell's exemp-tion, the forest's sacred shadowed dapple could soon yield up a whole host of self-professed churches, with legions of prayerful hermits kneeling to thank their respective almighty deities for being blessed with freedom from taxes.

Though granting the exemption was likely to ring a death knell for the town's ability to provide municipal services, Connell seemed to have no prob-lem with this scenario.

"We have freedom of religion in this country, supposedly," he said. "We don't need the government to tell us which ones they accept and which ones they do not."

And in fact, Connell's claim couldn't be dismissed lightly. America is home to many legitimate religious organizations that don't fit the popular public mold of a church, which is why the federal government gets pretty loosey-goosey in defining the "advancement of religion" mission that is key to waiving a church organization's federal income taxes.

One way a municipality can safely identify legit charitable organizations is by following the lead of the Internal Revenue Service, which formally recognizes 501(c)3 nonprofit organizations, a designation that includes both churches and secular public charities. To get an idea of how broadly the rules define "public charity," consider that the American public supports, through tax exemption, the National Hockey League, the National Rifle Association, the US Chamber of Commerce, and a rogues' gallery of fringe hate groups that have taken up the ever-ennobling charitable mission of promoting white supremacy, nazism, and ISIS.

The town told Connell that, if the IRS recognized the Peaceful Assembly Church as a public charity, it would give the town grounds to approve his tax exemption application without opening the floodgates to a tsunami of frivolous claims. Grafton officials were eager to put the matter to rest because by now it seemed that every time the issue was raised in public, two or three people would threaten to declare that their own houses were churches too.

But Connell had just one small problem with clearing the low bar that the town set out. To apply for nonprofit status with the IRS, he would have to first correspond with the IRS. And to correspond with the IRS, he would have to accept that the IRS was a legal authority, which he most emphatically did not.

Connell tied his ambivalence about the IRS to his stance against violence. He believed, as many libertarians believe, that all government directives carry with them the implied threat of a gun to the head. In fact, Connell found it objectionable to form any sort of legal entity beyond his own personhood.

"This church was not created by the government," he said. "This church is God's church, not the government's church."

With the discussion seemingly at an impasse, the town rejected Connell's tax exemption claim.

But Connell wasn't done.

After first asking not to pay taxes, he moved forward with the second part of the two-step plan pioneered by Grafton settlers 230 years before: he simply didn't pay them.

Over the next two years, the town sent him more tax bills, accompanied by letters that described ever-stiffer legal consequences for continued nonpayment. When he was interviewed for a video promoting libertarian causes in New Hampshire, the subject got him heated. He started gesticulating and, at one point, clenched his hands:

"I cannot and will not do the things that the government is demanding that I do in order for them to accept that this is a church."

A moment later, he made a dark prediction.

"They will be coming to steal this church eventually. I can promise only one thing." He added great emphasis to his next words as he vowed in his rough voice that there would "not be violence coming from inside this church. Ain't gonna happen."

But no one had suggested that it would.

4

THE CAMPFIRE CLASH

"A deplorably constituted creature, that rugged person," he said, as he walked along the street; "he is an atrocity that carries its own punishment along with it—a bear that gnaws himself."

—Charles Dickens, *Barnaby Rudge*, 1841

Once they'd declared Grafton a Free Town, the libertarian activists began flexing their muscles in an ongoing game of resistance against town authorities.

John Connell was doing his part by refusing to pay taxes. Jeremy Olson, Tom Ploszaj, John Babiarz, and Bob Hull were all doing their part by suing the town over things like planning board elections and law enforcement over marijuana.

But often the opportunity to defend freedom came serendipitously, on the street. That was the method preferred by Mike Barskey, a man in his late thirties who came to Grafton from California around 2009. Barskey's rapid-fire speech and boundless bravado fit right into the Free Towner community—his new Grafton friends saw him as a habitual and polished defender of freedoms. He even carried three recording devices on him at all times to document the various little injustices that always seemed to erupt around him.

Barskey was also partial to the type of ambitious theorizing that underpinned so much of the Free Town Project's frenetic energy. Soon after arriving in Grafton, in a nod to Rand's fictional utopia, he unveiled a plan to construct a building called the "Grafton Gulch." It would be owned by Barskey but used as a private clubhouse where libertarians could engage in unrestricted commerce with one another. The libertarians seized upon the idea, and Hull, who by then lived with a group of Free Towners on Grafton's Liberty Lane, sold Barskey a suitable property along Route 4 in Grafton Center. Located about a mile north of Connell's Peaceful Assembly Church, the three-acre tract, vacant save for a shed and some materials left over from a previously aborted development plan, sloped down from Route 4 and toward the old railroad line.

In late May of 2010, Barskey, Connell, and a handful of Free Towners assembled beneath blue skies and bright sunshine to help clear brush from the site and break ground on Grafton Gulch. Around noon, the work crew lit a small cooking fire in a rock-lined fire pit so that they could roast hot dogs for lunch.

That's when a deputy fire warden from the neighboring town of Enfield pulled over on Route 4 and told Barskey that the unpermitted fire could accidentally ignite either the nearby shed or a pile of wood chips. Barskey declined to snuff the fire, on the theory that the actual danger was very small and their desire to roast hot dogs was very great. The warden left, but he contacted Grafton's gray-haired police chief, Merle Kenyon, who arrived on the scene and also told Barskey to put the fire out. Barskey once again refused. After a testy exchange in which Barskey accused the police chief of being more interested in controlling innocent citizens than public safety, and the police chief accused Barskey and his friends of being pathetic, Chief Kenyon contacted the Grafton Volunteer Fire Department to come put the fire out. With the Grafton fire station only a few miles away, the response should have been lightning-quick, but the station had no paid staff, and the only available volunteers were not trained to drive the fire truck. And so a call went out to Babiarz; as he headed toward Grafton from out of town, Barskey was already embroiled in an acrimonious defense of freedom against Chief Kenyon.

With Barskey's recorder rolling, the two squared off in a contest of composure. They leaned against the car of one of the work crew members, talking with performative, insincere civility, each waiting for the other to slip up.

"So, Merle," Barskey said, faux-causally. "Did you get permission to lean against this car?"

"No, I didn't," Chief Kenyon answered, his hands folded casually over his gut. Though bigger than Barskey, he was not generally an intimidating presence, with his earnest hooded eyes set over a watermelon slice of a nose. His tone was folksy, low-key.

"I did," said Barskey, who evidently preferred very specific one-upmanship to low-key folksiness.

"Hey, that's nice," said Chief Kenyon, patronizingly.

Barskey, the consummate freedom fighter, needed to provoke without being provocative. He sought to frame the exchange as a defense of his friend's vehicle against the tyranny of being leaned on.

"So, uh, you going to scratch it up with your gun or your utility belt or anything?" asked Barskey.

"I'm not planning on it," Chief Kenyon replied. "I'm really not planning on hassling anybody."

Barskey pivoted. Chief Kenyon's own vehicle was parked nearby, on the roadside.

"So," Barskey asked Chief Kenyon, "can I go lean up against yours?"

Chief Kenyon refused to take the bait.

"If you have to," he said, with that same mild, "knock yerself out" placidity.

Over many years of freedom fighting, Barskey had honed a strategy for arguing with people who weren't arguing back. He deployed it.

"No," he said weightily. "Not if I have to."

He quickly followed up with the next provocation. "Are you going to threaten or arrest me, or take me away to jail if I do?"

The question put Chief Kenyon in a difficult position. He couldn't very well promise not to take action, with Barskey so clearly looking for a line to cross. But Chief Kenyon also didn't want to open himself to an accusation of hypocrisy. He settled on vague.

"I don't plan on it," he repeated, his vocal cords now weighted with just a tiny hint of strain.

"You don't plan on it?" Barskey parroted. He switched to a new tactic, issuing an order and daring the chief to disobey.

"Tell you what," said Barskey. "How about if you don't lean against his car, please."

At this point, Chief Kenyon could have simply shifted upright, thereby taking the whole issue of car-leaning off the table, but instead his eyebrows snapped downward, his irritation finally bubbling to the surface. He thought Barskey had finally overreached.

"Whose car is it?" he asked.

"It's one of those people," Barskey answered, indicating his work crew, "who I asked for permission."

One could see the chain of thoughts flit across the chief's face. If he refused, he'd have to keep leaning against the car like an ass, until the owner invariably asked him to move, all with Barskey's recorder rolling. So Chief Kenyon took the only face-saving measure he could. He pushed himself away from the hood of the car, holding out one hand toward Barskey in a palm-down gesture that was both placating and derisive.

"Whatever you say," he said.

"No, not whatever I say," repeated Barskey, evidently rediscovering his arguing trick. "I *asked* you. I didn't *say* anything."

"I mean," said Chief Kenyon, his face contorted into a taut parody of accommodation, "I wouldn't want to—"

"Scratch the car, which isn't yours," Barskey interjected, finishing Chief Kenyon's sentence with his own, likely unrelated, thought.

The police chief went on to finish his sentence in his own words, but those words are lost to history because Barskey edited the rest of the exchange out of the video. In the judgment of the libertarians, the video documented a great success in the struggle to defend freedom. Or, if not that, then at least a fine example of Barskey getting Chief Kenyon's goat.

Scenes like this were playing out constantly in Grafton, with infinitely variable details coursing through the same wearying dynamic. Every time a Free Towner was pulled over for a traffic infraction, or came to the town office, or appeared before a judge, or was sent a formal letter, they took the opportunity to vigorously defend their freedoms, typically sapping already strained public resources in the process.

The disagreement over the campfire took a critical turn with the arrival of Babiarz. As the libertarian fire chief parked the fire truck, partially blocking the traffic on Route 4, Barskey and his work crew perked up. Barskey and Babiarz had been at a libertarian potluck together just the week before, and now the would-be governor was in a position to denounce what Barskey saw as blatant state meddling.

Babiarz dragged one end of a fire hose over to the weenie roast, walking past Barskey without making eye contact.

"Hi, John," said Barskey. "How come you don't want to say hi?"

In the background, one of Barskey's friends, another libertarian named Russell Kanning, said, "You know, Mike, I don't know if you even want to keep talking to that guy."

As Kanning spoke, Babiarz stopped and smiled quizzically at Barskey, trying to suss out whether the words from his fellow libertarians were in jest or in earnest. Somewhat awkwardly, Babiarz explained that he intended to extinguish the cooking fire.

"This is a Class 2 fire danger day. It's kind of dry here," Babiarz said. He gestured toward the nearby shed. "And the law says this has to be at least fifty feet away from the building if it's a campfire."

"It's not a campfire," offered Kanning.

"What is it?" asked Babiarz.

"I am burning debris," replied Kanning, who at that very moment was roasting a hot dog over the flames.

Babiarz left the hose, flaccid, on the ground and walked back toward the truck. Kanning and Barskey expressed surprise that Babiarz didn't seem to be defending their freedom.

"So Babiarz didn't just offer a permit. Hmm," said Barskey.

Babiarz returned with a soaking attachment for the nozzle and, with Chief Kenyon helping to steady the now-pressurized hose, was soon thoroughly drowning both the flames and the hot coals in a mix of water and fire-retardant foam, while the libertarian work crew watched.

"In case anybody is wondering," said Kanning, though almost certainly nobody was, "this is unwelcome intrusion into our lives."

———

ONCE THE VIDEO was posted online, news of the extinguished campfire spread. Connell started a discussion thread on the libertarian freedom forums about the Enfield fire warden who'd touched off the enforcement action. The warden, Connell wrote, "was simply on a huge power trip and he wanted desperately to introduce GUNS . . . into the situation!"

But most people weren't focused on the warden. They were focused on Babiarz. The libertarian-themed website "New Hampshire Free Press" carried an article (written by Kanning's wife) that said Babiarz had "shown that elected libertarians will, in a pinch, act just like every other bureaucrat in order to keep their positions of power."

The post unlocked a flood of criticism of Babiarz, who was in the midst of his third campaign for governor. Former libertarian supporters savaged him as a petty, corrupt, jackboot-wearing, authoritarian, control-freak thug, with a hard-on for paper permits. (Libertarians reserve a special disdain for pieces of paper that hold power over their actions.)

When some suggested that Babiarz owed Barskey money for putting polluting chemicals on his land, Barskey generously declined fiscal compensation and instead laid out a four-point plan for what would constitute an acceptable public apology, including an assurance that Babiarz would re-frain from extinguishing future fires in similar circumstances. If Babiarz hit all four criteria *and* seemed sincere about it, Barskey allowed that he would "likely" deign to talk to him socially again and give him a chance to earn back his trust.

But for Babiarz, who had no intention of apologizing, the whole incident had crossed the line from all-in-good-fun freedom-fighting to something more sinister.

"They thought it was a joke," he said, recalling the incident years later. Babiarz has a fun, even goofy, side to him, but when it comes to fires, his tone is always somber. "No, it was serious. It was a high danger day. They were burning too close to a building."

Though he was publicly stalwart, the dispute with Barskey put Babiarz in an odd position. For years, his nonlibertarian Grafton neighbors had cas-tigated him for his role in the launch of the Free Town Project, so he had grown used to being criticized from the left. But now the libertarians were describing him in the same terms they used to describe their worst left-wing enemies.

"The word of a petty little Statist like him is worth . . . what, exactly?" Joseph Brown, a particularly argumentative Free Towner, wrote in the free-dom forums.

Babiarz tried not to take that kind of sentiment seriously.

"If you think I'm a statist," he said, "you have no idea of the guy who's going to replace me."

The fallout from the campfire incident may have had an effect on the upcoming gubernatorial election. Babiarz hoped to hit 4 percent in the vote, enough to guarantee the party ballot access for future elections. He'd come close the last time he ran, in 2002, when he'd gotten 2.9 percent, or thirteen thousand votes. But after the campfire incident, he lost ground, netting only ten thousand votes (2.2 percent).

Though Babiarz felt that his core principles hadn't changed, there seemed to be a growing gap between himself and a certain subset of Free Towners. Did the cause of freedom really boil down to knock-down debates over campfires? He later talked to me about "flamethrowers" within the movement, the ideological descendants of Larry Pendarvis, whose destruc-tive advocacy undermined the very causes they sought to uphold and pro-fessed loyalty to.

Babiarz saw himself differently. He increasingly described his political goals as defensive rather than offensive. He wanted to prevent America from sliding into Nazi-like authoritarianism, while holding the line on taxes and government encroachment.

Too many of the Free Towners that he and his wife had invited to Grafton seemed to be creating more problems than they solved. But the Babiarzes could only stand and watch helplessly as the gap between them grew.

"They don't get the responsibility side of being libertarians," said Rosalie Babiarz. "They don't want anybody to impose anything on them, but they want to impose their ideas on everyone else." Many libertarians felt that the root cause of Babiarz's "corruption" was that the fire department was funded through taxes, which they considered blood money. The freedom forums lit up with a debate over how Grafton could privatize its fire services, with some suggesting that a voluntary fee of $7 per month could replace the involuntary $7 in monthly taxes that went toward supporting the existing department. This was objected to on the basis that some people might not voluntarily pay the fee, and then where would they be?

It was difficult for the logic-bound debaters to navigate the very tricky business of referring to a semi-compulsory fee as something other than a tax, but the discussion was happily aborted when one poster announced that donations could be sent to Hull's alleged private fire department, which was equipped with a forestry fire truck.

Connell, who was friends with Babiarz, declined to join in on the general bashing, but he did suggest that the choice between a tax-funded fire department and a privately run fire department was a false dichotomy.

"Maybe a 3rd option," he wrote, "is to put out the fire oneself?"

The highly visible conflict between Barskey and Babiarz signaled a trend emerging among the Free Towners. Several months after the campfire incident, Babiarz was at Bob Hull's compound when Barskey came over to dispute ownership of some concrete forms that had been taken from his Grafton Gulch property. (It turned out that the concrete forms had already been returned.) A muscular volunteer firefighter named Jay Boucher ordered him to leave and then got physical, shoving Barskey violently multiple times in an effort to drive him from the property. Barskey, who of course had his recorders handy, posted another video of this incident, and finger-pointing camps emerged on both sides of the issue. Free Towner Joe Brown (the same man who had accused Babiarz of being a statist) accused both Barskey and

Boucher of allowing the situation to escalate unnecessarily before they got all the facts. "Figure it out, before you confront someone," he said.

But the Free Towners were finding that the situations that had been so easy to problem-solve in the abstract medium of message boards were difficult to resolve in person. Bickering was breaking out. Whenever a couple within the community split up, people took sides, framing the actions of the nonfavored spouse as statist. When a young man staying at a Free Towner's home was found in questionable circumstances with a preteen, he was asked to leave in an impolite manner involving a very visibly wielded baseball bat. Even John Connell drew fire after someone accused him of inappropriate behavior that would likely be libelous to repeat in print. Chief Kenyon's annually reported call statistics showed that, by 2010, the number of civil issues he responded to more than doubled, and the number of neighbor disputes nearly quadrupled, as compared to the years before the Free Town Project started.

In late 2010, Barskey completed construction of Grafton Gulch and opened its doors in what was meant to be a watershed moment in the movement. Visiting libertarians could drive past the old shipping container sitting alongside the driveway, park near a large camper, and enter the structure, which had concrete walls topped by wood. Once they came inside, Barskey, who now lived on the property, served them breakfast burritos, burgers, and ice cream, all flavored with the sweet taste of freedom. But the free enterprise proved to be short-lived. Within months a woman from the food protection section of the New Hampshire Department of Health and Human Services came by and told Barskey that he needed to conform to the same licensing and health requirements as anywhere else that served prepared food. In the spring of 2011, less than a year after opening the Gulch, Barskey announced that he was closing it, permanently. The shuttering of the Gulch left Connell's Peaceful Assembly Church as the only large-scale community project serving the libertarians. It wasn't exactly commerce, but it did manage to pull off some successful programming, including a Sunday service that drew anywhere from one to eight people a week.

A few libertarians began to question whether the Free Town Project was indeed a worthwhile endeavor after all.

"It's too late for some," wrote one jaded libertarian, "but if anyone is out there thinking of moving to Grafton because they also are under the illusion that it is some kind of libertarian utopia, try to grasp some reality."

But to the substantial number of Free Towners who kept the faith, infighting was not the main problem. The main problem, they maintained, was that taxes were too high, rules too suffocating, statism too overbearing, and authority too abundantly wielded. Though daily life was getting more difficult, they were, at heart, idealists and romantics.

Things would improve, they insisted. They just needed more freedom.

5

A DELUGE OF DOUGHNUTS

One tablespoonful of honey will attract friend Bruin more than half a dozen barrels of first choice malt vinegar. Bear's buzz bothers bees.

But of this apart. At another time we may resume.

—James Joyce, *Ulysses*, 1922

The first time Doughnut Lady saw a bear behind her house had been back when Princess was still alive. One morning she was dragging a sled filled with grain and hay and water out to the cows when she spied a bear walking right toward her, on a logging road that ran through the property. Doughnut Lady abandoned her sled and hurried back to the safety of the house.

Though the encounter made her heart pound, Doughnut Lady also noticed how thin the bear was. Almost gaunt. No wonder it had acted so boldly—the poor thing was desperate for a meal.

Not much later, after going out of town for a pizza dinner, Doughnut Lady pulled into her driveway and the headlights illuminated a mother with three cubs sitting on a large rock. They looked hungry too.

"I just felt they needed something, you know?"

When the bears began raiding the sunflower seeds in her cylindrical bird feeders, her main reaction was to hope they would help the mother bear pack on a bit of fat for the upcoming winter. Soon she progressed to dumping a pile of sunflower seeds directly onto the ground. When the bear came, Doughnut Lady sat, delighted, on her second-floor porch, watching from among the potted flowers.

The bear would flop down onto its belly while eating the seeds. Its soft, pink tongue lapped them up delicately, seemingly one at a time.

Every day, on her way to feed her cows, Doughnut Lady began taking out a separate bucket for the bear. Sunflower seed was expensive—bears eat more than birds, after all—so she switched to grain.

Over time Doughnut Lady began to feel closer to the bear in her backyard. And that made sense, because she *was* closer to the bear. It had begun to anticipate her regularly scheduled delivery, and she could see it, watching and waiting on the periphery of the forest as she upended the grain bucket beneath a tree.

Over the years things spiraled in various directions. The number of bears spiraled up, the inhibitions between woman and beast spiraled down, and the cost of the food spiraled out of control.

It's not clear how exactly word of Doughnut Lady's largesse was being circulated throughout the bear community, but it quickly became clear that quite a few woodland bears were in need of help. She began taking out two buckets of grain per day; then four, with one feeding at sunrise and another in the late afternoon. She doesn't want to say how much the enterprise was costing her.

"I'm embarrassed," she said, "I really am." She admitted only that it represented a significant portion of her monthly budget. People have told me that she had to back up her truck to a loading dock to receive the grain.

Rather than lurking on the forest's edge, the bears began to wait closer and closer to Doughnut Lady's makeshift feeding stations as she tottered outside, her weight steadied by two buckets full of grain. She carefully upended one beneath each of two trees, topping the steering wheel–sized piles with a dozen sugared donuts, the cheap kind from Market Basket.

Inevitably, the bears got to the point where they were waiting expectantly when she arrived, jockeying for position like cats anticipating that a dinner bowl is about to be set down.

That's when she began to give the bears voice commands. She would shoo them off, in the way someone might warn a dog off a dropped bit of steak.

"Go away!" said Doughnut Lady, withholding the grain until they had given her enough space for her to feel comfortable.

"Go away, go away!"

The definition of "enough space" shrank until her shooing only moved the bears a few feet from the feeding station. There they sat, like rotund and feral wood-gods demanding tribute, on patches of grass wilted by the shuffling of a thousand paw steps.

Doughnut Lady's endless stream of grain was repaid with an endless stream of entertainment. Every day she got a close-up view of multiple bears standing shoulder to shoulder, eating and huffing and snorting. How many people could say that? And along with the bears came other animals—coyotes and foxes emerged like silent forest spirits to share in the bounty.

Best of all were the cubs. When their mother sent them up a tree, their claws made a pleasant scratching sound as they scampered up the bark. One of the trees had Doughnut Lady's satellite dish mounted on it. Sometimes the cubs edged onto the slick plastic surface until they slipped comically off, tumbling back down.

The bears, which were routinely killing livestock in various other Grafton yards, never laid a claw on Buttercup or Princess or, when he came, Monty.

"They all got along," Doughnut Lady said. Sure, she had to begin keeping her cats indoors after some disappeared in the wood, but she didn't associate that with the bears, not specifically.

Once a year an echo of the last Ice Age blows across the Northeast in the form of a New England winter. For most bears, the thickening layer of snow and the absence of foraging opportunities trigger the energy-conserving magic trick of hibernation. But in Grafton, no seasonal slumber was more tempting than the sugar and fat on offer during Doughnut Lady's twice-daily bear parties.

She was tenacious, feeding the bears in good weather and bad. Sometimes the snow melted, condensed, and refroze, turning the meadow behind Doughnut Lady's house into a precariously slick sheet of ice.

Wasn't she worried, I asked, that her feet might shoot out from under her, leaving her on her back and looking helplessly up at the bears towering above?

In a tone that suggested I was being silly, Doughnut Lady told me this did not worry her. Not because she was so sure-footed, she said. But because it had already happened.

"I was falling all the time," she said.

Even when Doughnut Lady fell, the bears were content to wait patiently until she regained her feet and dispensed the grain. Their bond was growing. Doughnut Lady's husband began taking pictures of the bears, and extended family would watch during visits. Over time people from outside the family began to hear about the trusting relationship between Doughnut Lady and her bears. It sounded like something out of a fairy tale.

That's when, at the top of the sloping meadow outside her home, neighbors, or people visiting neighbors, began gathering in ones or twos or little knots, watching the bears eat from a distance that felt (but wasn't) safe.

Though she was not a Free Towner herself, Doughnut Lady was friends with some of them, like Bob Hull, and her bear-feeding habit was very much in line with libertarian doctrine.

Libertarians believe that a landowner like Doughnut Lady owns any natural resources on that property—oil deposits, trees, and even wandering wildlife, like bears or endangered species. In Grafton, I was told, four or five families were intentionally feeding the bears, and the libertarian community saw this as their absolute right.

In 2009, when Alaskan authorities fined a man named Charlie Vandergaw $20,000 for illegally feeding game, Grafton's Free Towners saw it as one more example of a victimless crime being targeted by "control freak government parasites."

"Fish and Game is not for the protection of animals, it is for prosecuting the people that love animals," said one. "I hope they never find out that I feed the wild turkeys, gray foxes, deer, and bear here in my own yard."

———

MOST AMERICANS, INCLUDING many people in Grafton, like bears.

Bears are burdened with every anthropogenic trope that the collective psyche can heap upon their broad, shaggy backs—one story depicts them as roly-poly, bumbling buffoons, while the next describes fierce and toothsome man-eaters. Perhaps the only area of broad agreement is that bears symbolize the wild places that endure beyond the boundaries of human development.

But in fact, the idea that America's undeveloped places are a pristine wilderness—a faithful echo of the prehistoric era—is pure myth. We can preserve an individual butterfly by pinning its corpse to a corkboard, but as naturalists like Bernd Heinrich note, we can never pin down anything so complex and dynamic as an ecosystem.

The forest creeping in on Grafton is only superficially similar to the one that was hacked down by the European settlers. Before they came, the Abenaki hunted bear with bows and arrows, pulled silver trout from New Hampshire waterways, and competed with wolves to stalk the mighty half-ton Eastern elk that used to pace the deer trails. They flushed heath hens from the undergrowth, beneath skies that were literally darkened by massive flocks of passenger pigeons.

Today New Hampshire has no silver trout, wolves, Eastern elk, heath hens, or passenger pigeons, and the forest itself has seen many of its tree species wither away. Bur oaks and American chestnut, both of which were once critical food sources for bears, have all but disappeared beneath the onslaught of introduced blights, as have bog birches and black maple. Tree species under attack by invasive bugs include white pine (white pine blister rust), hemlock (hemlock woolly adelgid), ash (emerald ash borer), and balsam (balsam woolly adelgid). In all, people have documented 268 invasive species in Grafton County, a subset of the 525 that have been found in the state.

Rather than evolving in its place over eons, the components of the ecosystem that supports Grafton's bears were thrown together haphazardly over the past few hundred years.

And if we turn the clock back further, we see that America's indigenous humans established themselves as the deadliest invasive species by far, as recounted by Yuval Noah Harari in his book *Sapiens*. Long before they invented the wheel, North America's first human interlopers waged a two-millennium-long campaign of environmental degradation that resulted in the wholesale destruction of every big, meaty megafauna animal on the continent. The death list includes American mastodons and wooly mammoths, giant ancient bison, *Aiolornis incredibilis* (a fifty-pound bird of prey with an eighteen-foot wingspan), the woodland musk ox, and a large American camel. (A *Camelops* fossil was found at the site of a planned Arizona Walmart by a construction foreman named John Babiarz, no relation.) Early humans also eliminated North America's two-ton armadillos, twenty-foot-tall sloths, six-hundred-pound saber-toothed tigers, dire wolves, and bear-sized rodents.

Not to mention the bear-sized bears. Genetic testing suggests that bears first arrived in North America between 3 and 3.5 million years ago, and evolved into several distinct species that occupied different ecological niches. When human hunters unleashed their spears on the continent, most bears were just as hapless as all the other large mammals. Over the past eleven thousand years, *H. sapiens* have hounded to extinction the largest bear ever—the short-faced bear, which stood twelve feet tall and weighed more than a ton. We have also killed off the whale-scavenging California grizzly, the seven-hundred-pound Mexican grizzly (which hung on until the 1960s), and the Florida cave bear. But while carnivorous and other specialized-diet bears have failed to survive things like the Ice Age and the arrival of humans, black bears have endured because of their ability to problem-solve, work together, and adapt to almost any food source.

But that very propensity for adaptation has made Grafton's modern-day black bears very different from the black bears that roamed the woods in ages past. People reject the genetic modification of animals in the laboratory as artificial and unseemly, but in fact there is a much less controlled genetic experiment happening in a continent-sized laboratory: the unintended natural selection of the bears that are trying to survive alongside modern humans.

Today's New Hampshire bruins are so different from their forebears of just five hundred years ago that they might be mistaken for another species. They are, for better and for worse, civilized. Civilization is a mighty force; it turned fierce paleolithic hunter-gatherers into a flabby technocracy in which the most-retweeted English-language Twitter post is an appeal for chicken nuggets that reads: "HELP ME PLEASE. A MAN NEEDS HIS NUGGS."

Modern black bears, once placid and undisputed kings of the forest, have been similarly twisted by the topsy-turvy world that humans have created. Unlike their diurnal ancestors, modern bears forage all night, not for the grubs and wild berries of the woods, but for their version of "nuggs"—the kitchen scraps and cornfields that tend to be less well guarded at night. Access to nuggs also explains why all ten of the heaviest bears ever recorded in New Hampshire were spotted (and shot) in 1997 or later. (They each weighed between 493 and 552 pounds.) A 2019 study found that some wild black bears with access to sugary human foods (like doughnuts) are skipping seasonal hibernation; these bears also showed advanced aging at the cellular level.

Because bear ranges are now dictated by roads and human food sources, they are susceptible to being fragmented into isolated islands of habitat, which can have dramatic consequences for their gene pools. A handful of New Hampshire bears were recently diagnosed with gangliosidosis, a genetic disease that affects brain development; in humans its symptoms include exaggerated startle reflexes and dementia. Researchers say that the number of New England bears with the disease indicates that they may be experiencing the "founder effect," which happens when a population of animals has been genetically isolated from other groups and is thus susceptible to a lack of genetic diversity.

And the attitude of modern bears is also different. Whereas an ancestral bear might have spent the entire day grazing contentedly, secure in the knowledge that it had no natural predators, a modern specimen is always on guard against men and trained dogs, packs of which deplete the bears' calories and time resources by harrying them for hours at a time.

The overall effect is a bear torn between the unique dangers and caloric payloads that humans provide—they are more sleep-deprived, more anxious, more desperate, and more twitchy than the bear that nature produced.

Though modern-day humans and conservationists pay well-intended lip service to the idea that they are restoring the woodlands' most magnificent ambassador to its rightful arboreal throne, in truth they are more like Dr. Victor Frankenstein—stitching together the elements of life they have at hand in the hope that the resultant creation will serve the needs of humanity, rather than turn against its maker.

When I heard about Doughnut Lady's experiences, I was a little envious. As a lifelong animal lover, I could easily imagine the sheer joy of seeing bear cubs tumbling around while their mother watched, relaxing in the sunshine.

But I would eventually learn that Doughnut Lady's story was less like a Disney movie and more like *The Odd Couple*. It's the story of one old woman thoughtlessly leaving bears all over another old woman's lawn and front porch.

6
THE SURVIVALISTS STRUGGLE

> It was but a step on either hand to the grim, untrodden wilderness, whose tangled labyrinth of living, fallen, and decaying trees only the deer and moose, the bear and wolf, can easily penetrate.
>
> —Henry David Thoreau, *The Maine Woods*, 1864

Adam Franz leads me through the trees to the survivalist camp that he once dreamed of, now made real. Up above us, along the height of the dirt road, scarecrows stand sentinel duty in a ragged row, wearing anarchic Guy Fawkes masks and holding empty beer cans to ward off both order and sobriety.

Adam says the survivalists achieved critical mass only after a few false starts with different groups of friends. Eventually, his permanently parked camper was joined in the woods by a few tents, and then a few more. Sometimes a Free Towner would come by asking for a place to live. Adam always said yes.

"This," he says, "is Tent City."

He waves toward a clump of tents, lawn chairs, barbecue grills, plastic containers, tarps, and assorted campground detritus sitting on a relatively flat stretch of leaf-carpeted soil. "Sometimes, depending on how many people, we get more tents. The weekends here, it can get kind of crazy."

I find that, when one walks toward Tent City, one also walks away from civilization. The shared assumptions that underpin society—television ratings and the Dow Jones Industrial Average and presidential polls and, yes, even taxes—fade away, replaced by the tangible objects within the immediate viewshed. Here, a cast-iron pot for cooking; there, a gnarled root for stepping over; in the air, patterns of light for making the drab leaf litter mesmerizing, the whole ground rippling like water every time the breeze shifts the treetops.

Out here I am not in society but in the world. Though some part of me is fully aware that I'm within fifteen miles of a Subway eatery, when I stand in the woods with Adam, survivalism sounds much less nutty than it did when I woke up that morning. Out here what seems nutty is that people spend the workweek doing things they hate in exchange for white pieces of paper that represent green pieces of paper that used to represent yellow metal but now represent only a collective delusion of value. Out here it's easier to be seduced by the apocalyptic survivalist notion that, instead of nature being inevitably steamrolled by the tide of progress, the natural world will bleed back into our lives, outlast our frail constructs, and carpet the world in moss and bramble.

Grafton is more than halfway there already, and the more time Adam spends in Tent City, the more his strategic response to the postcollapse world mimics the bears of the woods. There's no garden in Tent City because a garden, or any storehouse of food, would have to be protected. Adam says he isn't looking to re-create the agricultural revolution; he wants to go full paleolithic.

"Why put the effort in if you can just go pick it off the tree? There's a lot of land back here on this property, and there's plenty of blueberries and raspberries and blackberries. I think there's even strawberries out there, not to mention all the mushrooms, all the other edible plants, plenty of beech trees and things like that."

The art of living primitively has not come easily for Adam and his companions. The best they can achieve so far is a kind of semi-ferality, because they keep running into logistical difficulties. For example, it would be logistically difficult for Adam to give up his car.

"We live in the real world still. I still need fuel to get to where I'm going and stuff," Adam says. To pay for such things, most residents of Tent City still have some sort of job, though Adam would prefer that they meet their nagging financial needs by turning the natural resources of the property into something that could be sold, like rustic log furniture. Though lots of Graftonites tend patches of marijuana, he's refrained, because growing pot carries the risk of having the property taken from him under drug seizure laws.

Another logistical difficulty facing the survivalists is that most or all of them lack most or all of the survival skills they would need to get most or all of their food from the forest.

"I'm meeting up with a guy who's going to teach me all about mushrooms," Adam says. But, he admits, he isn't confident about picking up the skill. "The problem is, I'm color-blind."

In fact, the more I see of Tent City, the more apparent it is that, outside of burning wood for heat, the hard work of survivalism is mostly a theoretical discussion point that occupies the airspace over campfires during bouts of partying.

Adam leads me beyond the tents, and I become aware that a constant low-pitched whine in the background is growing into a dull roar. It's a gas-powered generator, hidden somewhere amid a vaguely circular arrangement of wooden cabins the size of garden sheds, no two alike in design. One has a worn bearskin tacked to the outer wall. Another is decorated with a tattered and fading Confederate flag.

Adam says the flag is a sign of the diversity of political opinion here on the fringe of society. Though he himself is staunchly anticapitalist, some of the people who live here are libertarians; others identify primarily as gun rights activists.

"So this is probably the only place in the world that has a Confederate flag and a Bernie sign," he says, referring to the socialist senator of Vermont (and would-be US president).

Tent City's crowning architectural achievement is "the Orb," a Quonset hut of a structure that, thanks to the generator, is wired and therefore has a functioning television, DVD player, electric cooking range, and lights. As Adam leads me toward the Orb, I see that it's in even worse shape than Adam's camper. It looks like the kind of thing someone would hammer together out of an old carport and some siding.

"We hammered it together out of an old carport and some siding," says Adam.

Suddenly, the roar of the generator ceases, leaving a moment of odd silence before birdsong fills the void. A dark-haired woman appears in the doorway of the Orb.

"That the last of the gas, Annie?" Adam asks her. Annie lives here with her boyfriend Mark and her teenage daughter.

"Yeah. I got five bucks to go down to get some more," she says.

"I'll go down in a little while," says Adam. In keeping with his communist leanings, no one owns the perks that come with the Orb's electrical resources—the structure is available to each according to their need, and the gas that fuels its luxuries comes from each according to their ability.

All things considered, Annie likes living beneath Tent City's protective canopy. She enjoys the camaraderie and the sense of distance from the world's headaches.

She does have one concern, though.

"It's just the fact that I've never been that close to an animal like that," she says, almost apologetically. "And they're big."

She is referring, of course, to bears. For the survivalists, eating the fauna may be mostly theoretical, but being eaten by the fauna is a real and present danger. Bears have always been a nighttime presence in Tent City, knocking over a grill, cracking open a sealed container of corn, raiding the garbage, or taking a big dump in the middle of camp. One pile of bear scat looked particularly unhealthy to Adam, whose time in the woods has given him an eye for such things. It reminded him of when his mother-in-law's dog ate a bag of Adderall.

"That dog did not have a fun time," he says.

For most of Tent City's existence, the bears were easy to shrug off because they were experienced as occasional hairy shadows that quickly fled into the eventide woods. But this summer the shadows became corporeal, and less flight-prone. When a survivalist drove into the camp, the bears in the trash area lacked the common decency to scatter in the headlights. Instead, they sat stubbornly, daring the humans to escalate things.

Around the Fourth of July, Adam says, there was an unusually bear-free week. He eventually figured out why.

"I have some five-gallon containers of fry grease. Because my car runs off fry grease, you know. And we found two or three containers that they had drug off into the woods."

"Drank it," Annie says, stepping on his punch line. Though, to be fair, she has probably relived this moment several times already.

"Bit into and drank every last fuckin' drop of fry grease," Adam says, as if he hadn't heard her. "Can you imagine? And it had been sitting for a couple of years."

Next, the bears started showing up in the daytime. They could be glimpsed prowling around Tent City's margins, checking in as if they were fur traders walking a trapline. Annie began to get the feeling that one of the bears was paying her special attention. When she came out of her cabin in the morning, she often felt his eyes on her before she spotted him in the woods.

"He's usually just sitting down there, looking at me," she says.

The survivalists, beginning to get uneasy, decided to respond. First they posted a sign by the trash bins that read No Bears Allowed. It seemed unlikely that the bears could read, but you never knew, right? Bears had recently torn down and broken a man's tree-mounted game cameras four times, as if they were convenience store burglars disabling the security camera system. So maybe a three-word sign wasn't beyond their capabilities. Anyway, the sign boosted morale and solidarity among Tent City's humans by reminding them that the bears, not the survivalists, were the interlopers here.

The more realistic line of defense was Adam's "bear gun," the Taurus Judge, which he began wearing most of the time. Annie and the others were comforted by the sight of Adam charging around camp with the oversized .410 in his hand. But though Adam often threatened to shoot the bears, he never actually pulled the trigger. His reluctance stemmed in part from being sympathetic to the bears, and in part from knowing that dead bears could draw unwelcome official attention. The survivalists, like most Graftonites, prioritized staying under the radar of state authorities.

But just waiting around for disaster to strike also seemed imprudent, given the several well-documented cases of American campers being dragged from their tents and killed in the middle of the night by black bears.

As they cast around for ideas about how to defend Tent City, the survivalists got advice from the town's other armed camps, each of which repelled bears in its own way. As Adam ticks down the list—cayenne pepper, electrified fencing, motion sensors, booby traps, and radios that constantly blasted out disembodied voices—I wonder what subtle forces work behind human perceptions to make an entire encampment of people develop such a high tolerance for bears and for bear protection devices. In Tent City, the residents finally came up with a unique, high-risk, middling-reward strategy. Adam went shopping for a secret weapon.

It didn't take long for said secret weapon to be deployed. It started one morning when Adam, sleeping in the decaying camper, heard Annie calling from clear across Tent City. He rocked himself off the bed and shouted out of the camper's tiny screen window.

"Annie, is that you? You need help?"

It sounded like Annie did need help. He didn't have time to dress, but he grabbed his new bear deterrent and burst out of the camper in his underwear.

"And there's a bear. He's right there, past that dying tree there," Adam tells me, pointing to a spot in the woods about twenty feet away from the center of camp. "Sitting on the ground. Just kind of looking at us."

Adam picked up a cowbell, which he says the survivalists ring only for "emergencies," and started tolling it to drive the bear away. The bell roused the bear to its feet, but instead of leaving, it walked directly toward Adam, as if he were ringing a dinner bell.

Adam, unnerved, started shouting.

"Go away!" said Adam, taking a step backward and scolding the bear like he would a dog. He shook the bell more vigorously.

"Go away, go away!"

When the bear remained undeterred, Adam flicked open a lighter and touched the flame to the fuse of his new weapon: a packet of firecrackers. When the first firecracker in the line exploded with a sharp report, the bear started violently, momentarily confused. As more explosions filled the air, the bear ran—thankfully, away from Adam.

"He run like twenty feet and he stopped," Adam says. "Because the firecrackers stopped. And he kind of sat up there thirty, thirty-five feet away, and he started watching us." Finally, the bear reluctantly wandered off. The survivalists, heartened by the win, made immediate plans to expand their arsenal.

"I also think we should get bottle rockets," Adam says, "so we can send them his way so he feels like he's under attack."

Annie, meanwhile, worked to overcome her natural fears. When the bears were not physically present, it was easier for her to see their boldness as mere friendliness. She worried that the too-chummy bears were going to make them easy targets for hunters. So she too began throwing firecrackers at them. Adam is proud of her progress.

"Now that she's been within twenty feet of the bears several times, I think she's getting more used to—she realizes this isn't some wild animal rearing up aggressive, ready to kill her," he says. I have my doubts about this framing. Many times I've heard that it's dangerous to let bears get acclimated to people. I've never been told what now seems clear to me—that it's at least equally dangerous to let people get acclimated to bears.

Not until later did I realize that Adam and Doughnut Lady, who lived relatively close to each other, had both tried to communicate with what were almost certainly the same exact bears using the same exact words—"Go away! Go away!" But while Adam intended for the bears he shouted at to retreat, Doughnut Lady intended for them to simply be patient for an imminent snack time.

This underscored just how confusing Grafton's people must have seemed to its problem-solving bears. Every house was a potential source of calories, but the people who inhabited them might flee, or sic a llama on them, or offer food, or throw firecrackers at their head. It was a lot to sort out.

Before I leave Tent City, I ask Adam whether a better resolution might be to call the state Fish and Game Department to come address their bear woes.

"I would never cut my own throat by calling Fish and Game," Adam says. With Grafton as thick with bears as it is, he seems a bit mystified that wardens haven't shown up of their own accord.

"The fact that I'm not seeing them," he says, "makes me think they're understaffed."

On this point, Adam was right.

7

A BUREAUCRACY OF BEARS

THE AUTHOR submitted that it could be most fully and satisfactorily accomplished, if Her Majesty's Government would cause to be brought over to England, and maintained at the public expense, and for the public amusement, such a number of bears as would enable every quarter of the town to be visited—say at least by three bears a week. No difficulty whatever need be experienced in providing a fitting place for the reception of these animals, as a commodious bear-garden could be erected in the immediate neighbourhood of both Houses of Parliament; obviously the most proper and eligible spot for such an establishment.

—Charles Dickens, "Full Report of the Second Meeting of the Mudfog Association for the Advancement of Everything," 1837

In one sense, Grafton's bears came from the woods, and in another sense, they came lumbering out of a distant prehistoric era. But in yet another, equally true, sense, they came from the Commonwealth of New Hampshire.

Each bear in Grafton was put there, on purpose, by active changes to state policies that previously supported a bear-free landscape. By the time the Free Town Project began, Grafton was just one tiny part of a vast landscape in the midst of a great sixty-year bear expansion that was cheered by wildlife conservationists, photographers, and recreational hunters.

Despite all of Grafton's best efforts to unmoor itself from centralized authority, the town is deeply affected by what happens in the gold-domed New Hampshire statehouse, located less than an hour away, in Concord.

This is where the state's best and brightest, vetted by the voting public, gather to resolve all of society's issues, including bear issues. In the 1700s, lawmakers issued bounties meant to extirpate bears from the area; as a result, most of the state was bear-free by the mid-1900s, with a few isolated survivors up in the mountains, where people rarely ventured.

After the state ended the bounty system in 1955 and began funding crude bear census counts in 1956, officials found, not surprisingly, that the number of bears living in New Hampshire was growing.

The 1960s and early '70s were boom years for environmentalism. Particularly in New England, conservation enjoyed the support of a truly bipartisan coalition that included hunters, hippies, and pretty much everyone in between. It may seem unthinkable today, but the Environmental Protection Agency was created by a Republican president, Richard Nixon, just forty-five years before another Republican president, Donald Trump, pledged to "get rid of" it.

During this era, New Hampshire bears were transformed from a public threat into a resource to be managed by the state for the common good. In 1978, New Hampshire hired its first dedicated bear biologist, who used a punch-card computing system to track hunter bear kill statistics.

Under the new paradigm, bears thrived. By 1989 the state had successfully grown the bear population to about 3,000, and by 2010 or so New Hampshire was simply awash in bear, with more than 6,100 bruins benefiting from reforestation, regulated hunting, and, all too often, access to human food sources.

If researchers like "bear whisperer" Ben Kilham might be criticized for relying too heavily on a qualitative analysis of bears, the state may have erred on the other end of the scientific spectrum by relying on data sets to drive bear policy decisions. For decades the New Hampshire Fish and Game Department has drafted bear reports full of statistics—the average bear age, hunting licenses issued, chicken attacks, and so on—to inform its bear management plans. Each year state statisticians use complex algorithms to generate estimates of the number of bears per square mile in dozens of distinct management districts. The data set, amassed over decades, is very impressive. But also kind of misleading.

One problem is the narrow scope of the data: policymakers who rely on the reports can easily get an estimate of how many pounds of bear there are in any given township, but other than the abundance of natural food crops, the reports don't track traits that could influence bear behavior. No one measures the availability of human food garbage, for instance, or whatever extra-legal hunting and trapping activities might go on in the woods. Almost all of

Grafton's notable bear-relevant activities, from doughnut runs to firecracker assaults, seem to fall outside of the data.

And if the quantitative approach has certain blind spots about bears, it has even bigger blind spots about people. The state assumes that there is a direct correlation between bear complaints and bear problems, but in fact different people have very different levels of tolerance for bears—and very different levels of tolerance for state officials. A bear's first visit to a neighborhood's trash cans might generate dozens of calls, but its tenth visit to that very same neighborhood might generate zero.

And in Grafton, where the state is widely reviled and freedom-seekers are chomping at the bit to manage their own bear encounters, the number of calls to Fish and Game is likely to dramatically lowball the number of worrisome bear encounters.

In effect, Grafton seems to have a don't-ask-don't-tell bear policy, based in part on the reasonable suspicion that state-issued one-size-fits-all bear management advice could even, in some cases, increase the risk of a bear attack.

Fortunately, the state's Fish and Game Department does have one tool that makes up for the weakness inherent in the data-reliant approach: it employs a staff of trained game wardens who can be dispatched to investigate bear problems. A warden on the ground, who has had the benefit of studying hundreds of bear encounters, can interview people and survey the area for relevant information to determine whether anything unusual is going on.

In the 1970s, when bears and people were relatively few in number, this system worked, even though there were only fifty wardens covering the entire state. But by 2002 the department's traditional funding formula, which relied heavily on fishing and hunting permit fees, was beginning to break down. With taxpayers unwilling to make up for waning permit sales, the department was forced to cut staff, shut down facilities, defer equipment maintenance, and boost the cost of black bear hunting licenses.

By 2007 New Hampshire employed only 32 game wardens (compared to the neighboring state of Maine, which has 130). Each warden covered an average of three hundred square miles of territory—unless there were open positions, someone was sick, or someone was on vacation (which was every day), in which case the ratio was even worse. The 34 percent staff reduction was even more dramatic than it seems considering that in 2007 New Hampshire had twice as many people, and six times as many bears, as it did in 1970.

The state fields an average of 635 bear complaints each year, but they command only a small slice of department resources, because game wardens have so many nonbear worries—their duties have expanded to include everything from monitoring boat launches to leading hiker rescue operations.

Fortunately, someone has the power to fix all of this: the New Hampshire State Legislature, where representatives of the voting public craft laws and direct resources to solve societal problems.

If the state wanted to, it could dramatically reduce the number of problematic bear encounters. One way would be to dramatically reduce the number of bears, at least in those areas where human population densities are most likely to create conflict. Another way would be to codify all the best bear practices—force people to manage their garbage and bird feeders more responsibly, adopt strict zoning that would shape development in ways that are less likely to attract bears, and stiffen penalties for those who feed wild bears. And yet a third way would be to fund the Fish and Game Department to the level needed to problem-shoot effectively, so that game wardens would have more time to exercise their judgment in specific situations, and to educate the public.

I would expect all of these measures to be the subject of intense discussion among lawmakers, who have drafted at least fifteen bear-related bills over the past twenty years.

But the fifteen bills are largely unconcerned with bear conflict. Two of the bills—the only ones that became law—increased the fee for bear-hunting licenses. Most of the rest sought to tweak the rules of bear hunting in order to strike a better balance between the interests of hunters and trappers, and the ethical considerations raised by progressive activists.

Not until 2013 did lawmakers take up a bill to reduce bear conflict by requiring owners of wildlife-attracting garbage "to store or dispose of such solid waste in a wildlife resistant manner (i.e., bear-proof dumpsters and garbage cans)."

Such measures have proven to be effective in tamping down bear complaints in national parks, but to many New Hampshirites, the bill stank of statism and taxes. The legislative Fish and Game and Resources Committee heard a man testify, without evidence, that the heavier components of bear-proof garbage cans posed a threat: children might get trapped inside, or beheaded by a slamming lid (or both trapped and beheaded). But the most-cited concern was that waste haulers and property owners could not be expected to pay for more expensive cans. Two months after taking it up, the committee voted 14–0 to kill the measure.

The Fish and Game Department doesn't always have to look to lawmakers—it can also take action via administrative rules. For example, in 2014, when four bears died in an outbreak of mass chocolate toxicosis, wildlife officials, somberly noting that the case "likely represents the most significant case of chocolate-induced mortality ever," made it illegal to feed bears chocolate. But no such speedy resolution to human-bear conflicts has been proposed, and until someone comes up with an idea that costs no money and is politically palatable, the cash-starved Fish and Game Department has developed a budget-friendly stance on bear conflicts: it's not him, it's you.

That's the primary message underpinning Fish and Game's ongoing public education campaign: "Something's Bruin in New Hampshire—Learn to Live with Bears," which, since 1996, has tried to "enhance public tolerance toward bears" and is based on the assumption that a lot of people are afraid of bears for no good reason.

The primary thrust of the campaign is to help people manage their garbage and bird feeders in ways that are less likely to attract bears. These are valuable lessons, but also convenient for the state, because they deflect bear complaints back onto the complainant, or the complainant's neighbors, rather than on the state policies that have effectively stocked the woods with bears.

Telling people to change their behavior is far cheaper than investing in an effective trapping and relocation process (for the bears, not the owners).

In a very real way, the Fish and Game Department depends on bears, both for the bear-hunting permit fees and for the goodwill that comes with managing a banner species for conservation. There is little wonder, then, that the department pushes the upper limits of each area's "carrying capacity" so that as many places as possible are populated with as many bears as possible.

There are also troubling indicators that, even when Fish and Game wants to reduce the number of bears, it has struggled to do so. As was the case in the days when bears were considered an imminent threat to the region's settlers, the state doesn't have the funds or the manpower to physically control the bear population, and so it outsources the work (though it now charges, rather than pays, hunters for the service).

In 1990, with a healthy population of 3,500 bears living in New Hampshire's woodlands, Fish and Game opened most of the state to bear hunting for the first time in decades. Over the next several years, it sold tens of thousands of bear-hunting permits, peaking at about 17,000 permits around 2001.

Hunters were happy, money was flowing in—and the bears were still thriving. Though people killed nearly 1,500 bears between 2003 and 2004 alone, bears outbred them, attaining an all-time population high of 4,830 bears in 2005.

Figuring that was enough bears, the department decided to bring the numbers down by encouraging more people to hunt bears for more days of the year. The plan of New Hampshire's bureaucrats was to stabilize the number at 5,100.

But the plan of New Hampshire's bears was slightly different: to make a thousand more bears.

The bears prevailed. Between 2006 and 2013, their ranks increased by another 1,140 animals.

Though they had previously worried that bear populations were too fragile to withstand hunting, Fish and Game officials were learning that the bears were more resilient than they had imagined.

"It has become evident that the state's robust bear population can withstand occasional periods of increased harvest," they noted in an annual report. And so the state really ramped up hunter permissions. It authorized more than 10,000 bear-hunting licenses, some of which allowed deer hunters to take advantage of an unexpected opportunity to shoot any bear unlucky enough to wander through. The state also gave out 1,400 bait permits, creating a network of feeding stations, loaded with piles of (then-legal) chocolate and gummy worms, where hunters lay in wait to assassinate hungry bruins. Hundreds more permits allowed hunters to use trained dogs equipped with GPS collars to track the bears down for slaughter.

The state was practically serving the bears up to hunters on a silver platter, and the hunting community responded enthusiastically. Beginning in 2013, the number of bears taken by hunters statewide (not counting illegal kills) increased from 558 to an all-time high of 1,083 in 2018.

And yet the bear market remained quite bullish. In 2016, the executive director of the Fish and Game Department reported, without the slightest hint of worry, that the bear population had increased yet again, to 6,500. By 2018, even using the generous targets employed by the state, the bear density was considered too high in almost every county. In the wildlife management region that includes Grafton, bears doubled in number between 1998 and 2013; by 2018, they outpaced their intended numbers by more than 50 percent.

In Grafton, the fundamental disconnect between the bear-tolerant Fish and Game Department and the bear-plagued but state-avoidant local residents created a world of possibilities for managing bears.

This was the sort of dynamic that informed a libertarian discussion in 2005 on whether to organize a formal, armed state militia that would be focused on performing community services, such as "wild animal handling," when it came to New Hampshire's bears and mountain lions.

The idea, like so many others proposed within the Free Town Project, never got off the ground, and that's probably for the best. But something had to be done. Some people—including Jessica Soule of Bungtown—were finding the bears to be altogether too much to handle.

8

THE CARETAKER CONFINED

Nothing moved amid the solemn vistas of stupendous trunks,
fading away into the darkness which held us in. Once some
bandy-legged, lurching creature, an ant-eater or a bear, scuttled
clumsily amid the shadows. It was the only sign of earth life
which I saw in this great Amazonian forest.

—Arthur Conan Doyle, *The Lost World*, 1912

When the Unification Church left Grafton, Jessica Soule stayed behind;
she had grown to love driving through Bungtown in her truck, bumping over stones in the road with windows down and sunshine in her hair. The farmhouse she'd purchased had two separate heating systems that covered different zones of the house, and a woodstove to boot, one of several quirky marks of the previous owner. Another was the back porch—it had a kitchen sink, enough space for two picnic tables, and a hole cut into the wall of the main house so that food and plates could be passed directly from the kitchen to the porch.

After the bear snatched her kittens in 1999, that direct access to the back porch became important for Amber and the other cats, because Soule no longer allowed them to go outside. There was a countertop on the porch that could be folded up and locked into place to cover the hole, but Soule left it open during the warmer months, so that the felines could wander in and out at will to enjoy the breeze of the screened-in porch.

For a while, Soule maintained strong ties to the church. In 2000, Reverend Moon helped pay for Soule to meet him in Seoul, South Korea, where he was opening a medical center that blended Eastern and Western medicinal practices. But by then, Moon was getting on in years and his children were exerting their own influence on the church. As the power structures changed, Soule's daily involvement with church activities waned.

By 2003, she was also experiencing severe medical problems. She'd always suffered from seizures, which had caused nerve damage to her legs when she was younger; she'd been able to maintain her ability to walk after an intense self-prescribed course of physical therapy. Now she felt her legs weakening again. She began relying on a cane to get around, particularly on the uneven footing of the ground outside the house. The bear-on-kitten attack had left her nervous about lingering outdoors on her shaky legs, so Soule now indulged her love of the outdoors by opening her screened windows and doors. Each breeze felt like a spring cleaning as it swept through the traditional New England mudroom at the front of the house, then whisked through her living room and on out the back porch.

When it was warm enough, she ate supper on the back porch, thinking about old friends at the church and the little tasks around the house that might keep her busy. From there, she could see the deer and moose passing through to visit the little brook out back. The cats joined her or not, using the tunnel-shaped hole above the kitchen counter to come in and out repeatedly over the course of a leisurely meal.

One day Soule was sitting in the living room, chatting with a friend, when the conversation was interrupted by the sound of her cats fighting on the back porch. But when Soule opened the door, instead of cats, she found two startled bear cubs staring at her in wide-eyed terror. Soule had just enough time to take in the wreckage—torn screens, the back door partially ripped off its hinges, chairs and potted plants scattered like bowling pins.

"I didn't take any long-term pictures with my eyeballs," she said. "I slammed the door. I said oh-my-God-oh-my-God."

Soule jerked the deadbolt into place and beelined for the kitchen. She didn't know what would be worse to find there—a glimpse of the tail of one of her beloved cats as it slipped through the hole to investigate or a bright-eyed cub trying to push its way in.

The reality was worse than either possibility. A bear paw—an adult bear paw—poked through the hole in the wall and was now groping blindly around the kitchen counter, thick claws knocking over cups and food containers in the pantry, unable to grab anything.

Soule had no desire to see the body of the bear pressed up against the other side of the wall. On the kitchen side, the hole could be closed by a small sliding door that perched above it; Soule screamed and slammed it down. The wooden frame of the door came down on the bear's arm like a guillotine but was nowhere near sharp enough to do any real harm. Still, the sudden motion startled the bear, which withdrew its paw long enough for Soule to slide the door into place. As she held it closed, she felt the pressure as the bear tentatively pushed its nose against the thin wooden barrier that had suddenly materialized between them. Then she heard its claws scritching across the wood, in gentle exploration.

Soule shouted at her friend to grab a hammer and nails from a nearby tool drawer. The moment Soule smacked the first nail with her hammer, the bear stopped pushing against the wood. Within minutes, the door had been nailed into place, and the porch had gone silent.

"Go count my cats," Soule told her friend.

Once she'd confirmed that each cat was accounted for, Soule went out to the porch and flipped the wooden counter up to cover the hole from that side.

"I nailed it shut," Soule said. "And it stayed shut. I never did fix it."

Within a week, Soule had also hired someone to board up the back porch. The boards blocked the bears, but they also blocked the sunlight, the breeze, the view of the moose and the deer and the little brook. She tried eating out there once, but there was nothing to look at but the washer and dryer, a depressing reminder of laundry to be done.

It was a trade-off, but Soule felt safer.

Years passed.

Soule's mobility slowly worsened, and her social circle shrank. She found it more and more difficult to tolerate the cold and spent too much of the winter sitting in her living room, covered in blankets and cats. She called doctors to help her walk, and a propane company to help her stay warm, but there was no getting around the fact that both legs and heating systems were, despite her best efforts, aging beyond use in the old farmhouse.

In the winter of 2011, she hunkered down as a parade of particularly unpleasant weather systems marched through the skies above Grafton—storms and cold snaps and nor'easters scattering sleet and snow into the air like confetti. For Soule, the cold wasn't just a temperature, but an actual ache, deep in her bones. After being diagnosed with both lupus and osteoporosis, she traded her cane for a walker, then the walker for a wheelchair.

Meanwhile, ongoing fighting with the VA began to wear Soule down. Though she'd won the lawsuit over her benefits, now she felt like the VA was targeting her, intentionally avoiding its responsibility to make her home fully accessible. She couldn't get up the stairs in her wheelchair and it didn't clear the edge of the bathroom shower so that she could get to the toilet, but they denied her request for a chairlift and a bathroom reconfiguration. She could still kind of creep around on the first floor, but her increasingly brittle bones left her terrified by the prospect of a fall—she'd stumbled against the wall once and broken her elbow. So she put piles of clothing on the bathroom floor, strategically placed to cushion her if she fell. Every day she moved shakily from wheelchair to toilet, grabbing door knobs and sink counters like an ancient Tarzan, humbled by age.

As she wheeled herself into the mudroom one day, she could feel the scented spring air through the screen door and windows, not enough to tousle her hair, but a light, sweet-smelling caress on her face, reminding her of old times. It was part of an unusually warm and dry spring that drove the ache right out of her bones and promised better days ahead.

Soule no longer trusted herself outside with the walker, so she used the wheelchair for even the briefest of errands. The high point of her day was often going to check the mail, a small but important outing that always let her taste the weather and held the possibility of an envelope bearing some sort of good news.

She opened the mudroom's front door, and a shaft of bright sunlight hit her, warm and wonderful and blinding, stretching beyond her and into the gloom of her home. As she navigated out of the darkness and over the bump of the door frame, she felt that familiar little rush of freedom and independence. She hooked the door into place and started down her ramp to get the mail, eyes adjusting to the brightness.

By then, the bear was only ten feet away. It had been nosing around the garbage can she kept near the bottom of the ramp, but now it was staring at her, trying to make sense of this human, sitting and gliding along at eye level.

Soule, startled, realized that she was completely in the bear's power.

There was an eerie silence. In the distance, Soule made out the faint sound of a truck rumbling down Route 4, but she knew it was highly unlikely that anyone would hear her if she screamed. Something told her that, as long as the bear stayed still, she shouldn't say a word or make any sudden movements.

"He wasn't huge, but he was big enough," she said. "He wasn't sure if he could take me."

Moving slowly, Soule reversed course, gliding backward inch by inch. The bear watched as she bumped gently against, and then over, the door frame, then slid back into her screened porch. When she unhooked the screen door, it closed with a mild bang, blocking her view of the bear and breaking the strange silence. She locked it. It was only a flimsy hook and eye, but it made her feel better. Realizing she had been holding her breath, she let it out, not in a whoosh, but slowly, quietly. As soon as it lost sight of Soule, the bear came closer. Its head appeared, framed by the top half of the screen door. They stared at each other through the screen, still in silence.

Soule hoped the bear wouldn't probe the screen and discover how flimsy it was. She maneuvered her chair as close as she could to the interior door and then risked a glance behind her, to get herself lined up properly with the opening to her house. It only took a second, but when she turned forward again, the bear was gone.

Of the dozens of people I spoke to in Grafton, only two had called the New Hampshire Fish and Game Department to report their worrisome bear encounters. One was Soule, and she didn't waste any time that day; the blood was still surging through her veins while she waited on hold. In a sign of the broader disconnect between the department and Graftonites, she was unhappy with the response she got.

"They said, don't bother the bears," Soule remembered later. "If you do anything to them, you're not allowed to shoot them. I said, if it does it again, it's going to die. They said, you will get arrested if you shoot a bear."

So Soule took other measures to protect herself. Her next call was to Grafton's postmaster, the rough-voiced but aggressively cheerful Debbie Clough. Clough agreed to have the mail delivered directly inside her porch, rather than at the mailbox.

Soule installed glass windows and a heavier door on the front porch to make the mudroom more secure, but now there was no longer even a hint of a breeze, and she didn't dare leave the door open. She began keeping her garbage inside, only putting it out a few hours before the private trash service she'd hired came to pick it up. From then on, if she had to venture out to her front yard for any reason, she carried her gun.

In September of 2012, despite Soule's prayers, Reverend Moon died at the age of ninety-two. Soule felt like she'd lost a parent, and as Moon's family began to squabble over his wealth and authority, she disengaged from the church.

Over the next few years, Soule continued to struggle with the same problems—declining health, the aching cold of winter, failing heating systems, and battles with the VA that never seemed to resolve anything. Her feelings of isolation intensified. After the libertarians stepped up the pressure on the town budget, she said, her road was no longer certain to be plowed, especially during late-winter storms, when the annual winter maintenance budget ran out.

"They would literally stop plowing," she said.

Soule entered a kind of hazy reality, a suspense film in which the first two acts ran on an endless loop. Tension ebbed and rose without ever achieving a climactic relief. She began to sleep only four or five hours a night. Sometimes she heard or glimpsed a bear moving around outside her house. She held her cats tight. Her seizures began getting worse, and she rarely opened the windows anymore, for fear that the bears would scent her garbage, or her food, or her cats, and try to force their way in.

In 2016, she called her local newspaper to see whether they could shame the VA into making her home accessible. That's when the phone on my desk rang.

I drove in on Route 4 that fall. It was my first visit to Grafton. The road bisected the forest, which was intact save for a few bogs where dead trees, their feet in stagnant water, jabbed accusingly at the sky above.

Soule's Bungtown house was covered in white siding, and the metal wheelchair ramp out front creaked beneath my weight. It took her a few minutes to answer the door in her motorized wheelchair. By then, she had been living as a virtual shut-in for four years. She wore a button-up shirt under two sweaters, one shoulder crossed by a neat feminine braid that softened her face, which age, worry, and outrage were slowly pinching into androgyny. She had dropped a lot of weight and was down to something like 100 pounds.

"I was barely maintaining a good front. I was at wit's end," she later said. "I probably would have gone back to jumping in front of the bus if I hadn't been so well educated in the divine principle."

As my eyes adjusted, I saw dark wooden walls with idiosyncratic angles. The closed windows left the air cloistered and heavy with the smell of the cats that milled around Soule, jockeying for space on her lap as she transferred herself to a chair in the living room. I sat on an unusually lumpy couch with a quilt spread over it. While we chatted, Soule used a phrase that struck me as odd: "before the bears came."

"I used to let my cats outdoors, but that was before the bears came."

It was my first sign that something unusual was happening in Grafton, that something fundamental had changed. Soule explained that, for her, the

eating of Bungtown's cats was the moment bear-human relations had irrevo-
cably broken down.

I asked Soule what had ever happened to Amber, the third kitten that
survived that 1999 attack by huddling beneath the leaf cover.

"She's right here," Soule said, pointing to a cat-colored cat nestled in
the center of her lap, like feline royalty. The milky-eyed cat and I assessed
each other. Amber was so rough-coated that she looked taxidermied, like a
child's favorite stuffed toy stubbornly patched over into adulthood. She was
so decrepit that she could no longer retract her claws, but she was unques-
tionably, indisputably, alive, making her the oldest survivor of Bungtown's
storied cat-bear war. My follow-up question was interrupted when one of the
lumps on the couch I was sitting on moved, startling me. It turned out to be
another cat.

"He's hiding," said Soule.

I wound up writing multiple stories about Soule for the newspaper; the
VA publicly said that it would look into her case, and she got a few offers
of help from third parties. But when the dust settled, she was still unable
to safely access her bathroom or her upstairs bedroom. Soule had come to
Grafton seeking freedom, but somehow she felt more trapped than ever. She
began to feel that the town was literally killing her.

"I love my home," she said, looking about herself helplessly. "But I love
living. And I want as much life as possible."

9

THE HIDDEN HITCHHIKER

I had a line about my waist and followed obediently after the
sea-cook, who held the loose end of the rope, now in his free
hand, now between his powerful teeth. For all the world, I was
led like a dancing bear.

—Robert Louis Stevenson, *Treasure Island*, 1883

I f there is a scientific explanation for the increasingly strange behavior of
Grafton's human and ursine residents, it begins in 1902, when a passenger
ship docked on the southern shore of the Tyrrhenian Sea and a Frenchman
herded his young family down the gangway to step for the first time onto the
sunbaked Tunisian shore.

There are few photographs of thirty-six-year-old Charles Nicolle (mostly
because, in those days, no one considered him worth photographing), but he
was described as tall and lean, polite and attentive, with a mustache, a domed
head, and the sort of precisely professional fashion sense that hinted at his
preference that you go a little heavy on the starch in his crisp white shirts.

Nicolle's nattiness contrasted sharply with Tunis, the Arab-dominated
capital city in which he now stood, where a swirling cauldron of political
forces and disease considerably upped one's chances of meeting a messy death
in the streets. Beyond the city lay untold miles of a harsh, arid climate that
bore little resemblance to Nicolle's memories of the green, rolling hills of
France. His career in France had been beset by friction that culminated when
his tenure with the University of Rouen was terminated by a political rival.
And so he had come with his wife, Alice, and two sons, Marcel, age seven,
and five-year-old Pierre, to accept a job that his elder (and more celebrated)

scientist brother had just turned down: director of the Pasteur Institute of Tunis, a satellite of the Parisian Pasteur Institute.

From the moment he set foot in Tunis, Nicolle enthusiastically pushed Pasteur's counterintuitive idea that tiny bacteria can cause mammoth problems, including mass human casualties. He saw himself as a soldier taking the fight to a formidable enemy. "[If] these micro-organisms . . . would have any understanding, or a minimal intelligence," he told a colleague, "they would be able to promptly destroy and annihilate human populations on this planet."

Nicolle considered typhus Africa's most dangerous game. Widespread among the rural poor, it had a trio of symptoms—fever, rash, stupor—and often blossomed into deadly epidemics in the close living conditions of prisons and army encampments.

Wearing a white lab coat over a clunkily knotted patterned tie, Nicolle spent long hours sitting with mortar and pestle, a microscope, wooden swabs, a gas-line-fed Bunsen burner, a collection of stoppered beakers and jars filled with clear fluids, and his most beloved tool: the hypodermic needle.

The needle was like a glass-bellied parasite with a tapered tubular snout; in Nicolle's hand, it came alive, withdrawing blood from one vein and disgorging it into the next. First, he used it to inject typhus-tainted human blood into a macaque monkey; then he ground up some insects and injected their remains into more monkeys.

Between injections, Nicolle wrote an urgent letter to Paris, asking them to send him a chimpanzee. When it arrived, he injected the poor creature with more typhus-laden human blood. After the chimp got sick with typhus, Nicolle saved it—not the animal proper, but its infected blood, which he drew into his trusty syringe and then injected into yet more monkeys, successfully giving them typhus.

At some point, all of this needlework gave Nicolle great insight into a fundamental truth in experimental science: injecting primates with fatal diseases is expensive. And so he turned to rodents, which he found could be injected with typhus at a very reasonable price.

From then on, Nicolle's labs were always well stocked with small, chirping gundis, a rodent so well adapted to the arid terrain of North Africa that it can go its entire life without a single sip of water. To prevent the gundis from escaping, Nicolle also populated his labs with free-ranging security cats, which served the same function as the sharks in the seas surrounding the island prison of Alcatraz.

In 1903, when a prison about fifty miles south of Tunis reported a typhus outbreak, Nicolle planned a visit with two other doctors. He didn't make it in one sense—having caught a cold, he canceled at the last minute—while the other two doctors didn't make it in a much more permanent sense: they visited the prison, contracted typhus, and died. In all, one-third of Tunisia's doctors were dying of typhus.

Though prisons now seemed too risky for the cautious Nicolle to visit, he wanted to see how typhus affected a population rather than an individual. And so the next time an epidemic swept through the country, he went to where the action was: Sadiki Hospital.

———

NICOLLE'S TUNISIA WAS more like Grafton than appearances might suggest. To get a hint of their common political dynamic, look to prolific French author Guy de Maupassant, who, fifteen years before Nicolle's arrival, furnished the French public with a vivid description of Sadiki Hospital, a former army barracks with a Moorish bath that functioned at the time as an insane asylum.

Maupassant found that the African and Arab madmen held at Sadiki had developed a different, and more terrifying, level of madness than could be found in sedate European asylums. He described men at Sadiki whose "faces were livid and ghastly," who were "jumping up and down in their respective cells, like animals in a menagerie," voicing "a continuous laughter with a menacing air." One old man, he wrote, "laughs and shouts, dancing like a bear." In his account, which was enthusiastically repeated in psychiatric journals throughout France, he reported that most of the Arabs had brought their madness upon themselves by choosing to smoke the narcotic hashish. Maupassant even found their state of mind to be infectious: he himself felt "a breath of unreason penetrating into my soul, a contagious and terrifying emanation." (And indeed, six years later, a syphilis-induced paranoia drove Maupassant to try to cut his own throat, after which he was confined to just the sort of genteel Parisian madhouse that he preferred.)

Maupassant's florid, and somewhat savage, depiction of Africa's mentally ill was very convenient for the French, who had come by Tunisia only recently, and under questionable circumstances. After bargaining for control of the country at the 1878 Congress of Berlin, France used a Tunisian tribal raid on French-occupied Algeria as an excuse to send in thirty-six thousand troops and establish a formal protectorate there in 1881.

None of this pleased the Tunisians, who had been looking forward to independence after the collapse of their previous colonial rulers, the Ottoman Empire. But they were hard-pressed to argue their case for self-rule when people like Maupassant were describing Tunis, their capital, with a lopsided focus on its asylums and brothels, as well as their sewage systems (which, he wrote, were "dragging their slow and nauseous mire through a land impregnated with filth").

Nicolle was part of an invasion of well-meaning French administrators who were eager to bring Tunisia's Moorish savages up to the high standards of France. (In but one example of France's high standards, the government had recently been induced, under pressure of violent public demonstrations, to cap the legal workday at eleven hours for French women and children.)

Tunisians, understandably unhappy with their new Gallic masters, embarked on a protracted campaign of organized resistance, with freedom fighters employing tactics that ranged from assassination attempts to violence in the streets.

The dynamics of French-occupied Tunisia were hardly unique, or even uncommon, as noted by scholars of colonialism like Professor Daniel Butt of the University of Oxford. Many think that colonialism is a thing of the past, a dark stain on human history. But Butt heads down a different path by defining colonialism as having three key features that persist into modernity. First, the colonial oppressors subjugate a group of people, typically by limiting their say in political and criminal justice decisions. In this case, France defanged the Tunisian government by populating it with French appointees and French allies.

Second, the oppressors (according to Butt) wipe out the indigenous culture and replace it with the imposed customs of the colonists. The French achieved this by installing an array of schools where Arab and African children were taught the French language and European culture.

Butt cracks down on the notion of benevolent colonialism with his third defining feature: the oppressors exploit their wards, such as through the levying of unfair taxes. France helped itself to Tunisia's natural resources to fund a public health network (including the Pasteur Institute of Tunis), government offices, and roads. All three characteristics, taken together, make this very serious theory of colonialism, proposed by Professor Butt, whole.

These hallmarks of colonialism would sound very familiar in Grafton, where free-minded people have long chafed under the rule of oppression, though whether the oppressors have been the settlers who pushed out the Abenaki, the Free Towners who sought to colonize existing residents, or the US government continuing to assert its authority over an increasingly feral Grafton depends very much on one's point of view.

AT SADIKI HOSPITAL, Nicolle discovered the connection between head lice and typhus, which gave the world a magic bullet in the war on typhus: kill the louse, end the contagion. Though reservoirs of typhus persisted in rural Tunisia, where any solution proposed by the French authorities was met with distrust, the global impact of his discovery earned Nicolle the Nobel Prize for Medicine. The Pasteur Institute of Tunis has accomplished nothing so notable since.

The once-cautious Nicolle became increasingly likely to push back against the medical establishment and to pursue personal freedom. He divorced his wife and, over her strenuous objections, sent his family back to France. He traveled abroad, handing out diseased gundis as a sort of party favor for his scientist hosts. He began harshly criticizing the Pasteur Institute of Paris in particular, and the centralization of medical power and resources in general.

"Some revolutions are useful. The worst may be necessary," he wrote. "When a machine is rusty or a mechanic foolish, egotistical, or impotent, one must change the former, cast out the latter. The process will only be brutal if it meets with resistance."

At some point, Nicolle's newfound appetite for risk increased, and his passion for the needle took a darker turn. In pursuit of a typhus vaccine, he got downright foolhardy with a home brew of typhus-infected blood and a few other ingredients.

"I injected myself with the mixture," he later announced. It is remarkable that he was even alive to make an announcement, but he reported that he had suffered no ill effects whatsoever. Unfortunately, this response had emboldened him.

"I then injected a few children . . . ," he wrote. "You can imagine how frightened I was when they developed typhus."

Happily for Nicolle, the children (whom Nicolle did not identify) recovered. But unhappily, he never did get the typhus vaccine figured out, and credit eventually went to a Polish scientist familiar with Nicolle's work.

Though Nicolle is primarily remembered for typhus, a much less her-
alded piece of his research would prove to be just as important, for both Grafton and the world.

It started with a minor mystery. In 1908, after some of the gundis in his
lab died unexpectedly, Nicolle found an intriguing bow-shaped pathogen in
their liver tissue. He and a colleague eventually learned that they were looking at a microscopic, never-before-described parasite. They named it *Toxoplasma gondii*. This was a misnomer, based on Nicolle's mistaken belief that
his lab was stocked with gondis, rather than gundis; had he gotten it right,
the correct name for the parasite would have been *Toxoplasma gundii*. Gondi
or gundi, it was a consequential find.

Other researchers would eventually demonstrate that *T. gondii* did not
exist in Tunisia's free-roaming gundis. This raised a perplexing question: if
the pathogen hadn't come from the wild, and it hadn't come from Nicolle's
trusty needle, then how had it gotten into the isolated population of gundis
in his Tunisian laboratory? But Nicolle, swept up in his typhus studies, never
returned in any significant way to *T. gondii*, and the question remained unanswered for another sixty years. When scientists did finally figure it out,
Nicolle had very little to say about the matter—probably because by then he
was long dead of typhus himself.

In the meantime, scientists learned that *T. gondii* was killing not just
gundis but all sorts of animals in all sorts of places—otters in the sea, rab-
bits in Brazil, a cat in New York, sheep in New Zealand, and dogs in France,
India, Tunisia, and the United States. Though the public was largely ignorant of its existence, *T. gondii* became known among scientists as one of the
world's most versatile parasites, able to storm the internal organs of almost
any warm-blooded animal on the planet.

Including humans.

Though toxoplasmosis (*T. gondii*'s resultant infection) was linked to a variety of very serious symptoms in people (including death), it kept a relatively
low profile because most healthy people seemed to simply take the parasite on
as a hitchhiker, with no apparent ill effects. And because no one knew of any
T. gondii–specific modes of transmission, the best protection was thoroughly
cooking one's meat, which people were already doing anyway, for protection
against various other bugs.

The answer to the infected gundis finally came in 1972, when researchers
at the Pacific Southwest Research Station headquartered in Honolulu found

that isolated populations of rats, bats, and birds living on small atolls were infected with *T. gondii*—but only if cats lived there too. Other researchers confirmed that cat-free islands in Australia and the United States were also free of the parasite.

The nature of the cat-parasite relationship slowly emerged. Though *T. gondii* hatches from eggs into larvae in nearly any mammal, it can't breed and lay more eggs until it gets inside the guts of a cat; its eggs are then disseminated to the world via cat poop. Other animals that interact with that poop (including humans, who have been living in close quarters with domesticated cats for the last nine thousand years or so) pick up the eggs and become hosts for more parasites.

Had someone told Nicolle in 1908, it's likely that he would have identified his gundi-patrolling lab cats as the probable source of the *T. gondii* in his gundis (or gondis).

The revelation that cats were carrying around potentially fatal parasites led to a new generation of public health warnings designed to keep pregnant women away from cat litter and other sources of cat feces. But around 2005, the research literature took an odd turn.

Accessing a cat is a challenge for a parasite living inside a rodent, which tends to flee from the scent of cat urine. But researchers discovered that rats infected with toxoplasmosis showed no fear in the presence of cat urine—in fact, the scent seemed to attract and even arouse them.

This manipulation—which serves the parasite's interests perfectly and the rat's interests not at all—happens when the parasite forms cysts in the brain of its rat host; those cysts affect the production of an enzyme called tyrosine hydroxylase, which plays an important role in making the brain-affecting chemical dopamine. Controlling dopamine levels doesn't allow the parasite to direct the muscles of the rat, but it does something even better—it changes what feels good to the rat.

News of the parasite that controls rat brains quickly spread through the world via headlines, which were read by primates who had little inkling that, as they scanned their smartphones, their own brains might be susceptible to the very same parasite.

One such primate was Robert Sapolsky, a neuroendocrinologist at Stanford University who has studied *T. gondii*'s effects on the brain.

"You take a toxo-infected rat, and it does some dumbass thing which it should innately be skittish about, which is go right up to cats' mouths," he said. "And maybe, you take a toxo-infected human, and they start having the proclivity towards doing a dumbass thing that we should be naturally averse to."

Rats don't have a monopoly on tyrosine hydroxolase, or on dopamine either—it turns out that all mammalian brains, including the ones nestled inside human skulls, use dopamine to control what social scientists call "motivational salience." It's the all-important cognitive process that motivates us to move toward desirable and pleasurable outcomes, like hugs and cheesecake, and to move away from dangers, like gunfire and Reddit forums.

For example, Sapolsky cited research proving that toxo-infected people are three to four times more likely to be killed in car accidents that involve reckless speeding.

Other researchers have found that toxoplasmosis increases a person's chance of enjoying bondage and masochism in the bedroom. Infected men have higher levels of testosterone and are more likely to disregard the rule of law (like zoning laws and bear management regulations, to take two completely random examples), while a study of woman veterans found that the infected are more likely to exhibit depression, confusion, anger, and dysphoria. And because they have less fear of negative consequences, toxo-infected people are also more likely to commit suicide and engage in binge eating. Some people believe that vaccines cause autism, or that water is alive. Now, I developed my own crackpot theory—that toxoplasmosis was playing an unusually robust role in the Free Town.

Are parasites really bashing Grafton's humans around like so many sandbox toys? The answer is elusive. Toxoplasmosis researchers have never studied infestation rates among Graftonites, so the evidence is necessarily circumstantial. But if you tried to imagine a community that was particularly susceptible to a *T. gondii* epidemic, you would come up with something very like Grafton—a territory where people live in nontraditional housing that features substandard sewage and water systems and cats moving freely between gardens, woods, and bedrooms. The culture would include a disregard for expert advice from wildlife and public health agencies and therefore less reinforcement of societal norms like hand-washing and thorough cooking of game meat.

And if you were to next imagine the impact of high infection rates, you might again come up with something very like Grafton—a general disdain for authority, people engaged in high-risk behavior, more neuroticism in women, and more testosterone-driven brinkmanship in men.

We might dismiss the notion of a toxoplasmosis-infested town as a mere cocktail party hypothetical, and maybe we should. But keep in mind that the parasite is almost certainly at the party too, sharing stomach space with the guests' raspberry margaritas and smoked salmon crostinis. Toxoplasmosis isn't a rarity that affects a few crazy cat-loving individuals at the fringe. It's mainstream enough to shape society, culture, and national economies.

Researchers estimate that one in three humans on the planet are toxo-infected, and some populations of humans have much higher rates, probably based on things like cat ownership, cultural hygiene practices, and access to modern infrastructure. In the United States, the estimated infection rate is 11 percent, while other countries have rates as high as 60 percent. One 2018 study found that countries with high levels of infection had correspondingly high levels of entrepreneurship, presumably because the parasite short-circuited the part of the brain that would otherwise instill a fear of business failure.

While reading the research, I wondered whether Grafton's libertarian colonizers would find the parasite's actions to be an infringement on their freedoms or something more like consensual cannibalism, the unfortunate result of an active decision to expose oneself to cat poop.

This disturbing thought was backburnered by an even more disturbing thought: could *T. gondii* infect bears?

I soon found myself reading studies by US Department of Agriculture researchers who, in 1995, asked hunters to cut out the hearts of their black bear kills and send them to its Beltsville, Maryland, research lab for testing. When some of the hearts tested positive for *T. gondii*, the researchers threw a batch of infected meat into a blender and then fed it to cats, to see whether any parasites in the bear were viable for completing their life cycle inside the cats. That may sound cruel and creepy, and it is—but less so when compared to the USDA toxoplasmosis program's other practices. In 2019, the lab was shut down after journalists revealed that, over the course of thirty-seven years, the lab had purchased dead cats and dogs from Asian meat markets and fed them to the kittens it bred on-site, and that it had also euthanized and incinerated thousands of cats and kittens.

Despite the ghoulish methods, the bear heart study yielded interesting results. The presence of toxoplasmosis in black bears was expected—by that point, *T. gondii* had already shown up in everything from boars to kangaroos. But the thing that surprised me was how *many* of the bears had parasites floating around their bodily fluids.

No animal on the planet has infection rates as high as certain populations of black bears—80 percent in one Pennsylvania study, 84 percent in a population in North Carolina, and near 100 percent in other populations.

The tendency of bears to snuffle, mouth, snort, and swallow everything they can get their greedy claws into probably has them gulping down lots of things that contain *T. gondii*.

How does the risk-inducing parasite affect the behavior of a 350-pound bear that can literally smell a candy bar in your pocket from a mile away? No one knows, because most of the science is conducted from a public health standpoint that largely ignores the unhealthiness of being attacked by a bear. Instead, the research buttresses public health advice based on the assumption that the bears are the ones being attacked and concerned with managing the kills in a sanitary manner—handling the meat appropriately and cooking it thoroughly. Other scientists are trying to protect the public health by developing a *T. gondii* vaccine.

But efforts to reduce the spread of *T. gondii* will depend on politics as much as science. Back when Nicolle first unlocked the secret of typhus transmission, the deep divisions between the French colonialists and the Tunisian freedom fighters allowed reservoirs of typhus to continue to thrive in rural areas where governmental advice was largely ignored. And in modern-day America, different communities and demographic groups are affected by parasites and other infectious diseases differently. We may develop vaccines and learn how to make hunting practices more sanitary, but public vaccination efforts and the micromanagement of hunting practices are exactly the sort of thing that many Graftonites think of as government overreach.

Libertarianism is entirely built upon the appeal of exercising free choice to own a gun, marry indiscriminately, commit suicide, shoot bears, curse in polite society, or buy unhealthy amounts of soda in New York City. That appeal is decidedly less palpable if those choices are actually the product of a parasite.

And it's likely, Sapolsky notes, that *T. gondii* is not the only parasite out there. Sapolsky has become a standard-bearer for a theory that free will is more or less something people have made up rather than face the far less satisfying reality that most of our decisions are driven by culture, chemical processes within the brain, bacteria in the gut, and, not least, parasites.

10

THE PASTOR'S PLAN

Dares the bear slouch into the lion's den?
One downward plunge of his paw would rend away
Eyesight and manhood, life itself, from thee.
Go, lest I blast thee with anathema,
And make thee a world's horror.

—Alfred Lord Tennyson, *Becket*, 1884

The same brutal winter that made Jessica Soule ache in early 2012 was also keenly felt by John Connell.

By day, Connell enjoyed the way the thick layers of fallen snow warped the landscape into something that was both pristine and playful. Free to spend his hours as he chose, he walked through the silent icy cathedrals of the pine forests and climbed hilltops on snowshoes to see the shining winter landscape laid out beneath him. Closer to home, he exercised by shoveling out the church parking lot until his face glowed beet-red beneath his whitening hair, the tip of his nose burning with the cold. He piled up slabs of ice to create Zen-like art sculptures and snapped pictures of them, displaying the eye of an amateur photographer with artistic aspirations.

Those types of activities kept hot blood pumping through his every extremity, but the cold was harder to deal with when he was inside at night. Right from the beginning, he'd learned that the church building's walls functioned like a sieve: a large percentage of the warm air generated by the ancient furnace bled straight to the frozen world outside, leaving him chilled. He spent many hours shivering beneath the drafty roof of the Peaceful Assembly Church in his guitar-strewn sleeping quarters, which adjoined the large cluttered space of the main meeting room on one side and a small food pantry on the other.

He was rapidly running out of money to pay for the building's utilities. In fact, he was rapidly running out of money to pay for anything. He sent out a message on social media channels, warning supporters of the church that his funds were dwindling.

"This will not last," he said.

To make matters worse, the town's municipal government seemed intent on dragging Connell deeper into financial trouble. In December, he'd received a $2,186 tax bill, and he knew there were many more bills on the way. Once again, he submitted a form to the town seeking a tax exemption, and once again, without IRS-sanctioned nonprofit status, the town's selectboard voted to reject the application.

It seemed a no-win situation.

He posted frequently on social media and freedom forums, railing against town officials to his supporters.

"This is for real," he wrote. After sacrificing his retirement savings to fund the church, he said he was more than willing to put all that he had left—"my life, my fortune and my sacred honor"—on the line in the battle against taxes.

All along, Connell kept trying to build up the church's activities. On a Thursday evening, he hosted a choir practice for Rich "Dick Angel" Angell and friends to rehearse "Weeda Claus's Chronic Christmas Carols," a series of parodic songs that subbed libertarian-themed lyrics into Christmas classics.

When winter finally began to loosen its grasp, springtime brought Connell not only warmth but hope. His salvation came, as it often seemed to, from above.

God spoke to Connell, using that same inner voice with which he'd instructed the former factory worker to purchase the church.

When God spoke directly into Connell's mind, they were using a well-established communication method among the faithful called interior locution, which, the Catholic Church firmly believes, allows one to hear directly from God. The biggest pitfall, though, is that not all of the voices one hears are divinely inspired. Some people can't differentiate the legitimate messages from "spurious locutions," which either come from evil spirits or arise subconsciously from their own human desires.

Though interior locutions have sparked worldwide religious movements (including the Unification Church, which revolved around revelations God made to Reverend Moon), the words that God offered to John Connell were much more limited in scope.

Connell had made the natural assumption that, when God told him to abandon all concern for the future and invest his life savings in the church, he would live out his days in said church, doing the work of God.

But in the summer of 2012, as heat and drought began to stir the bears of the forest into a sweltering desperation, Connell received a message that the Peaceful Assembly Church's pure mission was not, in fact, a long-term deal. It was only meant to last for about three years, two of which had already passed.

The time line laid out in Connell's interior locutions neatly corresponded with August 1, 2013, which he understood to be the date the town could exercise its authority to seize the church property for unpaid taxes.

Connell received more messages. He should prepare to give everything away rather than let the "Gov-Almighty worshiping, thug allies" (as God called them, according to Connell's posts on internet freedom forums) steal from Connell.

As Connell explained it, God then got very specific. He told Connell not to actually give things away—just to be prepared to do so. When the time came, God would pass the word to Connell, and then he could execute the plan to divest himself of all his earthly possessions. God also told him not to set a deadline for the individual members of the town selectboard (who God, with divine wit, referred to as "select-thugs") to do the right thing.

God also had a little emotional messaging for Connell. When he'd told Connell to buy the church, the message had been: *Don't worry.*

And Connell hadn't worried.

Now God said to him: *Be patient and still.*

So Connell resolved to be patient and still. As he began to mull over what he knew of God's plan, any trepidation he might have felt must have melted away. The plan wasn't going to leave him homeless and penniless; instead, it would allow him to escape the pressures of his tax bill and stick it to the government officials who had been harrying him for the past two years.

Here's how it would work: Connell's principles prohibited him from dealing with the IRS directly. But perhaps he could do an end run around those principles by giving the church to someone else, someone who did not share his concerns about dealing with a federal agency.

If he could find a trustworthy group to form a nonprofit, they would be able to jump through the paperwork hoops necessary to establish the Peaceful Assembly Church as a nonprofit, thereby skirting the tax issue.

The idea seems to have first come up in a conversation Connell had with Jeremy Olson, a computer engineer who moved to the area from Massachusetts in 2007. Olson was a rising star within the libertarian activist community; he had updated his résumé to include everything from planning motorbike events at the Canaan Lions Club to directing research for the New Hampshire Liberty Alliance. He was also a director for the Citizens for Criminal Justice Reform and held a couple of minor public positions in Grafton's town government—he served as a trustee of the town's small portfolio of trust funds and as an alternate to the planning board.

Olson helped Connell come up with a list of people who would join him in forming a nonprofit and serve as its board of directors; he suggested people who were connected to the Free Town Project. They settled on Free Town "founder" Bob Hull, whose taciturn nature had earned him the nickname Silent Bob; Jay Boucher, who lived on Hull's property and was a volunteer firefighter for Babiarz (Boucher was the man who'd violently shoved Mike Barskey in a dispute about concrete forms the previous fall); Tom Ploszaj, who was not a libertarian but who always seemed to find himself involved in libertarian causes; and thirty-two-year-old James Reiher, another local activist who often showed up at libertarian gatherings.

The plan seemed such a perfect escape hatch that Connell was soon waxing enthusiastically about the idea, even in public. Though he was still waiting for the word from God to make it happen, he began letting people know that he was planning "changes in organizational structure."

Connell wanted to make sure that, in the event God did tell him to sign away the church building, he would be able to continue his spiritual work. As Connell would later recount, during continued discussions with Olson and the others, he told them that he wanted ironclad assurances built into their agreement. They would have to let him live out his days as the resident pastor and sexton of the church, with free rein to continue his religious activities there. If they ever found that they couldn't coexist alongside Connell's activities, they would have the option to simply sign the property back over to him. And to make it more difficult for the board to deviate from this agreement, any changes would have to be agreed upon unanimously, by all the board members, rather than simply put to a majority vote.

It seemed like Connell had covered all his bases. Conveying all of that detail—lifetime appointments, unanimous decision-making process, exit clauses that would return the property to Connell—in a contract was a complicated enough endeavor to keep a professional lawyer busy for many hours. But that smacked of governmental bureaucratic jibber-jabber.

So instead, to consummate their agreement, they shook on it.

11

A BEAR'S BELLIGERENCE

While he was going up on the way, some small boys came out of the city and jeered at him, saying, "Go up, you baldhead! Go up, you baldhead!" And he turned around, and when he saw them, he cursed them in the name of the Lord. And two she-bears came out of the woods and tore forty-two of the boys.

—2 Kings 2:23–24

In early 2012, the snow stopped falling, but the rains never began. The spring was among the driest ever recorded in New Hampshire, and after a century of relentlessly marching upon the people of Grafton, the dark forest that ringed the town paused. Deeply buried roots of oak and beech were denied in their ceaseless quest for water, and the trees, lacking nutrients and fluids, entered a sort of drowsy senescence, declining to put out their usual energy-intensive offerings of beechnut and acorn.

The bears that relied on the mast as a dietary staple must have looked longingly at the bare branches and all the other signs of thirst in what is normally a lush forest landscape of food. Without water, there were fewer grubs, fewer berries, fewer grasses and succulent shoots. But there was one natural resource in ample abundance: hunger.

The drought was widespread. Across the state, phones on the desks of wildlife officials began to ring insistently. Populations of bears were at an all-time high, and now they were descending from the forest, all seeking to offset a dearth of natural foods with a human-related smorgasbord. More than a thousand people called with bear complaints that year, sometimes describing the bears around their homes as bolder, more desperate, and less responsive to scare tactics.

These were the conditions that led to Soule staring down the black bear she found on her wheelchair ramp. A little farther up Wild Meadow Road, a neighbor's dog chained to a steel stake in the middle of the yard disappeared in the night, leaving behind only a bit of blood. Elsewhere in Grafton, bears threatened a small dog on a leash and pushed into vacant homes through screen windows. No one was hurt, but everywhere, there was a sense of mounting unease.

Even Dianne Burrington, Hurricane the llama's commanding owner, grew worried. By 2012, she had been blackberrying along Grafton's decommissioned dirt roads hundreds of times; when she saw a bear, her usual response was to simply give it space by moving to another nearby patch. But that year she ran up against a bear that didn't seem to want the space.

"She wasn't afraid of me at all. That's what did bother me," Burrington said. "I hollered at her when she was far enough away from me, but she kept kind of circling back down to where I was."

Burrington, spooked, backed up toward her truck, and left.

It was only a matter of time, it seemed, before someone got hurt.

———

TRACEY COLBURN HAD always lived in relative harmony with the bears around her little yellow house, a mobile home standing isolated in the middle of the woods. She got a little thrill when she saw them on the trail near the edge of her yard or climbing her trees, and she laughed when they raided her compost pile, chucking aside the cabbage in a humorous show of contempt.

Tracey, who quit her job as administrative assistant to the selectmen when things got weird in the Free Town era, looks a little like Anna Kendrick, if Anna Kendrick were over forty, had taken a shot at college that was cut short by breast cancer, and found herself struggling through a long string of clerical and municipal jobs in the backwoods of New Hampshire. Tracey was a little confused and wounded by most people's failure to return the kindness and trust that she tried to put out into the world.

By June 2012, Tracey was out of work, and money was tight. But she found a few dollars to buy a print at a thrift store in Meredith to give to her father on Father's Day. It was a print of a painting by a Canadian artist, R. A. Fox, of a mother bear with two cubs.

She also scraped together a few dollars for a small pot roast to feed Kai, the Husky-Lab mix she'd gotten from the shelter. Kai had developed an allergy to wheat and corn, and she was trying to get him off the cheap dog food. On Friday, she cooked the pot roast.

The skies had finally let loose enough water to end the drought, but it was too late to alleviate the natural food shortage, so the practical effect was mostly to add so much moisture to the heat that the air itself seemed to sweat.

Saturday was Tracey's first day on a new job, a greenhouse at a hardware store down in Bristol. By the time she left work, she was exhausted, drained by the heat. When she got home, she opened her windows and decided she'd better go ahead and slice up Kai's pot roast before she collapsed into bed. Afterward, she opened the glass French door to let Kai outside to pee.

The porch was small, just eight feet by ten. And it was, she says, "just full of bear."

———

TWO BEARS, YOUNG ones she estimates were two hundred pounds each, crouched to her left on all fours, noses to the wood of the deck, sniffing, while another, much larger, three-hundred-pound bear was right in front of her. Had a hidden parasite emboldened them to creep onto the porch? There was no way to tell.

Before Tracey could react, Kai rocketed onto the porch and, as the two smaller bears scrambled off the sides of the deck, launched his sixty-five pounds at the big bear. Dog and bear tumbled down the porch steps, biting at one another furiously. At the bottom of the stairs, the bear tried to catch Kai with her claws, but Kai kept finding her rear, turning in tight little circles as he snapped at the backs of her legs.

Shouting at a bear is often the best way to drive it away, and so Tracey let out a wordless, primal wail. But in this case, the sow's exit was blocked by Kai, and Tracey's screams seemed like a war cry.

Tracey didn't see the bear charge until it was upon her.

"They can move so fast that you can't—they are not slow," Tracey said later. "They move like lightning. That bear was on me about, I think it was one second literally, and they run like a deer. They are so fast."

The bear lashed out at Tracey, raking at her face and torso with the five heavy claws of its left front paw. Tracey turned her face away and threw up her hands in a defensive gesture, palms in. The bear's claws ripped the skin of her right forearm and the back of Tracey's right hand, badly, continued across the width of her body, and stripped more skin from her left forearm, with such force that Tracey was knocked off her feet and thrown backwards onto the ground.

Twisting onto her back, Tracey tried to use her feet to propel herself backwards into the house, but somehow she'd shut the door behind her, and her head thumped against the glass.

She reached up toward the doorknob with her right hand, but the bear charged again. Tracey was close enough to smell and hear the bear's breath, but she remembers no smell, no sound, just that silent-movie image of the bear's enormous shaggy head, dark eyes, and pointed teeth eclipsing her world.

"She was going to frickin' kill me, and I knew she was going to, I just knew it. Because her face was right here," Tracey said, holding her hand about eight inches in front of her. "I was looking right into her eyes."

Kai must have bit the bear's rear legs then, because it jerked away from Tracey and threw itself at the dog again. There was another explosive round of teeth and claws, and then the bear dashed into the woods, Kai snarling right behind.

Tracey gained her feet and scrambled inside, already shaking from the flood of adrenaline.

Shit. I'm hurt, she thought. *And I don't know how hurt I am, and my dog is missing.*

She opened the door a crack to see Kai beelining toward her from the woods.

"Huskies prance," Tracey said. "He come prancing out of the shadows, big grin on his face. Like it was the most wonderful thing he's ever done. For him, it was like his, his one big, you know, showdown with bear."

Tracey looked at her right hand for the first time. There was not much pain—not yet—but her stomach turned. The bear had unwrapped the skin from the back of her hand like it was a Christmas present. The gaping hole showed ligaments, muscles, and gore.

Tracey looked around her kitchen helplessly before picking up a clean dishcloth and wrapping it firmly around the wound. Instantly, red roses began to bloom on its surface.

Tracey didn't know if the bear was waiting in the pitch-black night on the other side of the flimsy door, but she had no cell reception at her home and she couldn't afford a landline.

Nor could she wait for the relative safety that would come when daylight filtered through the heavy foliage to illuminate the dirt road on Sargent

Hill. Dawn was seven hours away, and Tracey was losing too much blood—already it soaked her T-shirt and shorts, streaked the white skin of her bare legs, pooled like spilled wine across the small dining room floor, stained the buffet red.

Her car, an old white Subaru, was all the way on the other side of her yard, where the trees blotted out the starlight, and the dark shadows hid who-knew-what. She wished she'd parked closer. But there was nothing to be done about it now. Getting to the car was her only chance.

She prepared to step out onto her blood-spattered deck. The night air was still hot, but she couldn't stop shivering. The shudders radiated outward to her left hand, which now gripped a trembling lead pipe, and her right hand, which was cradled against her chest, the dish towel tied pathetically around the gaping wound.

Not until later, after the news had broken, did anyone ask how it had come to this: Tracey Colburn, a 120-pound woman and the forty-six-year-old former administrative assistant to the Grafton town clerk, having to open her door, step into blackness, and run toward where she had last seen three black bears.

Moments later, she locked the car door and turned the key in the ignition. When the car roared to life, she revved the motor, honked the horn triumphantly, and flooded the area in front of her with a white blaze of headlights, seeking to frighten the bears.

That was when Tracey realized she couldn't drive the car. It had a manual transmission, and her mangled right hand, which was beginning to throb, couldn't grasp the gearshift. She sat in the car, honking, and thinking, and bleeding.

THE IMPASSE DIDN'T last long. Tracey got the old Subaru into first gear by reaching awkwardly across her body with her less-badly-injured left hand. She puttered out of her driveway and onto the pitch-black, rutted dirt road, pain levels rising and blood levels dropping.

Worried that she couldn't make it all the way to town, she pulled into the driveway of Bob, a guy she knew who lived down the road.

When she rang the doorbell, his head popped out of the window.

"I've just been attacked by the bear," she called up to him. "I need to go to the hospital. I want you to drive me."

He squinted at her shivering form in the darkness.

"Hold on."

His head disappeared. Tracey stood awkwardly, bleeding and wondering if she should get back into her car.

Bob's head popped back out.

"Uh. Ah." His voice was thick with sleep. He didn't seem to understand what was happening. "Well, you're kidding, right?"

Tracey began to shout.

"No, I'm not kidding, and now I'm in a lot of pain and I'm going to frickin' pass out if you don't get down here and get in the car right now!"

It was unclear whether Bob was absorbing anything.

"Hold on," he said.

He disappeared from view again.

━━━━━

ONCE BOB'S HEAD had cleared, he drove Tracey to the fire station, a little oasis of light. There, Fire Chief John Babiarz was on duty. No fan of bears, he was showing the excitement of a man who'd finally been called to respond to the crisis he'd long been anticipating.

"Those goddamn bears!"

He repeated himself, louder.

"Those GODDAMN bears!"

Within minutes, emergency responders flooded the fire station while Babiarz called the New Hampshire Fish and Game Department. For an awful, awkward moment, two worldviews of bear management collided. The man who answered the phone sounded doubtful.

"It's been a century since we've had a bear attack on a person," he said.

But the quantitative statistics the man was citing did not match the qualitative experience unfolding in Grafton. So Babiarz shouted at him too.

"I'm HERE!" he said. "I see the BLOOD!"

In the ambulance, an EMT named Kathy cooed sympathetically at Tracey as she poured saline and tugged at the dishcloth, now deeply embedded in the mass of clotted blood forming between Tracey's ligaments and muscles.

"I'm so sorry I have to do this," she said, "but I have to get this off."

Each centimeter caused Tracey's by now agonizing pain to flare. It was torture.

"Oh God!"

She finally began to cry, talking through tears.

"You know," she wailed, "I've already been through a lot."

She didn't mean the events of the night. She meant the events of her life in Grafton. The breast cancer, the sweltering greenhouse, the pay-by-the-minute cell phone that wouldn't work in her house, the coyotes dogging her steps when she went for a walk.

"And now I've had a fuckin' bear attack!"

Tracey sobbed.

"I can't believe it."

———

IN THE WEEKS and months that followed, Grafton was awash in a sweaty, boiling anger that was stupid in its willingness to cast blame indiscriminately and pardon no one for their faults. Everyone, it seemed, wrestled endless demons of fur and heat: John Connell, still waiting to hear whether God wanted him to sell his church for zero dollars, got into an argument with the police chief over whether enforcement of victimless crimes was harassment; Jessica Soule rolled down her wheelchair ramp, a garbage bag in one hand and a gun in the other; Tracey Colburn lay awake on sweat-soaked sheets, listening to the bear outside her house. Burglary rates were up, drug crimes were up, and two different groups of people began talking seriously about how to address the area's bear surplus: state officials discussed a ten-year population reduction plan, while a group of Graftonites discussed blowing the heads off of every bear in town.

Throughout it all, Doughnut Lady and a handful of libertarians continued to feed the bears, which needed the food more than ever—after all, it was a drought year.

BOOK THREE
BOUNDLESS RUINS

I have given you bear and bison,
I have given you roe and reindeer,
I have given you brant and beaver,
Filled the marshes full of wild-fowl,
Filled the rivers full of fishes:
Why then are you not contented?
Why then will you hunt each other?
I am weary of your quarrels

—Henry Wadsworth Longfellow, The Song of Hiawatha, 1855

1

A HUDDLE OF HUNTERS

A change, a great change, is coming in society; but, haply, it may not be the change the bear anticipates. The bear has said that he will crush us.

What if we crush the bear?

—Jack London, *The Iron Heel*, 1908

No matter how many phone calls I make, no matter how many doors I knock on, every answer I dredge from the depths of Grafton's deep pool of secrets is encumbered by three or four questions, steadfast as barnacles, mute and intriguingly shaped.

This is never more true than when I fish for information about illegal bear hunting. Under state law, it is generally only legal to kill a bear in season, with a hunting permit, and when following a long list of rules that govern which bears can be hunted, how to report the kill, and what weapon can be used. The deployment of chocolate is, of course, strictly verboten.

Outside of these state-sanctioned hunting practices, the first rule for killing a bear is pretty much the same as the first rule for killing a human: it can only be done in defense (though when it comes to killing a bear, defense of one's dogs or chickens counts).

And yet, I hear whispers that, behind this veneer of sensible rules, an ugly, clandestine bear killing has taken place. One man tells me, with palpable anger, that he found a wounded bear in his backyard out of season, its jaw shattered so badly by a bullet that it couldn't eat.

And so every time I pull my notebook from my pocket for an impromptu interview, an illegal bear hunt is one of the topics I try to broach. Has one happened? Who did it? And why?

The why was of particular interest—if Grafton's men were killing bears because they felt threatened, it would be the ultimate return to that Revolutionary-era past so revered by the Free Towners, when the flames of freedom burned hot and bright and manhood was measured in pelts.

All this is on my mind when I climb a steep, overgrown driveway not far from where Tracey Colburn was attacked. I can see that the tree-crowded mobile home will soon be completely swallowed by the forest. The last line of defense against this eventuality is Tim Bowen, who's got a doughnut of a face, sweet and soft. He tells me he's thirty, though he sounds twenty and looks forty. He is not a Free Town interloper, but a native-born Grafton libertarian.

"We have the media and Hollywood," he says, sitting on his porch. "The liberal party or Democratic Party, they're too busy telling you how to run your life. You know the media is going to sell you some kind of product. Well, I don't give a crap about any product."

He takes a breath, lets out something between a moan and a sigh.

"Unless it's cheese. I don't care. Cheese is one of my favorite things. If Cabot was to become world-famous or something, I would love that."

Bowen's career litters the yard. I can see the two beaters that he drove to four years' worth of graveyard shifts at Walmart, before they finally crapped out and forced him to quit. Now he does yard work, he says, nodding at a bevy of rusting rakes and hoes leaning up against the trailer but offering no explanation as to why his own yard is covered in a messy tangle of dogshit-studded grass.

I gently steer the conversation. Many people, I observe, seem to feel unsafe around so much bear activity. Some, I venture, might even feel so unsafe that they would feel compelled to take action. Bowen agrees instantly. He has no love for game wardens, mind you, but he finds it upsetting when people shoot bears illegally.

"It's like being a German in Nazi Germany and not wanting to kill the Jews," he says—presumably with an underlying recognition that there is no moral comparison to be had between the shooting of bears and genocide. "You hear about it and you know it's happening, but you just don't want to think about it."

Bowen would like to speak out against the practice, but he worries that to do so would place him between two dangerous adversaries. As a pacifist, he doesn't relish the thought of being shot, or eaten.

Bowen's take on bear killing piques my interest. He's describing not just a single instance of bear poaching but what sounds like an ongoing pattern.

When I ask for names and dates, Bowen goes briefly mute, then returns to the subject of Fish and Game, which he says charges a scalding $35 for a hunting license.

"Thirty-five dollars is a lot of money," he says. "I can make that in half a day's work, but still, I'm a smoker and I like to drink beer, so I have my other expenses on top of other bills. And you can't live without cheese."

Bowen may be the only one choosing between cheese and hunting permits. But others are similarly reticent about illegal bear hunts.

When I bring up the subject with Tom Ploszaj, he gives me a staple of Grafton's small-talk playbook: Friendly Advice. When Ploszaj first came to the community, he says, he got Friendly Advice of his own when he started asking too many questions about how things worked and who had done what to whom.

"There's a lot of places around here where they'll never put a shovel into the dirt," he tells me now, his tone mild. "You don't want to find one of those places."

When I don't respond, he clarifies, holding my eyes with his.

"If you ask too many questions, you might be in a hole in the woods and no one's going to find you."

Friendly Advice took many forms in Grafton. Sometimes a phrase like "I'm a proud gun owner" was slipped innocuously between a description of one's pets and an observation on the weather. Sometimes it took the trappings of gossip, as in, "That guy knows not to break into my home because he knows I have guns," presumably implying that I too should now know not to break into that home, for the same reason. Or somebody like Ploszaj's friend, the free-wheeling John Redman, would sometimes just slap a gun clip down on your car console.

In all cases, the common denominator was someone taking special pains to communicate to me that there were guns in an easily accessible, but undisclosed, location, and that those guns could be employed against me.

You know, if it came to that.

———

MY QUESTIONS ABOUT bear hunts take a sharper focus during a visit to the town's last remaining retail business, the general store on Route 4. It has the same uneven wooden flooring that it had during Grafton's more prosperous days, though the barrels of soda crackers have faded away. In their place are lamp-heated terrariums full of rotating slices of pizza that were born in the freezer and are doomed to die of dehydration. Even this store, Grafton's last bit of commerce, is in a state of decline; months later, in the library, I will overhear women tsking over how Graftonites are lining up at Canaan's more modern gas station rather than supporting their hometown store. (Though, in a counter-tsk, they then note that the Grafton general store is not helping its cause any in failing to correct a spelling deficiency in its signage that consistently identifies the "regular" grade of gasoline as "rugular.")

As I exit the store, a drink in hand, I strike up a conversation about bears with a pair of older men on the wooden front porch. They tell me that, in the recent past, a posse of Grafton men hunted and killed thirteen bears in one day. At first, they sound happy about it, in a those-damn-bears-had-it-coming kind of way, but to me the news is an absolute bombshell, and my reaction must have shown on my face. When I pull out my notebook and press for details, the men exchange a look and stop talking.

That idea of bear killing—a mass execution, not for sport, nor for food, but because the bears had it coming—becomes the center of my attention. Now that I know what to ask about, I start to pick up other little bits of information, and a picture of a massive bear hunt in the recent past slowly emerges.

It was triggered, of course, by the events of 2012, when the attack on Tracey Colburn pushed drought-desperate bears and heat-crazed humans to the brink of crisis.

As media outlets picked up and repeated the Colburn story, it became a subject of heated debate around town. Many in Grafton held the bear blameless, but a sizable minority saw it as a call to arms to defend the community. After Tracey was released from the hospital, she ventured onto her porch with a friend and watched as a pickup with a large wooden box in the truck bed bumped up her remote dirt road. Though bear-hunting season was still months away, the cab bristled with men and guns; the box, hammered together out of plywood, was filled with dogs sticking their heads out of holes, noses twitching in the open air to pick up scents.

When hunters use trained dogs to hunt bears, they wait until the hounds bay and then release them, using GPS collars to follow behind. Often the bear is swarmed on the ground by the dogs, an encounter that can be fatal for both bear and dog; sometimes the bear seeks refuge in a tree, at which point the hunter typically catches up and shoots it down. The men driving past Tracey's house didn't acknowledge her, and though the humid air was good for holding scent, their hounds did not bay. She never saw them again.

Months passed. It was a long, hot, wet summer, and tensions continued to simmer. The bears continued to be far more active than in a nondrought year, but there were no more attacks. When fall came, both temperatures and moods cooled.

That year's dearth of natural foods kept most bears leaner than usual; when the autumn chill came, most allowed themselves to grow sleepy, rather than burn fat all winter. By late fall, barbecue grills were withdrawn, the forest was stripped bare of acorns, and most bears had taken to their dens, where they could sleep and dream their bear dreams.

That's when the men struck.

In Grafton during hunting season, people have grown accustomed to the chatter of gunfire emanating from the woods, telling stories of battles lost and won. There is the single smug crack of the expert marksman, and the awful, misery-laden silence spanning two shots (the second one a mercy). The hills might ring with the sound of a hunter chasing fleeting glory, a triple staccato as irregular as a frantic heartbeat, or the lazy, endless patter of a mass beer bottle execution, cruel in that the targets until quite recently performed their beverage-holding service ably and well. But in late 2012, as hunting season ended and the cold descended, a novel bullet-told tale began booming out of the woods.

In November, Cheryl Senter, a photojournalist from out of town, was preparing for an estate sale in the home of her mother, who had died during the summer heat. Senter was going through the sprawling historic farmhouse, making small decisions about furniture and tools and larger decisions about life. She knew it made financial sense to sell the property, but it was also where the family had spent their summers during her childhood years. As sentimental and practical values wrestled with one another, her thoughts were interrupted by a bang exploding from the woods beyond the farmhouse. By the time she registered that it was a gunshot, there had been three more, all in quick succession.

"I'm used to gunfire where I live," she said. But she'd never heard anything like this. There were more shots, then more again. "It sounded like a war going on up in the woods."

Panicked, Senter moved away from the windows and stood listening to the ongoing fusillade. It sounded like a firing squad had invaded her mother's property. "Just so many guns firing. It just kept going on and on and on."

When the actual noise yielded to echoes in her mind, Senter didn't go outside to investigate, nor did she call Fish and Game to report what she had heard. But when she left her mother's home, she was deeply unsettled.

Why was there so much gunfire? she asked herself. *Why did they need so much gunfire to get it?*

Others also noticed unusual fusillades of gunfire in the woods that year. They made little sense in the context of a legal hunt. Groups of hunters didn't typically cluster together, all shooting at the same target, at the same time, like a Revolutionary War company executing a defense from behind a stone wall.

But who were the shooters? The more questions I asked, the more I realized how well hidden the poachers were. It wasn't the dense tangle of leafy forest scrub or the crumbling rock walls that hid them—it was a thicket of social relations and a stony culture of resistance to outsiders. Sometimes, when I talked to a Grafton man, I got the feeling that his face was a mask, that a bear killer was peering out at me through the eyeholes. But I could never be sure.

What seemed clear was this: in a town that refused to allow the government to protect it from bears, vigilantism seemed the only option. Just as the libertarians wanted, it was every man, woman, and bear for themselves.

2

THE ASSAULT'S AFTERMATH

I must tell you Susie's last. She is sorely badgered with dreams; and her stock dream is that she is being eaten up by bears. She is a grave and thoughtful child, as you will remember.

. . . [W]ith the pathos of one who feels he has not been dealt by with even-handed fairness, [she] said "But Mamma, the trouble is, that I am never the bear, but always the person."

It would not have occurred to me that there might be an advantage, even in a dream, in occasionally being the eater, instead of always the party eaten.

—Mark Twain, letter to friends, 1878

It only took the one bear attack to convince Tracey Colburn to leave the little yellow house in the woods.

When I seek her out, I am led to the small home she rents. It lies among a dozen or so residential structures that flow south from the cluster of buildings that house Grafton's fire department, town offices, and library. If the wilderness is an unruly mob storming the castle of civilization, this neighborhood is Grafton's last civic stronghold, one of the few places where front-porch sitters from neighboring houses can see and draw comfort from one another's presence.

"I'm sorry for the garbage," Tracey apologizes, standing on her stoop in knee-length denim shorts in the strong summer sunshine. The wounds to her arms have been stitched into pale white scars. "I'm cleaning."

For a day or two after the attack, she says, a flurry of activity kept her busy—she fielded visits from local reporters, got rabies shots, and listened when a friend suggested, gently, that it was time to clean the crusted blood from her dining room. Kai, it turned out, had not escaped injury. Whenever Tracey walked from bedroom to bathroom to kitchen or any point in between, he crowded her every step, limping, but devoted and cheerful as ever.

After the attack, a state game warden asked her questions and erected a huge box trap in her yard. Once the bear entered, the heavy metal door would fall and lock into place, at which point the entire trap would become a cage for transport. After the warden left, Tracey and her friend peeked inside to see what they'd used for bait—a single little pink doughnut, resting inside.

Tracey didn't want to be home alone, and so she convinced her friend to sleep over. That night, as Tracey lay in bed, she heard a bear (the bear that got her, she was certain) banging on the side of the trap. She was sure the bear had been caught, but when they woke the next morning, it turned out that the wily bear had assaulted the trap from without, not within. The box lay empty, doughnut untouched. A few days later, the warden removed the trap and never returned.

Tracey often thought about the bear that had attacked her. She wondered how many times it had ventured into her yard, or onto her porch, how often it had watched her through the window. Not like a peeping Tom. Peeping Toms are people, and she had lost the ability to anthropomorphize wild animals. When that bear's head had eclipsed her night sky, the amiable cabbage-rolling bruins of her recent past had vanished entirely, replaced by something that measured risk and reward, pain and calories. She never wanted to find herself on the wrong side of that cold calculus again.

"If you look at their eyes, you understand," she says, "that they are completely alien to us."

In the weeks after the attack, Tracey replayed the scene in her mind, tweaking the script and then watching for different outcomes. In one version, she plays loud music, deterring the bears from investigating her porch. In another, she slides the door curtain aside before she opens the door and sees the bears outside. Or she sees herself running inside instead of screaming, and the bear doesn't charge her.

She also tweaked the script in the opposite direction. The bear crushes Kai with a single blow and then resumes its attack on her. It drags her out onto the ground, and the cubs circle back from the undergrowth, to learn from their mother how to kill the hairless primates living in their midst.

"I know that's a bizarre way of thinking, but they have that instinct," she says. "To teach their cubs."

In addition to failing to capture the bear, Fish and Game also failed to defend Tracey in the court of public opinion; instead, within hours of the attack, officials told media organizations across New England that the bear was attracted to the pot roast Tracey had been cooking at the time. That narrative shifted the blame away from the bear and also away from the state policies that led to a record-high number of drought-desperate bears in the woods of an increasingly lawless Grafton.

But even assuming that it is reckless to cook a pot roast in one's kitchen, Tracey wasn't cooking a pot roast on the night in question. She had simply removed a cold pot roast from her refrigerator and spent a minute or two slicing it on the kitchen counter.

Given that Tracey's harrowing encounter was the most dramatic example of bear conflict in New Hampshire since the state began nurturing bear populations, I was curious to see Fish and Game's reaction.

I wrote to Andrew Timmins, the state's leading bear biologist, with a request for copies of all paperwork related to the attack. But Timmins responded that there was no paperwork—no narrative of events, no analysis of the bear's actions, no correspondence among officials. The only formal record of the whole incident was a single check mark among many check marks in the tally of bear encounters associated with the presence of human food.

This is the end result—and the ultimate failing—of the quantitative approach: Tracey's potentially fatal experience was treated on paper no differently than a garbage can raid.

But I don't fault the department, which can't always afford to look beyond the data. Timmins, who was as kind and generous with his time as I could hope, responded to my request for information by offering me a summary of the five-year-old recollections of involved staff, including the game warden who set up the box trap.

The summary proved to be inaccurate, and inaccurate in a way that emphasized the blame assigned to Tracey. When I wrote Timmins back to ask about the lack of documentation and question the discrepancies, he acknowledged that the response had suffered under less-than-ideal resource constraints.

"Bottom line is that a handful of us handle hundreds of bear complaints each summer. Given the magnitude of the work, sometimes details slip through the cracks," he wrote. "I don't know why [the responding warden] did not fill out a detailed report with every minute detail. I can tell you from experience that there are times when I would not have time to do the same."

Though she didn't seek a medical diagnosis, Tracey exhibited symptoms associated with PTSD. Her heart fluttered without warning. She caught herself running her fingers lightly over the new seams that the bear attack had left on her wrists. At first, she sequestered herself inside her house, begging her circle of loyal friends and family not to leave her there alone. She tried to acclimate to the feel of adrenaline flooding her body.

As Tracey tried to hold herself together, a realization slowly dawned on her, one that left a sick feeling in the pit of her stomach. She had assumed that the Grafton community would sympathize with her. But in reality, many people blamed her.

As the summer wore on, colorful social niceties fell away like autumn leaves, revealing the stark black bark of human nature. Bear apologists came out of the woodwork, twisting facts to make Tracey seem more culpable.

Some accused Tracey of siccing Kai on the bear. They said the dog had torn open the bear's stomach and mauled the cubs, which grew smaller in each telling until they were helpless infants. Tracey had attracted the bears with birdseed, swatted them with a broom, gotten high, put hot beef stew on her open windowsill. Tracey felt like the victim of a sexual assault asked what she had done to provoke her attacker.

"They think, because it's an animal, you must have done something. And that's not true," Tracey says. "I did nothing but cut a cold roast on my counter."

She withdrew from the public.

I'm just staying away from people for a while, she told herself. *I've got to stay here and get healed up. . . . I don't care if there's vicious gossip. Don't care.*

If there is a silver lining to suffering trauma, it is the opportunity to learn about one's self, to trail mental fingers over a previously unrecognized core of inner strength.

It took weeks before Tracey got comfortable being home alone again. Around mid-July, she started venturing into her yard—not as far as the edges, where the rough maple trunks still looked ominously like scars, but toward the middle, where the sun shone and the grass grew.

The rushes of adrenaline became weaker, and fewer.

One might think that an early step, perhaps the first step, in Tracey's personal journey would involve a firm resolve to stay away from bears and, above all else, to abstain from bear-screaming.

In fact, she soon found herself within a few feet of another wild black bear, a much larger one. And—this is true—she screamed at it.

This happened at the house of a friend, who invited Tracey to see an old male bear that raided the suet from a bird feeder every two weeks, like clockwork. The friend convinced Tracey that it was an opportunity to confront her emotional trauma, on the same theory that convinces arachnophobes to allow fanged tarantulas to crawl along their naked wrists.

Soon, the bear—humongous, she says, the biggest she'd ever seen—was at the front door, unaware that Tracey was peering at it through the window, absorbing details. He looked calm enough.

We call him Teddy, her friend said. *He's all right.*

Tracey opened the window a crack.

"Teddy," she said, directing her comments at the bear. "You're not supposed to be there."

He ambled casually over to the window. She breathed. He was massive. But not threatening.

Until.

Suddenly and without warning, Teddy reared up on his hind legs, towering to his full height over her. Tracey screamed.

"Aaaah! My God!'" She turned and ran deeper into the house while the bear, startled, turned and bolted in the other direction.

Tracey was still screaming, but not in terror, not really. It was more like a roller coaster.

"Okay," she told her friend, laughing and trying to catch her breath.

"This is enough."

3

A PRESSING OF POACHERS

Bang! and she fell paralyzed and dying with a high shoulder
shot. And the three little cubs, not knowing what to do, ran
back to their Mother.

—Ernest Thompson Seton, *Biography of a Grizzly,* 1900

The woman asks me not to divulge her name, for fear of retribution from
the bear poachers.

"They'll burn your house right down," she says. "They've done it before."

Once I agree, she tells me about a knock that came at her door during
the 2012 winter, when Grafton's wooded slopes poured odd bursts of gunfire
down upon the valley.

A Grafton man was standing in her breezeway. They knew each other
well enough. She didn't see who was with him, she says, but the way he spoke
made her think there were four or five other men parked out of her sight,
down by the road.

The man said the group intended to kill a bear denning on her land.
The woman was familiar with both the den site and the animal, which had
emerged from the den with cubs a few times over the years. The poacher
didn't mention the attack on Tracey Colburn. He didn't have to.

"I got nothing to do with it," she replied.

The poacher asked the woman to cross the line from neutrality to
co-conspirator.

"We need to know if we can get on your property," he said.

In a world split between the law of the jungle and the law of the courtroom, between bear killers and bear protectors, everyone must weigh, in an

instant, whether the answer to a question might place them in the sights of one of these two opposing camps. It was a choice between fear and vigilantism, between the mouth of the bear and the mouth of the gun. The woman was loath to break the law, but the law was far away, and here the poacher stood, bearing unspoken promises of friendship, or enmity, as crumbs of snow fell from his boots onto her doorstep.

Besides, she had seen the toll the bears were exacting from Grafton's humans. *Something* had to be done.

So she answered quickly, lest he see her waver.

"What I don't know won't hurt me," she told him. "And I won't look out my window."

The gunfire came not long after, a lengthy barrage of vengeance, of blood taken for blood spilled. As she listened, the woman stayed away from her windows. She didn't want to see, she didn't want to be seen, and she definitely didn't want a stray bullet to turn her into a casualty of the quickening war on bears.

———

EVEN AFTER TALKING to the woman, it was hard for me to picture poachers killing a hibernating bear, an act that is grossly unethical by the standards of both the state and respectable hunting organizations. Because the practice is so widely and passionately condemned, it has taken place only in secret, without the public ever seeing footage of what it's really like.

Not until April 2018, that is, when an Alaskan game camera caught a man and his adult son storming a bear den in a remote rural location.

The video, which was popularized by the Humane Society of the United States, shows father and son standing side by side on cross-country skis. The son, wearing a fat goatee beneath handsome features, is bare-chested. The stubble-faced father is scruffy in jeans, a sleeveless down vest with no shirt, and a hunting cap that fails to hide the receding line of scraggle. They approach the darkness of a shallow bear den, partially hidden by needled pine branches that reach down to the snow.

In midwinter, while snugged away into the safe refuge of her den, a female black bear often gives birth to a pair of squirrel-sized young. For newborn and mother both, those first few months are the only time they will ever feel secure enough to enjoy a peaceful intimacy. The babies nurse until spring, when the mother, having lost up to 40 percent of her body weight, emerges on unsteady legs to search for her first meal of the spring. Unlike some animals, which go comatose all winter, black bears retain the ability to wake up, though when they do, they can be groggy and uncoordinated.

In the video, the son holds a revolver in a classic spread-legged Weaver shooting stance, while the father keeps his hunting rifle trained on the den opening; then both discharge their weapons into the bear den. A microphone attached to the game camera picks up the sounds—the crack of gunfire and the piteous squealing of two bear cubs. The father, now feet from the den, fires again, leaving just one crying orphan. While the son picks up three, four, five bullet casings from the snow—to remove evidence—the father takes careful aim and shoots yet another bullet into the den. The squalls cease immediately. After working together to drag the heavy corpse of the mother bear out of the den, father and son exchange a high-five, their hands smeared red with bear blood.

"They'll never be able to link it to us, I don't think," says the son.

The pair use knives to separate the mother bear's skin from the flesh and fat that, until recently, nurtured her young. They roll the skin up into a neat, practiced bundle.

"You and me don't fuck around," says the son, holding his two ski poles in one hand, while his father straps on a backpack bulging with flesh. "We pretty much—we go where we want, to kill shit."

The curse words are bleeped from the video, an absurd bit of propriety after the grisly violence that has just unfolded.

The two men are completely unaware of the game camera. It is still running when they return the next day to collect more bullet casings and the bodies of the two cubs, which they carry from the scene in a small sack. The footage eventually leads to convictions and punishments, including a three-month prison sentence for the father.

The woman tells me that something like this scene played out in Grafton on the day the men pressured her into giving them access to the bear den on her land. Now that I've seen the video of the father and son standing side by side, firearms extended, I can imagine how gunfire from many hunters standing in a semicircle around a single, stationary target embedded in a den might sound like the sustained barrages that people heard in Grafton that winter.

The next time the woman saw the posse member, he told her they had cleansed Grafton of bears that day. Every known den had been visited; every bear, adult and cub, had been dealt with.

"He said they got them, and emptied them out," the woman tells me. The number of bears he reported killing, she says, "was thirteen." I believe her. Thirteen is the kill tally I heard on the front porch of the general store. The figure suggests that they visited at least four or five bear family dens, and possibly more, that day. I have been critical of overreliance on statistics, but in this case the state's database of bear complaints yields up a number that corroborates the woman's story. Even in warden-wary Grafton, a handful of people, like Jessica Soule, do call Fish and Game with bear complaints each year. In most years, there are four or five such calls; in 2012, the year of the drought, there were a dozen (one of which was probably from Tracey Colburn).

There's only one year on record in which there were no bear complaints from Grafton—2013, the year after the posse's ursine genocide campaign.

The woman tells me something else that she has heard from posse members. Since I came to town, she says, they have heard that a journalist is asking too many questions about illegal bear hunts. They worry that my inquiries will lead to some sort of criminal prosecution or the revocation of their legally acquired hunting licenses.

"They agreed that they're not going to talk to you," she says. When I press her, however, she gives me a name. And I decide it can't hurt to ask.

———

AFTER I MATCH the name of the alleged bear poacher to his Bungtown address, I drive there to take a look at the rundown house, heated by the woodpile stacked against one wall; outside, the heavy wheels of some logging machinery have reduced much of the yard to mud, while inside a large dog barks portentously.

Even before my car rolls to a stop on the shoulder of the road outside his home, I realize that this is not the first time I've pulled up outside this house, planning to knock on this door.

Earlier this year, before I'd heard much about illegal bear hunts, I had stopped here to ask questions. At the time, the wary stance of the man who opened the door to me suggested deep distrust. I'd explained that I was trying to hear and document bear stories that took place in Grafton. Had he had any interesting bear encounters himself?

"I just moved here," he'd said, before closing the door. "I haven't seen any bears."

At the time, I considered it just one of several unfriendly rebuffs I'd received on doorsteps in town. But now I know his response was a lie—he was raised in Grafton, had a family deeply embedded in its community, and had lived alongside the town's bears for decades. Getting out of my car this time, I know I have questions that are far less innocuous, and I don't expect a warm reception. As I approach, he is standing in his yard, watching with eyes that glint like mica. He's rangy and muscled, with a straight-edge razor of a mouth. A sharp line divides the sun-browned skin of his forehead from the white skullcap of hair up top.

I don't want him to back himself into a corner by telling me, again, that he is new to the neighborhood, so I start talking as soon as I am in earshot. I call him by name and tell him, in the friendliest possible way, that I know who he is.

He listens and watches me, still as stone. He seems like a third party to the conversation, observing instead of participating. I fill the space between us with more words, explaining that I understand he may have had good reasons for the bear hunt and that I want to convey those reasons to readers.

When I run out of words, he finally engages with me, in a manner that is neither friendly nor unfriendly. He's never heard of the bear-hunting posse, he says, and wouldn't have taken part in any case, because he is part Cherokee and to kill bears would be a violation of that heritage.

I explain that I'm not trying to get his hunting license taken away. I want to describe the hunt, but not in a way that would identify him or get him in trouble.

"So I still ain't going to talk to anybody. I don't want nothing to do with it," he says. "You can explain it, but I don't want to get involved with it."

Though he won't explicitly admit to the hunt, he does offer me a certain brand of Friendly Advice.

"If you find out about this bear hunt that you keep mentioning, you're going to have a problem with that one, because they're going to say, 'Well, you ratted them out.' They're going to find out who started that and why they did it."

We talk for a while longer—he is critical of "fucking idiots" who leave their bird feeders out during bear season—but I realize that it is all I'm going to get out of him. I thank him for his time and leave.

"Just leave me out of it," he calls as I walk away. "Because then a war's going to come, and I'm going to be right in the middle of it."

Not long after, I call a friend of his, someone I heard was also part of the posse that gathered in the winter of 2013. When I get him on the phone, I identify myself and tell him I'm writing about bear encounters in the town of Grafton.

"I just moved here," he answers. "So I haven't seen any bears here, sorry."

Not only do I know this to be untrue, but he has uttered, almost word for word, the same untruth I got when I approached his friend. It seems rehearsed.

"Oh really?" I say, trying to mask my skepticism with the tone of friendly small talk. "When did you move to town?"

"I don't have to answer these questions," he says and hangs up.

I make other attempts to reach out to the poachers, to ask them to have a frank discussion with me. But this is the closest I ever get to an answer.

And anyway, their vigilantism hasn't helped, not really. It put a brief dent in the local bear population, but nothing more. With Fish and Game administrators still too overworked to step in, the woods soon teemed with more bears. Graftonites may have thought they had a bear problem, but you could equally say it was a problem caused by the retreat of their sworn enemy: taxes.

4

THE PASTOR IS PUSHED

Dost thou remember, Philip, the old fable
Told us when we were boys, in which the bear
Going for honey overturns the hive,
And is stung blind by bees? I am that beast

—Henry Wadsworth Longfellow, *Judas Maccabaeus*, 1872

On May 21, 2013, during a warm thunderstorm that rattled the roof of the Peaceful Assembly Church and drenched the canopy of the suddenly bear-free woods, God told John Connell that his period of waiting was at an end.

"The time has come," said God.

"Let go of everything," said God.

And so he did.

Up until the time God spoke, Connell had continued to struggle against the town's threats to repossess the church property. After a Facebook post in which he noted being 120 days from the final deadline, he got a text from his daughter, Theresa Rose Connell, who lived in Massachusetts.

"So this means . . . they can seize it? you'd have to sell it?" asked his daughter. "What's the plan?"

No plan, Connell replied. With his characteristic flair for allegorizing his own life, he added that they could take his possessions, but not his soul.

His daughter expressed solidarity, as well as sympathy for the stress he must be feeling.

"I'd give it away before they can get their greedy hands on it," said Connell. ". . . Pardon my putting it this way but—ummmmm—FUCK THEM! I've got better things on my mind than them. Like peace, love, and forgiveness."

"Keep me posted," said his daughter.

By the time the town was able to seize the property from Connell, Connell no longer had any property to seize. In August, he signed it over to a corporate entity called the Peaceful Assembly Church; its board of directors consisted exclusively of Free Towners and their allies—Jeremy Olson, Bob Hull, Tom Ploszaj, Jay Boucher, and James Reiher.

The church's new directors found it easy to convince town officials to give them more time to resolve the tax liens; even though the ultimate remedy of a town against recalcitrant taxpayers is to seize the property, the officials wanted the tax revenue much more than they wanted the property.

The freedom that Connell had found when he purchased the church was nothing compared to the freedom he felt when he gave it away. Suddenly liberated from legal entanglements, he pursued holy pursuits and devoted himself to devotion. And there were signs that he was gaining traction as a spiritual presence in the community. The church directors enlisted him in a statewide libertarian-connected program that donated Thanksgiving dinners to those in need; under the program, Connell gave out about a dozen baskets. He continued his monthly Bible studies and other programs. He launched a new arts initiative and developed a mentoring relationship with a young artist, who'd found in God the strength to distance himself from a life of drugs. Things were clicking for Connell.

But the respite didn't last.

THE FOLLOWING YEAR, in 2014, the three-member Grafton selectboard sat on folding chairs set up around a round plastic table to decide the church's fate. The fire station's fluorescent overhead lighting cast bleak shadows that gave no hint of the beautiful summer day outside.

A circuitous round of paperwork and negotiations between the selectboard and the church directors had yielded up no tax dollars. But it did yield a new tax exemption application that had to be duly considered, just as Connell's had.

If the selectboard rejected the new application before them, the town could renew efforts to seize the property—the exact scenario that Connell's divestment was intended to prevent.

Tom Ploszaj and Jeremy Olson, who had more of an appetite for paperwork than Connell, were eager to forestall a tax lien; they provided copies of their corporate registration, which demonstrated that they were a nonprofit entity in good standing with the state of New Hampshire.

But the debate shifted to whether the directors also needed formal recognition as a religious or charitable entity, a designation granted by the IRS to facilitate federal tax exemptions.

Olson, who was recording the proceedings, addressed the officials.

"When John was running the church himself, he had a position that he didn't want to deal with the federal government," Olson reminded them, speaking with a New York accent hard enough to ricochet off the fire station walls. "John did not want to be involved with the federal government. Doesn't want to talk to them. Doesn't want to sign their paperwork."

Now, though, the church was under new ownership and new leadership. Olson said that the new board of directors had investigated whether to file with the IRS, and they'd arrived at a decision.

"We're opposed to doing it as well. . . . The board decided to go with John's recommendation, that we don't have to file with the federal government."

Olson cited IRS regulations that he said showed that active churches didn't need to be individually recognized, as long as they were engaged in religious activities. He passed around copies of a list of community achievements—such as hosting Bible studies and working with the local Lutheran Ecumenical Council to distribute food to the poor—that he said demonstrated the church's religious and charitable nature.

In front of the selectboard, in a row of folding chairs, four grim-faced members of the public sat shoulder to shoulder, waiting to speak. They wore the solid-colored tops of women with a common fashion sense—dark purple, light purple, pink, and light green.

Dark Purple was opposed: "You're going to have a lot more people coming in and asking for the same thing. . . . Hell, I'll apply for it, if it's as easy as this."

Light Green was also opposed: "From what I know, I actually feel like it's just a scam. And I don't appreciate that at all, as someone who's paying my fair share."

Light Purple agreed: "It seems to me there's an ideological conflict. If you won't recognize the federal government, why should we [support you] recognizing your local government, to take from the taxpayers of the town?"

Pink said that she herself worked with the ecumenical council that Olson cited, and that she doubted Olson's assertion of an affiliation.

"I don't believe they're in it," she said. (What she did not mention was that Olson didn't even seem to know the name of the organization, which is the Mascoma Valley Ecumenical Council, and that it's interdenominational rather than Lutheran.)

Ploszaj leaned back in a folding chair with his arms clasped over the stomach of his clean white T-shirt. He had not yet adopted his "bum look" and instead sported neatly combed hair and a trimmed beard. Speaking with the tight voice of a parent who has been forced to explain himself to his wayward children, he objected to being judged by people who had never come to see the church's work in person.

"That church is open to everyone," he told the officials. "Of all faiths or no faiths. If they choose not to enter the door or step onto the property, we will not force them. We will not use force."

He spread his hands a bit while shrugging, as if the church not physically dragging uninterested people to its on-site activities was a great overlooked virtue.

"I'm being told we must do—must do—things that are not mandatory. That's all I'm going to say," he said. Then he immediately said more, delivering the latest in a string of only slightly veiled threats about what would happen if the town continued to try to tax the church.

"We have to go to the next step. . . . It might be legalese speak. None of us are lawyers, attorneys," he said.

When it came time for the three selectmen to vote, the first said that he favored the exemption, while the second was opposed. The tiebreaker, wearing a navy blue T-shirt and gray capris, had a blocky head perched on a narrow body, like a Pez dispenser. Though he sounded conflicted, he said that Ploszaj's talk of legal action "really turned me off."

"It kind of seems like putting up a cold shoulder to the community," he said, fidgeting in his seat. He uncrossed and recrossed his arms, waiting for the vote to be called.

With a majority of 2–1, the tax exemption was denied.

———

THE VOTE PUT Connell back in the same old position. The threat of property seizure hung over his head like the sword of Damocles, held back only by a fraying thread of legal arguments. As part of the Free Towners' ongoing pattern of taking government officials to court, the church directors were fully prepared to follow through with their threat of a legal battle. They told

Connell he needed to be deposed by their lawyers to help them in the upcoming courtroom fight.

Connell considered this directive an insult to his principles—after years of telling the town that he wouldn't fill out governmental paperwork, why would the directors expect him to reverse course? He reminded the directors that resolving the tax issue was their responsibility. He was opposed to, as he put it, "using government to protect the church from the government."

Anytime the directors brought up the issue, which was pretty much every time they talked to Connell, he shut the conversation down with a new catchphrase.

"I am relying on God—not men."

In April, after one of the monthly Sunday church services, the directors held a formal meeting outside the church building. Connell was surprised to find that they had invited a guest to introduce himself—John Redman.

I would eventually come to meet Redman, along with Ploszaj, on the day the ponytailed folk singer slapped his bullets down on the console of my car.

But the board had interest in a different side of Redman, who, like Connell, dabbled in both religious leadership (he had some religious training as a Quaker minister) and protests against the justice system (his favorite target was the police). The board of directors explained that if Redman was installed as a co-pastor, he might be able to help the tax situation by participating in some of the legal proceedings that Connell despised.

Connell, who already knew Redman as a supporter of the church, liked the idea. When the board voted to appoint Redman to the role of co-pastor, Connell sent out a warm, public introduction to church supporters (though, in an unsubtle marking of territory, he described Redman as assistant pastor, rather than co-pastor).

The first warning sign that things might not go well came early. One of Redman's first acts as co-pastor was what Connell felt was a ridiculously overdramatic display of the right to bear arms with a "very fancy" rifle, right outside the church. Connell didn't like the whiff of militarism emanating from so close to his massive peace dove painting, but trusting that things would resolve themselves, he held his tongue.

Besides, he had other worldly concerns. Perhaps he had envisioned that his basic needs would be served by the proceeds of the collection plate; if so, that never happened. In October, in a public call for donations, he said that he was unable to pay the church heating bills and was having a difficult time buying food.

"I've spent EVERYTHING I had, and I've been (for almost 4 ½ years) the UNPAID, FULL-TIME, VOLUTEER [sic] pastor and sexton to get Peaceful Assembly Church this far," he wrote.

When winter came, intermittent donations allowed Connell to scrape by, but just barely. At times, he said, he was forced to retreat into a small storage space with a ceiling less than four feet tall, because it was the only place in the church where he could get the temperature above 40 degrees.

"But, I am quite OK with suffering a bit to try to keep Peaceful Assembly Church going," he concluded. In May of 2015, he offered to sell his three favorite guitars to anyone who would offer a fair price.

If the winters were harsh, the long bright days of summers were good to Connell. He liked the way a hiking trail that followed the old railroad tracks running behind the church piped people right past his back door. Connell collected brush and whacked weeds to keep that stretch of the trail looking nice, and he often waylaid walkers with sculptures or face-to-face messages of peace and love. (That year the state of New Hampshire, which had a different definition of "looking nice," told Connell to remove his art from the public right-of-way along the trail.)

In June, he had an especially good day—working on his Zen garden, tidying up the hiking trail, talking spiritualism to people who came by, one of whom Connell described as being in a crisis. As the sun dipped below the horizon, a few more trail-walkers stopped to chat, and he brought out his guitar.

"Someone told me long ago, there's a calm before the storm," he began in his rough voice. "I know! It's been comin' for some time."

Connell's repertoire of what he called his peace songs was extensive, if tilted toward the years of his youth. He sang on to his small band of listeners, until the only lingering sign of the sun was vestigial warmth rising from the gravel of the rail bed.

When he finally bid them farewell and retired to the church, he was exultant.

"Forgiveness messages delivered—and received," he concluded, before he collapsed into bed.

Rosalie Babiarz remembered a time when she took some strawberries out of her greenhouse to Connell. Connell loved fruit; he always seemed to associate it with purity and goodness. They sat outside and ate together, savoring the soft seeded hulls and juicy flesh in the gentle sunshine. It was her favorite memory of him.

"He was a happy soul, and he wanted everybody to be happy," she said. "He wanted everybody to be free."

It was Connell's last summer in Grafton.

———

As THE SEASON's warmth ebbed, Connell and the freedom-loving church directors found more areas of disagreement. Though Connell's own religious activities were distinct from those of mainstream churches, he was aghast at the intermixing of firearms and faith and felt that the directors were drifting away from his central message of peace.

By September, relations had turned so sour and raw that the directors asked Connell to leave the church. He refused.

There were also other conflicts. During an October 5 deposition related to the tax issue, Redman went toe to toe with a friend of the church directors, Dave Kopacz, a baritone-voiced Second Amendment activist from Massachusetts, in the type of aggressive physical posturing that typically precedes a schoolyard fistfight.

Connell, meanwhile, unleashed a public barrage of attacks on Redman— he questioned his co-pastor's credentials, complained that Redman used the phrase "god-damned," and said Redman was being driven by "his demons." He accused Redman of training a laser light scope on the chests of people (which Redman denied) and also brought up the earlier firearms display on church property.

"Is the Peaceful Assembly Church," Connell asked, "moving from . . . 'Peace through Forgiveness' to 'Peace through superior fire power'?"

On October 29, he quoted an email in which Redman had fired back at him.

"You seem to have come unhinged," Redman said. ". . . You have not had good luck lately, nor managed to make things happen in Grafton."

Outside the church, Connell posed for a photograph, with no shirt on and a large target painted on his chest, the scarlet bull's-eye centered over his heart. It was a reference, he said, to Redman's supposed laser light scope antics.

"The target on my chest is my creative/artistic expression for what may be soon to come," he wrote to supporters on the freedom forums.

The harder Connell fought for freedom, the tighter the web of constraints drew around him. The days once more grew short and chilly, but he could afford neither propane nor heating oil. He began washing in cold water and wearing layers inside.

A week before Thanksgiving, Connell withdrew $30 from his last bank account. His remaining balance, he announced, was one dollar and one cent.

His war of words with the Free Towners escalated. He now called them "hypocrite takeover artists" to anyone who would listen, in person or in a series of posts on Facebook and the freedom forums.

"I have seen increasing amounts, of glimpses, of fear and hatred in some of the eyes and faces," he wrote. He accused one director of trying to intimidate him several times by flashing the butt of his concealed handgun.

Three days before Thanksgiving, for the first time that year, the temperature dipped below 20 degrees. The following day it barely got above freezing. Several years earlier, the libertarians had set up Porc411 (named for their iconic self-defense symbol, the porcupine) to connect freedom-lovers across the state.

Now Connell called Porc411 and, in a rambling, six-minute message to the community at large, accused the directors of abandoning the religious mission of the church in a "complete betrayal" of his agreement with them.

"They want a liberty clubhouse," he said. "They've been influenced by some very, very dark forces."

He said that, despite the cold weather and the oncoming holidays, Ploszaj and Olson were considering changing the locks on the church to force him out.

Connell added that he'd had a change of heart related to the town's tax liens on the church. Given the choice between the Free Towners or the town, he said, "I will tell the judge that this has been a complete fraud and that the government ought to take this building."

5

A NEIGHBOR ANNOYED

Bear and tiger skins covered the polished floor. There were lounging chairs and sofas, window seats covered with soft cushions of fantastic designs; there was one corner fitted in Persian fashion, with a huge canopy and a jeweled lamp beneath. Beyond, a door opened upon a bedroom, and beyond that was a swimming pool of the purest marble, that had cost about forty thousand dollars.

—Upton Sinclair, *The Jungle*, 1906

"Please. Do not! Write a story glorifying it."

The "it" that the older woman doesn't want me to glorify is the bear-feeding of her neighbor, who I know by now is Doughnut Lady. With a strained contempt that speaks of a more cosmopolitan upbringing, she has a way of referring to Doughnut Lady as if Doughnut Lady is an anonymous crowd.

"I think a lot of people," she says. "Have these illusions. That it's all fun and games. That it's entertainment for their guests."

I'll call her Beretta, because she gives me the by now standard Friendly Advice that if I ever break into her house, I could be shot, blah blah blah.

The years that Doughnut Lady has spent joyously bonding with the bears have been, from Beretta's perspective, fraught with peril. Whenever the bears came (which was every day, more than once), Beretta peered through the curtains and watched them loitering in the grass. When the bears broke the branches of Doughnut Lady's apple trees, no one cared, but when they did the same to Beretta's apple trees, she was furious.

A lot of Beretta's objections to the bears seemed to be based on their physique, which she describes in ways that make me uncomfortably aware of my own pudge-covered bulk.

They're "great big huge things," she tells me. "They look like sumo wrestlers. Big. Fat. All that."

Rather than foraging for berries and fish, the bears were eating doughnuts and other human foods, she says, which was very bad for them. Also, she says, looking at me archly, "if you read the labels. It's very bad for people."

"Very bad," I agree, meekly.

Though she likes animals, she is not in favor of the unnatural beasts in the woods of Grafton, the abnormally large coyotes and the invasive wild boars. In the 1970s, she says, Dartmouth researchers posted game cameras in the area, seeking evidence of Bigfoot. It was silly, she knows. She doesn't think Bigfoot is real. But she always remembered.

While Doughnut Lady was immersing herself in a Disney-tinged world of semi-tame bears, Beretta was trapped in a suspense film in which she was forever forestalling the final bloody scene (as heroines so often are).

"I don't want to get mauled by a bear," Beretta insists. "I really, truly don't."

Once, when she was preparing to leave the house to get to her volunteer shift at the hospital, she saw the bears outside. She called the police and asked for help to get to her car. The police dispatcher offered to stay on the phone until she got to her car safely. Beretta, correctly deducing that this was unlikely to lead to anything more helpful than an audio recording of her own dismemberment, instead hung up and dialed another number. She could not make it on time, she told the hospital, due to unforeseen bear.

———

THOUGH BEARS ARE perhaps the most immediate danger on Beretta's mind, they are not the only one. She has also been set on edge by the Free Town Project. She saw a crowd of them on election day.

"Somebody had a Doctor Seuss hat. And they were acting like crazy lunatics," she says. Though she's an independent voter, Beretta is an advocate for law and order.

"If all else failed, vigilante justice is okay. But I'm not for chaos," she says. "Who gave them the right? It's going to be the Hatfields or McCoys, maybe."

Ever since the Free Town Project got rolling, the sound of gunfire—AK-47s, she thinks—has filtered through the arboreal gloom surrounding her property. She doesn't like the idea of people spraying gunfire in the woods, or the growing lawlessness, in Grafton and elsewhere. She wonders sometimes what would happen if a mob formed here in town.

"I'm not suicidal. But I would sit in the bathtub. And slit my wrists. If they were coming up the hill," she says. "I always said we should put in a drawbridge at the bottom of the hill."

The bears began to take up an increasing amount of Beretta's time and attention. Every time she left the house for her car or garden, before she exited the safety of her doorway, she performed a brief bear check, just to make sure. After cooking a steak on her indoor grill (she name-drops it as a Jenn-Air brand, very chic), Beretta would quarantine herself for hours, worried that to go outside with the smell of steak clinging to her would lead to disaster.

That's not to say that Beretta is a shrinking violet in the face of danger. A woman of action, she has girded herself against the large and slovenly bears with a collection of firearms that are, like Beretta herself, small, neat, and orderly.

She has her "little Glock" and another "little pocket pistol."

"But!" she says, pausing to make sure I am listening. Her favorite is her "handy-dandy Beretta. Sixteen gauge."

I'm unclear on whether owning three guns makes one feel thrice as safe as one gun, or if gun ownership is, like potato chips and birthdays, subject to diminishing returns.

Over the course of years, Beretta began to think seriously about pulling out a gun (I am delighted to learn that, in the model of an Agatha Christie character, she keeps one stored in her umbrella stand) and shooting one of Doughnut Lady's bears. As we talk, it becomes clear that something other than fear is also motivating her thoughts of human-on-bear violence. In the spirit of making lemonade from lemons, Beretta has given thought to making a bearskin rug from the bears cavorting outside her door.

Like, serious thought.

Fresh bear corpses, she tells me, cost much less than a Jenn-Air grill.

"Getting the bear is nothing. It's one slug, if you're a good shot," she says.

No, the hard part would be transforming the bear pelt into the kind of rug with the lifeless head still attached to the skin, the look often associated with fancy ski chalets and parodies of fancy ski chalets.

Beretta relates these rugs to pictures of a luxurious lifestyle. She made some inquiries of taxidermists and learned that the price used to be $800.

"But now," she says, with a note of outrage. "It's over. A thousand dollars!"

The exorbitant price placed her dreams firmly out of reach. Beretta is, she explains, a woman of limited means.

"I would have to go without food for a couple of months," says Beretta. "Just to have a bearskin rug."

Beretta's next idea was to find a compromise between desire and means—perhaps a less lavish home decoration could be devised, one that would still include the all-important element of a partial bear carcass. Though a rug without a head was a nonstarter, she might settle for a head without a rug, positioned to greet visitors from a small display table in her breezeway.

But these hopes were short-lived. A bear head, she was told, would cost about the same as a bearskin rug, which seemed unfair.

And so she watched through her window as bear heads and bearskins lumbered through her yard, unpleasantly encumbered by all that bone, sinew, and doughnut-bolstered fat.

6
THE PASTOR'S PRICE

There were the silken colonists, sporting round their Maypole;
perhaps teaching a bear to dance. . . . Often, the whole colony
were playing at blindman's buff, magistrates and all, with their
eyes bandaged, except a single scapegoat, whom the blinded
sinners pursued by the tinkling of the bells at his garments.
Once, it is said, they were seen following a flower-decked
corpse, with merriment and festive music, to his grave. But did
the dead man laugh?

—Nathaniel Hawthorne, "The May-Pole of Merry Mount," 1832

A fter a tumultuous autumn for the purple-painted church, Connell worried that the end result would be violence.

Two centuries of storms had failed to rip the church's ancient, sacred
timbers out of the foundation and cast them to the wind, but now, outside,
gusts tore crimson-stained leaves from branches and scattered them to die
on the ground, while inside, whirlwinds of accusations, power plays, counter-
accusations, and legal threats were bloodying the reputations and wallets of
all involved.

The tug-of-war—which by then involved Connell, the directors, the
town, and a new group of historical preservationists who wanted to buy the
property and restore it to a pre-Connell state of being—was part and parcel
of the same fog of malcontent that was enveloping the entire Free Town community, setting neighbor against neighbor in pitched battles over who was
living free, but free in the right way.

In early winter, without warning, all the frenetic, destructive energy suddenly ceased. A calm descended over the church, as if the strife had been

frozen by the front of sterile Arctic air settling over the region. Town officials and libertarian lawyers disengaged from one another, setting aside their powerful pens in favor of holiday celebrations at home.

Connell's mood seemed to shift. In early December, he managed to get the furnace repaired and buy some heating oil. Though there was no clean resolution to the financial and legal problems that had ensnared him, he stopped lighting up the libertarian community with intensely personal attacks against the church directors, focusing instead on questions of theology.

As the winter of 2015 settled in, he took an interest in the work of Thieleman J. van Braght, a Dutch Anabaptist who lived in the 1600s and was part of the religious Reformation that swept Europe.

"The greatest danger to our souls today is not any particular denomination," Connell posted, quoting van Braght, "but any religious tradition that intertwines itself with the world system and relies on state support. . . . Convinced that we desperately need to drag ourselves from a slumber which rapidly looks more and more like death."

The quotation was from a 1660 book called *Martyrs Mirror of the Defenseless Christians*. The reference to a subset of Christians as "defenseless" is a nod to nonresistance, a trait that the Anabaptists believed was shared by the martyrs in the book, including Jesus.

During this lull in hostilities, the Anabaptist ideas of nonresistance may help explain Connell's newfound passivity. Having always lived his public life espousing the virtue of noncooperation, he was aware of the capacity of such traditions to inspire social change; his belief in the power of non-cooperation was what had once led him to show up at a courthouse without the means to pay his ticket, and to fast in solidarity with social causes.

But the Anabaptist doctrine of nonresistance goes further in walking the path of peace. It takes an almost Zen-like approach and does not support, for example, defending oneself in a lawsuit or lobbying the government. Defenseless martyrs, van Braght taught, completely abandon themselves to the will of God.

Connell's commitment to defenselessness was tested when, after a quiet holiday season, the peace was shattered. During its first meeting of 2016, the Grafton selectboard found that the church directors had exhausted all time lines to make good on back taxes, which by then totaled more than $14,000.

When the selectboard voted to initiate the proceedings to repossess the property, one of the church directors resigned; the remaining directors filled the vacancy with Dave Kopacz, the Second Amendment activist with whom

John Redman had exchanged schoolyard taunts during the October deposition. Rather than work with Kopacz, Redman resigned from his role as co-pastor.

Connell, perhaps thinking of the Anabaptist doctrine of nonresistance, gave no public comment on these developments. On a Sunday night, as his precious store of heating fuel created a little envelope of warmth in the church, he watched a lengthy video in which four religious leaders debated when, exactly, Jesus would once more walk upon the Earth and physically reign over humankind.

"What would you say or do to Jesus if you met him on the street?" he asked on Facebook.

There was just one response, from a friend: "Hi, want a beer?"

"I shoulda known," Connell wrote back.

On Monday, he posted a poem he'd written on multiple social media outlets.

"Christ ain't about the pistol and knife, my friends. Christ ain't about the riffle [sic] and sword," he wrote. He matched the poem with an image of a Bible carved into the shape of a gun.

"Read the Gospel, and read it well, my friends. Then, pick up your cross and follow," his song continued. "Pick up your cross, and follow Christ, my friends. Let us not wait until tomorrow."

———

ON TUESDAY, JANUARY 12, 2016, a cold front pushed temperatures down to 16, the coldest day of the winter. Strong winds blew in a cloud system from the north, hiding the crescent moon.

As dawn broke, the sun struggled to send a few rays of light earthward through the endless cloud banks; soon, it gave up the battle and was dimmed. Around 9:30, the winds calmed, and the murky skies cast down tiny floating sculptures of ice, ephemeral and endless. A gauzy scrim enshrouded the church, covering, for a while, the riot of color on the exterior and transforming it back into an idyllic New England building, both quaint and holy.

Outside the church, two men stood peering up at wisps of light smoke emanating from the second floor and drifting skyward.

When the call came in, John Babiarz hopped into the Grafton fire truck and sped up Route 4. As he came around the bend, he too saw the smoke seeping out of the second floor. The lack of visible flames made him cautiously optimistic that it might be a kitchen fire.

When entering a burning building, firefighters follow an OSHA "two-in, two-out" protocol: two responders enter together, keeping within sight of one another, while two more monitor them from outside, prepared to rescue the rescuers.

But Babiarz was alone. He could see that Connell's two vehicles were both parked outside, but there was no sign of the man. So Babiarz hurriedly shrugged on an oxygen tank, thirty minutes of life that he wore like a backpack, and put the snouted air mask over his face.

He went in through the front door. If the world outside was a gray limbo, the inside was a pitch-black hell. Waves of smoke and warmth emanated from unseen flames.

Babiarz called out, but got no response.

He didn't dare go more than a few steps into the church. The first floor was a maze of Connell's clutter, and the church had no insulation, meaning fire could race along the walls and floors with frightening speed. Once the rectangle of brightness behind him disappeared, there was a significant risk of becoming disoriented and getting trapped inside himself.

He needed backup.

And it was on its way. Outside, as John Redman rode toward Canaan on Route 4, wearing his trademark flat derby cap and John Lennon glasses, he passed a couple of fire trucks rushing past him.

Uh oh, Redman thought. He called Tom Ploszaj, but Ploszaj told him that he couldn't talk because he was already on the way to the fire scene from Center Harbor, a lake town about an hour away. Neither Redman nor Ploszaj knew where Connell was.

When the first wave of firefighters arrived from Canaan, they decided that they couldn't immediately reenter the building—best practices for entering burning buildings take into account that smoke inhalation can kill a victim in less than six minutes; within ten minutes, wooden trusses can fail, even in a newly built structure. In this case, there was an extra danger posed by a bronze bell, perched atop timbers that ran all the way to the ground. It was six feet in diameter and an estimated five thousand pounds, poised to impose a hasty death sentence on anyone who ventured inside.

By 10:00 a.m., firefighters were setting up a perimeter, cutting off electricity to the church and redirecting Route 4 traffic up toward Ruggles Mine. Redman was now at the scene, shivering in his fleece jacket as he began taking pictures.

The smoke pouring out of the second floor was thicker now. A firefighter went in through a window on the north side, away from the bell and near Connell's living quarters. He came back out a few minutes later. There was still no sign of Connell.

A second alarm was raised, to bring in more resources from more fire companies.

Lebanon and Hanover sent their expensive fire equipment down, trucks with extended tower ladders that dangled buckets off their ends. It was hard to tell where in the building the smoke was coming from before it escaped and blended into the gray sky above. Little knots of spectators began to form, standing in the snow and passing scraps of information back and forth.

They speculated on the church's flammability, and whether the huge open attic space was a help or a hindrance. One thing the church had going for it was its chestnut beams, which were slow to catch fire.

"There's probably a ten-thousand-pound bell hung up there by a fucking string," said someone.

At first, the fire seemed manageable. A firefighter laid a ladder on the roof and used a long pike to puncture it, striking over and over so that he could clear out enough space to let the heat escape. Once he opened it up, he used a hook on the end to drag out flaming pieces of wood that slid down the roof toward the gutter.

The firefighters became embroiled in a horrendous game of whack-a-mole. Each time they saw a hint of flame, they pried open shingles or siding to dump water in, only to see the blaze resurface in another part of the building. Two Hanover firefighters standing in the bucket used a chainsaw to cut through the siding; the released heat and smoke warped the bottom of the purple-painted window frame above it. Another pair stood in a raised bucket, using gloved hands to rip off slats of the shutters in the bell tower, where particles of soot levitated on thermal currents en masse.

John Babiarz spoke to one news crew in the early afternoon, his glasses and oversized white helmet giving him a boyishness immediately belied by his grave expression. He focused on a small silver lining: though he'd almost called in an excavator to knock the church down, he now felt that the building could be saved.

A short while later, he left the scene, and Rosalie Babiarz showed up, with Oreos and water for the firefighters. A neighbor came out and set up a hot chocolate station on his porch for anyone who wanted it.

In the early afternoon, rumors began to circulate that a body had been found in the kitchen, but the authorities wouldn't confirm it. When Police Chief Russell Poitras (Chief Kenyon had retired) drove slowly by, Redman called out to him until he stopped and put his window down.

"Do we know something yet?" asked Redman.

"I can't tell you anything," said Poitras.

"Who's going to identify?" asked Redman.

"That will be my task shortly," said Poitras, pulling away.

As soon as the chief was out of earshot, Redman laughed. Snow tangled in long, stray hairs from his ponytail.

"He can't tell me anything," he said derisively. "He told me everything!"

Above the firefighters' heads, two small gray birds, chimney swifts, entered and exited the belfry at will, apparently unbothered by the smoke and activity.

"I'm still holding out hope that it was just one of John's stupid fucking mannequins," said a libertarian who was watching.

"Well, it wasn't," said Redman. "Not when Russell just said what he said."

An onlooker plugged a recording device into the inverter of his Jeep, so he could document the loss of the historic resource.

Tom Warner, pastor of the Millbrook Church, stopped by. Before his congregation sold the church to Connell, he'd spent twenty-two years there, preaching a thousand sermons as its pastor.

"It's just too sad to hang around and continue to watch it burn," he said, before leaving the scene.

Dusk fell before the fire was extinguished. The fire crews set up huge spotlight arrays, the light glinting off the yellow and silver reflective striping of their turnout jackets.

That was about the time they removed the body. At first, they wouldn't identify it to the public.

"It's a male victim," said Deputy Fire Marshal Keith Rodenhiser, beefy and clean-shaven. "That's as far as we are willing to go."

Babiarz talked to the media again. His tone was level and professional, but beneath the snow-encrusted visor of his helmet, his eyes looked haunted. More snow gathered on his shoulders, unbrushed.

"I think we did a fantastic job with the mutual aid we had," he said, still emphasizing the positive. His eyes roved restlessly. "To, quote, hold the building together."

When the fire was finally extinguished, the building still stood, thanks in part to the chestnut beams, but it was blanketed in water, ash, and ice. Holes gaped; only the chimney swifts seemed not to mind.

A day or two after the fire, when the body was identified as Connell, the news rocked the Free Town community. It was eventually determined that he died of smoke inhalation. His three adult children expressed deep concern and shared the information from investigators that he did not have drugs or alcohol in his system. His daughter circulated a survey in which she asked people to weigh in on whether he had committed suicide, been the victim of a homicide, or been killed by an accident or an act of God. The results were inconclusive.

Three years later, state investigators still considered the case unsolved. It was unclear whether a strict adherence to fire codes—of the sort that both Connell and the Free Towners eschewed—might have made the difference in Connell's death.

Russell and Kat Kanning, who were particularly close to Connell, posted lengthy, heartfelt messages about the friend they'd lost. Joe Brown, the author of sometimes caustic posts on the freedom forums, also spoke effusively about Connell's devotion to peace.

"He was a man of honor, integrity, decency, and kindness. . . . He may not have turned my life around, since we were both walking in roughly the same direction . . . but someone walking the same direction can lend you a hand when the path is steep and rocky. . . . You were deeply loved, my friend, and you will never be forgotten by those who loved you," Brown wrote.

They were beautiful words, and they demonstrated how Connell, for all his quirks, served as a stabilizing influence in a Grafton community that was bearing a greater and greater resemblance to a Wild West town. Without Connell's constant calls for peace, the people he helped had one less reason to restrain themselves from the sort of street justice that sometimes accompanies the pursuit of rugged individualism.

Three years after Connell's death, Joe Brown got into a roadside altercation with another driver alongside Route 4. Both men had their young children in the car. The other driver reportedly punched Brown, after which Brown reportedly shot the other driver in the stomach.

The Free Town Project went on.

7

A PROPAGATION OF PREROGATIVE

But California had already been conquered by the Americans. In June, 1846, some three hundred American settlers, believing that war was imminent and fearing they would be attacked, revolted, adopted a flag on which was a grizzly bear, and declared California an independent republic.

—John Bach McMaster, *A Brief History of the United States*, 1909

The month after Connell died, in February of 2016, a Dartmouth lecturer took the podium before a group of about fifty libertarians and media reporters in a Radisson Hotel conference room in Manchester, New Hampshire.

The lecturer had the dark, floppy bangs of a Maltese and the face of a young pug, made even more boyish by his oversized dark suit and slim frame.

"This," he began, "is a great day in the history of human freedom." He paused while the audience cheered. "It sounds grandiose, but I really believe it's true."

This was Jason Sorens, a former Cato Institute intern famous for writing the 2001 essay that first exhorted the nation's libertarians to concentrate their voting power so that they could, as he reminded the audience, "exert the fullest practical effort toward the creation of a society in which the maximum role of government is protecting individual rights to life, liberty, and property."

Though the essay was the initial seed for the Free Town Project, when Sorens wrote it, he never intended that it would inspire libertarians to take over a town. No, he intended that it would inspire libertarians to take over an entire state. And a dozen years of clumsy, heavy-handed efforts in Grafton had done nothing to dissipate his enthusiasm.

The entire time that the Free Town Project was unfolding—from the moment Babiarz welcomed Larry Pendarvis into the firehouse in 2004 through the burning of the Peaceful Assembly Church in 2016—other libertarians were busily working on a much grander plan: the Free State Project.

Started in 2003, the project sought to take the idea of a utopian freedom zone from fuzzy concept to fully executed reality. A group of volunteers began urging libertarians to sign a solemn statement of intent to move to New Hampshire and reimagine the state's power structures and culture.

Under the plan, once twenty thousand people signed the pledge, the initiative would be "Triggered." No one knew exactly when, or if, the Free State Project might cross that lofty threshold, but once the Trigger was reached, all those who had signed on to the pledge were expected to actually move.

As they worked to sign people up, the Free Staters created a marketing campaign that promoted New Hampshire as *the* place to live. Their messaging was like any number of mainstream tourism advertisements, though prone to sudden hard right turns.

For example, a slick Free State Project website boasted of New Hampshire's breathtaking scenic views, numerous hiking opportunities along the Appalachian Trail, and state constitution that "expressly protects citizens' right to revolution and does not specifically prohibit secession."

Other features tailored to the liberty-sensitive included New Hampshire's many gun clubs, private shooting ranges, and black bear hunting opportunities; its lack of an income tax, general sales tax, or capital gains tax; and its status as the only state in the union that doesn't mandate automobile liability insurance or penalize the uninsured.

Bolstered by such arguments, the pledge proved to have an irresistible appeal. Signing it felt like an immediate, concrete step toward the creation of a libertarian state, a way to dream big at the stroke of a pen. Some early signers were driven by pot legalization, while others were anti-war, or anti-tax.

Many nursed personal grievances of oppression under the police state—they were the overtaxed, the overregulated, the wronged. Sorens told the audience that his own oppression started when a childhood bully pushed him, causing him to fall and chip a tooth on the pavement. Sorens says that he was forced to sign a piece of paper saying he had kicked the bully to provoke the attack, a miscarriage of justice that he attributed to the political connections of the bully, whose mother was on the school board. For Free State Project president Carla Gericke, oppression began with a frightening emergency drill at her South African all-girls boarding school during which police detonated firebombs. Every Free State pledger, it seemed, had had experiences that fit this general pattern of governmental overreach and oppression. People began signing—first dozens, then hundreds.

"We started to see a snowball rolling," Sorens said.

Over the first few years of the project launch, as more libertarians gravitated toward New Hampshire, it became the de facto center of the national libertarian community. A small army gathered there, the suffering victims of bullshit traffic tickets, alimony burdens imposed by unsympathetic divorce court judges, and school systems that were unfair to their kids. An annual freedom festival, PorcFest, swelled from a few dozen hard-core founders to one thousand attendees in 2007 (not counting the bears, which were reportedly seen roaming the campground that year) and more than two thousand by 2016—what Gericke called the largest gathering of libertarians in the world.

Though they had similar lineages, the Free State Project was markedly different in tone from the Free Town Project. Where the Free Towners were brash and extreme, the Free Staters were polished and sophisticated—an infinitely difficult demeanor to pull off given that libertarians are by definition on the political fringe and hold positions that have rarely been tempered by the burden of leadership.

Free State Project organizers tried to relieve this tension by disassociating themselves from the politically problematic Larry Pendarvises of the world. One such prominent Free Stater was Ian Freeman. On the plus side, Freeman hosted a popular liberty-themed podcast with an international reach that attracted many New Hampshire residents, but on the minus side, he had a long-standing belief that minors could consent to sexual relationships with adults. When a 2010 audio clip of his stating that view was publicized in 2016, the Free State Project canceled a mutual endorsement deal with his podcast and formally disinvited him from Free State Project events (though he remained a prominent figure in libertarian circles).

Another oust-worthy Free Stater was Chris Cantwell, who earned a national reputation for his role in the infamous 2017 "Unite the Right" rally in Charlottesville, during which white nationalist demonstrators marched with tiki torches, chanted hateful messages about Jewish people, assaulted people, and, in one case, drove a car into a crowd of counterprotesters and killed one of them. Cantwell was dubbed the "Crying Nazi," because he wept after he drew criminal charges for assaulting demonstrators with pepper gas. After Cantwell was kicked out of the Free State Project, Freeman interviewed him on his podcast. Freeman's main takeaway was that Cantwell had abandoned his libertarian principles and wanted to rule an authoritarian community—which, Freeman noted, would be far too statist.

The Free State organizers took care to keep people like Freeman and Cantwell on the fringe of the fringe. They even disavowed a controversial part of the Sorens essay suggesting that the libertarian state should use the threat of secession as a way to negotiate with the federal government. These and various other efforts to mainstream the movement paid dividends.

When Sorens took the podium in 2016, he was exuberant as he announced that, after thirteen years of pledge-peddling, a five-month burst of 2,500 new signers had put the Free State Project over the 20,000 mark. The Trigger had been reached, and it seemed only logical that the hard work of mainstreaming libertarianism was about to pay off.

"We are firing the starting gun on a mass migration of freedom lovers to New Hampshire!" he said.

The hotel audience was, in the best possible way, Triggered, and they maintained their enthusiasm when Gericke took the stage.

"We are a beacon of liberty for the rest of the world to emulate. The future of the Free State is very, very bright," said Gericke, to more applause. "I say: First New Hampshire. Then the world!"

Immediately after the press conference, the Free Staters implemented their post-Trigger plans, with organizers doing everything they could to smooth the way for their idealist fellows to enter the state. Volunteer-run phone banks called hundreds of signers at a time, trying to help them turn their pledge into action, while volunteer welcome wagons met newbies to help unpack their moving vans and connect them to others in the community.

Though the Free State Project had already attracted thousands to New Hampshire, the Trigger brought fresh life to the movement, and new political allies emerged.

One such ally was an independent presidential candidate named Vermin Supreme, who declared soon after the Trigger that he was switching to the Libertarian Party. Supreme, who has been running for president since the 1990s, is easily recognizable for his signature look—a long gray beard that forms a vague counterbalance to the boot he wears on his head.

"The Libertarian Party is the only party that aligns with my core principles of anti-state, anti-war, and anti-authority," Supreme declared. His platform consists largely of a mandatory tooth-brushing law, free ponies for every American, time travel research, and zombie apocalypse preparedness. In 2017, in a poll against seven other aspiring Libertarian presidential candidates, Supreme polled in third place, at 8.2 percent.

Though the presidency remains a long shot, the Free Staters have at long last entered the political mainstream in New Hampshire. They have managed to gain power and influence in the state legislature, in many cases running as Democrats or Republicans to make themselves more viable. Though state candidates like Tom Ploszaj, Jeremy Olson, Tim Condon, and Ian Freeman failed in their electoral bids, Bob Hull won a statehouse seat as a Republican, and the Free Staters claimed legislative victories with respect to several issues on which they shared common ground sometimes with the left and sometimes with the right, such as legalizing same-sex marriage, cutting the state budget, and expanding school choice.

After the Trigger, the libertarians quickly gained steam in the New Hampshire legislature. In 2017, three young state legislators—two Republicans and a Democrat—announced that they were switching their party affiliation to Libertarian, thereby creating a legislative caucus, and by 2019 the Free Staters counted twenty state representatives among their ranks, not to mention scores of school board, selectboard, and municipal committee seats.

With the support of its new Free State lawmakers, the New Hampshire State Legislature did away with licensing requirements to carry loaded, concealed firearms and abolished criminal penalties for small amounts of marijuana or hashish. It also passed measures to deregulate cryptocurrency, legalize home poker games, require police to get a warrant to track cell phones, exempt hair braiding from barber licensing requirements, legalize fireworks, allow brew pubs to make cider, cut taxes on business profits, and eliminate a staggering 1,600 state regulations, many of which were considered obsolete.

Outside of the statehouse, the libertarians have worked to build self-perpetuating cultural and economic infrastructures. The more tech-savvy members have helped make New Hampshire first in the nation, per capita, for Bitcoin use, while libertarians have started businesses like LBRY, which owns an internet information technology designed to evade government tracking. (Its protocol developer is Lex Berezhny, a Grafton firefighter and one of the few Free Towners who defended Babiarz during the campfire fiasco.)

In addition, with support from Ian Freeman, Russell Kanning (one of Babiarz's detractors in said fiasco) founded the Shire Society, whose projects include a chain of "Shire Free Church" parsonages that were inspired, in part, by Connell's Peaceful Assembly Church. At the Shire Society's Church of the Sword, in-church activities include hard cider communion, combat with foam swords, and a "Ritual of Pie," while out-of-church activities include lengthy legal battles over religious tax exemptions.

Despite their widespread influence, the New Hampshire libertarians, partially cloaked by their mainstream partisan labels, enjoyed an ability to operate largely under the radar. The average visitor to Murphy's, a Manchester bar, didn't realize that it was libertarian-owned and home to the world's first Bitcoin ATM. They didn't realize that if they walked into a local church service, they could be confronted with a foam sword fight. And they certainly didn't realize that, soon after the Trigger, Grafton's bear problems began to go statewide.

It is unfair to entirely blame the Trigger, but it does seem like 2016 was also a tipping point for a long-gestating problem of bear management that respected Free State boundaries. Neighboring Vermont, which has roughly the same number of bears and acres of land as New Hampshire, has about half the number of bear complaints.

Between 2013 and 2015, New Hampshire's Fish and Game Department killed a total of six bears that had exhibited worrisome behaviors, including one that entered someone's home. But post-Trigger, between 2016 and 2018, they killed twenty-seven bears, including fourteen that entered human homes.

But even that didn't satisfy people worried about the spike in bear activity—which may have been prompted in part by bear-feeding scofflaws, and some of which may have been prompted by a fresh bout of drought. People began taking matters into their own hands. In 2018, Cornish town police shot a bear that was acting in a threatening way on the property of a day-care owner, while a resident of another town shot and killed three bears as they tried to break open his beehives. During 2016 and 2017, the Fish and Game Department estimated that, through illegal hunts, car accidents, and citizen-led shootings, the public killed 120 bears. In 2019, several close encounters with bears caused federal officials to shut down a camping area within the White Mountain National Forest.

It seemed only a matter of time before a human-habituated bear came across an unarmed, non-bear-habituated human. It's just a shame that it had to happen to Apryl Rogers, a seventy-one-year-old woman who lived in a modest, one-floor home in Groton, less than twenty miles from Grafton.

At about 1:15 a.m., Rogers, who lived alone, heard noises in her kitchen. When she rolled herself into the kitchen in her wheelchair, she saw that the room was occupied by strewn trash, bear shit, and the shitting bear, which had apparently come in through an unlatched door.

Tracey Colburn was faulted for screaming at the bear, possibly causing it to feel attacked. Rogers did the opposite—when she saw the bear, she sat quietly in her wheelchair. "I tried to stay calm," she would say afterward. She remained calm as the bear approached her, sat down next to her, silent, and then began rocking its head from side to side. She was calm right up until the moment it attacked.

"All of a sudden," she said, "he just let me have it."

Unlike Colburn, Rogers didn't get her hands up in time to take the brunt of the blow.

"He just grabbed hold of my face and ripped it down," she said.

The bear tore large gashes on her cheek and scalp, broke facial bones, fractured the vertebrae in her neck, and destroyed her left eye.

Rogers doesn't remember what happened next, but the blood smears suggest that she dragged herself to the phone, which was found spattered in red, and then managed to close the door, presumably after the bear left the premises.

While Rogers was in the hospital for what would prove to be a month of rehab, Fish and Game sprang into action, once again spinning the event in a way that exonerated the bear and the state policy that helped put it there.

"First of all," Fish and Game major Jim Juneau told a reporter, "bear attacks are extremely rare. It's not really fair to call this a bear attack."

Speaking to another reporter, Juneau drew on all the blamelessness that passive sentence construction could provide. "The bear reacted in a panicked manner and unfortunately," he said, "she sustained some injuries."

A game warden, the same one who had responded to Tracey's attack, took care to note the home's food crimes, which were nonexistent.

"There was an empty bag of birdseed next to the front door," he said. "And there was some cat food in the house, and it obviously investigated that."

Though Rogers had neither bird feeder nor barbecue grill in her yard, the state also took the opportunity to tell people to remove those items, admonishing that "people need to be responsible when they know there are bears in the area." It's not so much that state officials or the freedom community are wrong in their approach to the question of bear management. It's just that the two approaches are totally incompatible, and neither side is in a position to effect change on the other side of the divide.

As the disconnect spread statewide, wildlife officials continued to push the limits of acceptable numbers of bears, and libertarians continued to promote a culture of civil disobedience and individual rights, including the right to feed or shoot the bears in one's backyard. The stage seemed set for more conflict, one that would involve more deaths for bears and perhaps human casualties as well.

Colburn and Rogers were both marginalized women living on fixed means in remote towns; neither was likely to make a fuss that could threaten the status quo. I wondered what would happen if the bears instead threatened privileged, politically connected people.

It didn't take long to find out.

8

THE RESPECTABLE RIOT

Ultimately, to satisfy the public, the fanciful name has to be discarded for a common-sense one, a manifestly descriptive one. The Great Bear remained the Great Bear—and unrecognizable as such—for thousands of years; and people complained about it all the time, and quite properly; but as soon as it became the property of the United States, Congress changed it to the Big Dipper, and now every body is satisfied, and there is no more talk about riots.

—Mark Twain, *Following the Equator*, 1897

If Grafton is New Hampshire's unruly stepchild, Hanover is its favorite daughter, the one that gets cookie after cookie pressed into her politely outstretched palms. The charming town of about eleven thousand people lies about thirty minutes and several income brackets north of Grafton; it benefits from politically connected town administrators and representatives who ensure that the town's soccer moms, racquetball dads, and stock portfolio managers receive largesse in the form of crisp roads, attentive environmental managers, and multimillion-dollar grants.

Hanover is the seat of Dartmouth College, where award-covered college deans churn out ribbon-covered graduates whose purpose is to funnel alumni donations back to their ivy-covered alma mater. Far from being plagued by *T. gondii*, researchers at Dartmouth's medical school are the ones who have studied and isolated different genetic strains of the parasite.

One of the nice things about Hanover (and the town is simply awash in nice things, from low-cost violin concertos to free public tours of the historic Shattuck Observatory) is that it has achieved, through aggressive zoning, a fantastic balance between development and green spaces. On Dartmouth's infamous fraternity row, one can witness the debauchery of undergraduate house parties while outside a deer and her fawn pick their way delicately along the neatly manicured lawn. Stately mansions are herded into compact residential neighborhoods bounded by forests that are made more appealing by the Appalachian Trail, the Connecticut River, and the meticulously tended trails of the Greensboro Ridge Nature Preserve.

Another natural resource in Hanover is Mink Brook, a cheerful little waterway that winds through the town's woodlands.

Right around the time Tracey Colburn was attacked in Grafton, a bear began climbing the steep bank that defined the Mink Brook Nature Preserve and sampling the bird feeders and compost bins of Hanover's upper crust.

Because the bear lived in Hanover, she was given a name, and because she favored the brook, the name she was given was Mink. The bear became a celebrity, a local media sensation.

With neighborhoods full of college students who were just about as careful with their discarded pizza and Chinese food containers as one might expect, Mink got very people-friendly, very quickly. She knocked down bird feeders. She climbed into dumpsters, sticking her head up from inside to watch warily as humans walked past.

Mink's boldness was largely attributed to an elderly realtor who liked to set out large piles of food to watch Mink eat. Eschewing the bargain basement grain and supermarket doughnuts that made do in Grafton, he put out high-quality black-hulled sunflower seeds and maple-glazed crullers purchased from the same diner bakery that fed Dartmouth professors. When her benefactor died in 2016, Mink began plaguing the rest of the town like an indigent widow, now with three young cubs in tow.

By then, Mink and her cubs were really pushing the limits of acceptable bear raiding. They wandered into and out of garages in search of food. Mink once sat beneath a zip line at Hanover High School, watching the kids pass above her head like a sumo wrestler keeping a close eye on a sushi conveyor belt. She attacked a dog, injuring it badly. One of the bear cubs even got into an outdoor hot tub, apparently not realizing that said tub was already occupied by a nine-year-old girl, who screamed bloody murder as both escaped uninjured.

Mink's riling of the rich led to a firestorm of indignation and histrionics—some of Hanover's choicest residents were outraged at the bear's incivility toward humans, while others were outraged at the outrage directed at an innocent wild creature. As the outrage cycle built, people looked down their noses from horses so high that they could barely be seen by the mere mortals crawling upon the surface of the earth.

But there was one thing every outraged individual understood: clearly something must be done about Mink, and the Fish and Game Department obliged.

In 2017, after a couple of the cubs entered a residential home in Hanover, Andy Timmins, New Hampshire's bear biologist, and other game wardens set traps to capture the whole family, with the intent of euthanizing them. Timmins, making the case for euthanasia, explained that once a bear has become accustomed to people, it can be extremely difficult to break it of its foraging habits. "When their behavior reaches a certain point, it is tough to be wild bears again."

The eminently reasonable explanation was met with, predictably, outrage.

It's unsurprising that no one liked the idea of bear euthanasia, a protocol that evolved in the shadows of wildlife management because of chronic underfunding. But no one had ever rubbed Hanover's nose in the ethical murk of killing a bear.

In short order, doctors were writing letters to area newspapers, asking that the bears be spared. Similar pleas appeared on popular Dartmouth College websites and in media sources, and two different "Save Mink" petitions gathered nearly thirteen thousand signatures.

In Grafton, public opinion had split between shooting and not shooting the bears. In Hanover, the schism was characteristically different—some people wanted the government to spend a lot of money to modify Mink's behavior, while other people wanted the government to spend a lot of money to capture and relocate Mink and her cubs to someone else's backyard.

It being Hanover, both sides got what they wanted.

With elite state players pulling all the political levers at their disposal, Governor Chris Sununu got involved. He countermanded his own state biologist's expert opinion and instructed Fish and Game to come up with a plan that would allow the bears to live.

And so, during Memorial Day weekend, the three yearling cubs were captured and relocated to Pittsburg, a remote town in northern New Hampshire along the Canadian border. Mink, meanwhile, disappeared from the area to find a mate.

The public furor died down until the spring of 2018, when Mink strolled back into town, this time with four new cubs trailing along behind her. She promptly began to raid bird feeders and garbage cans again, teaching her foraging tactics to her new brood. Euthanasia was even more strongly recommended now, but the idea was a proven nonstarter.

The outraged Hanoverites knew just what to do: spend more money.

And so, in 2018, an intergovernmental task force that included Hanover deputy fire chief Mike Hinsley, Timmins, and a federal official from the US Department of Agriculture's bear management program sedated Mink and fitted her with a radio tracking collar and a brightly colored ear tag so that her every movement could be tracked.

Some residential areas set up the equivalent of a neighborhood watch, but instead of looking out for criminal activity, they policed bird feeders and untidy garbage receptacles. When there were Mink sightings, Hanover town officials sent out a "Code Red" mass text to residents, asking them to be extra vigilant about attractants, and Dartmouth sent out similar messaging to its students. Residents were told to keep barbecue grills inside, take down bird feeders, and keep their trash cans secured until the morning of municipal trash pickups, rather than put them out the night before. These directives were enforced with a $500 fine, and the town also recommended that people consider bear-proof garbage containers, at a cost of $280.

Hinsley became the point man of the Mink-deterrent campaign. When my employer, the *Valley News*, sent me on a ride-along with Hinsley, we cruised slowly up and down residential streets in his SUV, looking for evidence of human food sources and talking with people on the street about Mink's latest movements.

At one point, he pulled over and set up an antenna and directional tracking system, which pinged at him with varying degrees of speed and strength, allowing him to zero in on Mink's location in real time.

Whenever he caught Mink straying into human neighborhoods, he confronted her, using methods taught to him by bear whisperer Ben Kilham—maintaining eye contact, talking firmly, and walking toward the bear to express dominance. Mink's potentially lethal naughtiness persisted into June, at which point she was captured and relocated about two hundred miles north. Her four new cubs were taken to a bear rehabilitation orphanage run by Kilham.

The contrast with bear management in Grafton could not be more stark. A bear's life in Hanover is threatened, and the state moves heaven and earth to find it and treat it in accordance with the wishes of the public. A bear threatens a woman's life in Grafton, and the state makes a half-hearted effort to capture it before the incident quickly fades from the public imagination.

In my correspondence with Andy Timmins, he acknowledged that there was nothing built into the state's bear management system that prioritized cases in which bears actually injured humans or dogs.

"We are hesitant to call these 'bear attacks,' because we don't view them as such," he said. "However, physical contact between a bear and a person is not the norm, and we should probably be putting those events in a file."

He said that, after my inquiries, he intended to create a specific form that would capture "not-attacks" by bears.

"For me, some of my delay in creating this form is my concern over the fact that a lot of people want to make bears into aggressive marauders," he said. "I maintain that they are not. My experience is that most of the time when bear-human contact has been made, people (often with dogs) have put bears in a position where they feel directly threatened and they react defensively (swiping, swatting)."

He also said that the lack of documentation regarding Colburn was due in part to how the data was structured—it was designed to track actions taken to alleviate bear conflict, not the severity of any particular conflict. In Hanover, the saga of Mink was, surprisingly, not over. Her radio collar showed that in 2019 she found her way back to Hanover by a very circuitous route that involved traveling more than a thousand miles and crossing the Connecticut River. The story made national news.

"I'm back bitches," said Mink (according to a Twitter account in her name). "Where the donuts at?"

After Mink made the long journey home, people were braced for more hijinks, but surprisingly, she exhibited no unusual behavior toward people this time. The months she spent traveling had apparently taught her to prefer a paleo diet that prioritized acorns over pizza crust.

Mink's story demonstrates that, in a place with strong civic engagement, aggressive enforcement of best practices with regard to human food attractants, and political will, even a worst-case scenario of human-habituated bears can be resolved in a way that makes everyone happy.

The problem is that state and local officials can't afford to leverage that kind of effort everywhere. And until they do, bears will be effectively managed only on the doorsteps of the elite.

9

AN EXPERIMENT ENDS

I am gone for ever.
[Exit, pursued by a bear]

—William Shakespeare, *The Winter's Tale*, 1623

Though no one saw it in the moment, the same Trigger that birthed the Free State was a death knell for the Free Town.

Grafton's libertarian colonists, who had charged into town twelve years earlier with unbridled optimism and enthusiasm, were already beset by various undermining forces. The infighting that surfaced around the time of Barskey's campfire continued, splitting people into factions and adding an air of tension to the formerly joyous flag-burnings and festivals. Another problem was that some of the project's most influential people were dying. In 2012, the movement lost Lloyd Danforth, a liberty stalwart from Hartford, Connecticut, who had nabbed a post as a Grafton registrar; Connell perished in the 2016 fire; and in early 2019, Bob Hull, Grafton's largest landowner and a state representative, died of cancer.

But nothing sapped the energy of the Free Town like the Free State. After years in which Grafton was the most visible and important landing point in the world for those who wanted to create a libertarian utopia, in the post-Trigger era, it became just another town in a state with many options.

The continuous trickle of incoming colonizers dried up as new Free Staters passed up Grafton in favor of places like Keene, a city of twenty-three thousand. Keene had triple Grafton's property tax rate, and restrictive zoning ordinances to boot, but apparently even libertarians were attracted to Keene's amenities—a baseball team, tennis and basketball courts, a village green with a musical bandstand, playgrounds, the restored historic Colonial Theater, manicured parks, and a bustling downtown strip, all underpinned by robust, tax-supported municipal services.

The "Free Keene" people, led by Ian Freeman, drew headlines for smoking marijuana in public every day at 4:20 p.m. and for harassing meter maids while plugging coins into parking meters, thereby saving the parkers from being ticketed.

With antics like that stealing the spotlight, Grafton was left with no more grand plans to be announced, no more Free Towners showing up to drag annual town meetings out to twelve-hour ordeals, no more video cameras pointed at the town clerk as she fielded aggressive questions about freedom and control.

As people packed up and left Grafton, no new recruits appeared to replace them. Stalwarts remained, but they had largely assimilated into Grafton's larger population. In the 2016 presidential election, just 33 people voted for the libertarian candidate, Gary Johnson. (The remainder favored Donald Trump over Hillary Clinton, 367–297.)

As the libertarian presence wilted, a hush descended.

In the newfound quiet, the survivors of America's first Free Town were left to assess the damage, as if they'd woken up after a smashing house party, only to remember, with growing horror, that it had taken place in their own home.

As I drove into Grafton early one morning in 2019, I had a little time to kill, so I took a tour of the changes wrought during the Free Town era. I drove south on Route 4, passing Peaceful Assembly Church, where the tarps stopped rainfall with about 90 percent efficiency and the only signs of life were the chimney swifts, who had graduated from the belfry to taking full advantage of the building interior.

Across the street from the church, I noted the homemade billboard that points visitors toward Grafton's most striking natural resource, the Ruggles Mine. The mine had yielded up $30 million in minerals over 215 years of continuous operation, and in the 1960s it became a lifeline for Grafton by serving as an improbable tourist destination. But in 2016 the local paper broke the news that the mine had been closed and put up for sale, sad tidings somewhat leavened by the clever headline "Mine Could Be Yours." As I drove along, even the weathered FOR SALE sign tacked to the billboard looked forlorn.

I continued south on Route 4, past the general store, which closed permanently in 2018, depriving customers of "rugular" gas. It stood vacant, save for a loyal clientele of dust mice, actual mice, and spiders.

Modest though they were, the Ruggles Mine and the general store were Grafton's two biggest employers. Such a loss would devastate most towns, but it seemed that few in Grafton were looking for work anyway. In 2018, town officials said they weren't sure what to do, because they could no longer find people to hire to plow and ditch roads for the highway department.

As I idled up and down rough dirt roads, I saw that the Ruggles Mine wasn't the only property in Grafton marked with a FOR SALE sign. Similar signs festooned the yards, wire frames topped by the smug, smiling faces of realtors from Canaan and other, more prosperous communities. Census estimates showed that nearly a third of Grafton's eight hundred housing units were vacant and that the population declined slightly between 2010 and 2017.

I cruised past Babiarz's little brick schoolhouse in Slab City and turned onto Dean Road, where I passed the home of a man named Danny Coutermarsh. In October 2017, when a state-led law enforcement task force executed a search warrant at the property, they found more than two dozen knives, which he was not supposed to own, because of his felonious history, and an Uzi submachine gun, which he was *really* not supposed to own.

The machine gun was an alarming discovery—although not entirely unexpected, given New Hampshire's high concentration of machine gun owners.

I bumped up a poorly tended dirt road marred by rocks and tree branches, until I got to Tent City, where Adam Franz had expounded on how he thought bears would fare under a libertarian society.

"One way or another, it wouldn't be a good thing," he had told me. "Whether they hunted them to extinction in the area, or they fuckin' let people feed them until they overpopulated, I don't think that would ever balance out."

Adam's own plans for a survivalist community had been sidetracked by all the bear activity. After his Judge and the fireworks failed to deter the bears effectively, the survivalists decided that more drastic action was warranted.

In a move that seemed strangely reminiscent of Donald Trump's efforts along the southern border of the United States, the anarcho-communists of Tent City decided to build a big, beautiful barrier to keep the bears at bay.

They scrounged some chain-link fencing, pallets, and other scraps of building materials and got to work. Looking past the scarecrow sentries and down the embankment, I could see the fruits of their labor in the woods. The cabins at the heart of Tent City were all joined together by a stockade that could, in theory, block bears from accessing the humans inside. Sections of chain fence were topped by soda cans filled with BBs, designed to rattle loudly if the bears tried to breach the walls in the night. Here, I thought, was another irony, in that those who had come to this patch of woods seeking the ultimate freedom were instead barricading themselves into a rudimentary fortress to attain some level of security that was not being provided by the government.

Though the living areas were bounded by the walls, the junk that the survivalists had somehow accumulated—lawn chairs, buckets, pieces of cars, and tarps hung from ropes—sprawled beyond them. In the past, it had looked like a back-to-nature encampment, but now it looked like a tornado had stolen away a hoarder's barn, leaving all of its contents to clutter the patch of woods.

What I didn't see was people. The same tidal forces that undermined the Free Town Project were also eroding Tent City.

Around 2016, Franz's life of freedom began butting up against reality in various inconvenient ways. An ardent champion of learning, he got himself elected as library trustee, but his personal eccentricities often created more friction than his devotion to learning might have alleviated, and some people began to complain that he was sleeping in the library. In mid-November 2017, he was picked up by police on a DUI, and he failed to appear for his court arraignment in February 2018, resulting in a decision to suspend his driver's license. Several months later, he formally resigned from the trustee position, and not long after, he moved out of Tent City and out of Grafton altogether.

As I pulled away from Tent City, I felt a bit sad to see it reduced to such a sorry state. I later heard that there were a couple of people still squatting on the land, but Adam was gone, the synergy with other camps was gone, and the bonfires and nighttime debaucheries were gone. For all intents and purposes, Tent City was dead, waiting to be slowly reclaimed by the forest.

WITH NO MORE time to waste, I drove on, past more FOR SALE signs, back out onto Route 4, and past the decrepit town offices. I pulled into one of the three parking spots outside my destination: the Grafton Public Library, which was open for three hours every Wednesday morning. Against the southern wall of the small building was a cracked porta potty that the town had purchased secondhand nine years earlier and patched up to working order.

The library was, perhaps, the community's best forward-looking link to aspirations of culture, education, and community. It served the town's home-schoolers and put on winter sliding parties and gingerbread house–building activities. With nowhere else to go, townies popped by to access the internet or borrow jigsaw puzzles while talking about the news of the day and eating a slice of the cakes that appeared like clockwork every Wednesday morning. The cakes were made by the librarian's sister, Onshin, a Buddhist Civil War reenactor who once told me that she was the oldest trick-or-treater in town. In short, the library was exactly the sort of tax-supported frill that the 2019 Baylor University study found glues communities together and makes people happier—part of the reason that, during a town meeting, civic-minded resident Sue Jukosky called it the "heart and soul of the community."

When I walked inside the library, I was greeted by the town librarian, Deb Clough, who also served as the town postmaster (the same one who agreed to deliver Jessica Soule's mail to her door so that she wouldn't have to leave her porch).

Owlish eyeglasses aside, Clough is not your stereotypical librarian. She is rough, bawdy, broad, and friendly, filling the tiny enclosed space of the library with an energetic stream of high-decibel patter on all manner of topics. She's also a stalwart at community events—when the 2018 Christmas tree lighting ceremony was threatened by a power outage, she saved the day by fetching her own fuel generator.

When the Free Town Project founders first came to town, she said, she was quickly labeled a statist.

"The rumor was that I was the head of the anti–Free Town movement, and I was basing my operations out of the library," Clough said.

As a rule, libertarians don't favor publicly funding libraries, and Clough's so-called statism virtually ensured that the library's fortunes would suffer during the Free Town era. When I asked Babiarz about the library, he wrinkled up his face.

"Does the library serve a purpose? Eh, it might," he said. "But with an internet connection, I can get the world's knowledge as long as I can type it in. Are you going to spend more on the library than the fire department? I don't think so. You have to have priorities."

Though the library building was built in 1921 for just $4,000, mostly out of concrete blocks, it has some nice architectural features, like hardwood flooring, wainscoting, and pressed tin on the upper wall and ceiling. Unfortunately, it hasn't been significantly updated since it was built a hundred years ago. I could see the cracks in the wall masonry and knew it was plagued with a leaky chimney, a crumbling slate roof, and a flood-prone basement.

Though Canaan spends $160,000 on its library each year, and the neighboring town of Enfield spends $180,000, the Grafton library gets only about $10,000 in cash—and an endless litany of complaints.

But anytime library supporters mount an effort to build a proper library or increase funding, they've run into stone walls and insults, both from libertarians and from tax-conscious town officials. During one town meeting, when Jeremy Olson was told that state law mandates wages for public library workers, he put forth an apparently serious proposal that the library do an end run around the law by paying its staff $1 an hour. Another library antagonist suggested that its free WiFi was opening the town to legal attacks over copyright infringement.

Town leaders haven't helped either. A 2010 municipal budget that included a small across-the-board increase to town departments redistributed the library's share elsewhere; another time, the selectboard instructed the library trustees to stop storing items for their annual yard sale in shared municipal storage space, recommending that they store items instead in its dank, crowded basement. And in June 2018, after a lengthy back-and-forth about the library's lack of a handicap ramp, Babiarz shut the library down, citing its lack of accessibility. (It was reopened after the ramp was installed.)

And still the library persists. As I sat and had a slice of cake and plugged in my laptop, I reflected that the public library could, just possibly, be the nucleus of a Grafton renaissance. Here, sheltered by books and amity, a tiny flame of civic pride burned bright, nursing a sentiment that might one day lead to reclaiming the town's wilted infrastructure and a rolling back of the wilderness pressing in on all sides.

Clough was hopeful that the library's prospects would brighten, now that the latest storm had been weathered. The Free Town era, she told me, was at an end.

"In the last few years, a lot of them have just disappeared off the face of the Earth," she said. "It's like we did with the Moonies back in the '80s. We chewed them up and spit them out. Grafton has a way of doing that."

10

A DENOUNCEMENT OF DOUGHNUTS

To whom do lions cast their gentle looks?
Not to the beast that would usurp their den.
Whose hand is that the forest bear doth lick?
Not his that spoils her young before her face.

—William Shakespeare, *Henry VI, Part 3*, 1591

One night in 2017, Beretta heard a sound at her door, like someone break-ing in.

She got her handy-dandy 16-gauge Beretta and prepared to fire on what-ever breached the door. But the noises soon went away, and she tried to go back to sleep. The following morning she went outside and found a footprint by the walkway.

Oh my God, she thought. *Was Bigfoot at my door?*

Her kids still tease her about that. She knew it wasn't Bigfoot, she says. She emphasizes the point, to make sure I know that she knew that it was not Bigfoot.

"At first, it looked just like the ones they show," she says. "On those silly TV shows."

She could see from the pawprints that the bear had prowled the perime-ter of her house, pausing outside her front and side doors.

Beretta called Chief Poitras to complain.

In general, Poitras (who is a bear hunter himself) maintains that the bears of Grafton are not a problem, outside of their tendency to raid chicken coops, beehives, and livestock pens. In the summer of 2015, while Poitras was putting up a swimming pool in his backyard, he heard a noise and peered around the deck to see that a bear had approached him from behind the barrier. But it didn't seem threatening to him. He and his wife wound up watching it as it stretched out in his driveway, relaxing.

"He was very docile," Poitras told me. "He was very comfortable with humans."

But this was exactly the sort of encounter that was driving Beretta to dark places and bear rug fantasies. When she called Poitras to complain about the definitely-not-Bigfoot probing her front door, he told her there was nothing he could do.

THE FIRST TIME I meet Doughnut Lady, she is still dealing with the aftermath of a visit from the Fish and Game Department.

I start with a slow drive-by of her home, pausing to scan the trees with binoculars. I've come at 8:00 a.m., which I've heard is the time of the morning feedings.

But I see nothing.

It seems too early to knock on the door, so I come back around ten. Knocking on doors in Grafton has left me with the nervous reflex of tensing up every time the door opens. You just never know when you're going to get Friendly Advice.

But in this case, the door swings back to reveal Doughnut Lady, looking as kindly as a fairy godmother. As she invites me into her home and introduces me to her cats, I feel a little wash of relief. The cats are Friendly, but they do not Advise.

Doughnut Lady shows me lots of evidence of her long-term love affair with the bears of Grafton. Here is the tree the cubs climbed to access the satellite dish. There are the two feeding stations, the grass worn away by years of bear visits. She hands me a homemade calendar featuring pictures of the bears, most of which were taken by her husband.

"My husband named one of them Darth Vader this year, and here's another one he called Mr. Big Stuff," she says. "Who we thought was a Mrs. Big Stuff."

But one thing Doughnut Lady does not show me is the bears themselves.

When I ask her about the specifics of feeding, she begins talking about the New Hampshire Fish and Game Department. Like many people, she refers to them as "F&G," but she puts her own little spin on it, so that it sounds like "effin' G."

As in "the effin' G came to attack me."

She still wasn't sure what, exactly, prompted the events of Labor Day 2016. After completing her 4:00 p.m. feeding of the bears, Doughnut Lady answered a knock at the door to find a uniformed game warden standing on her porch.

He asked her questions about her bear-feeding habits, questions to which he already seemed to know the answers. He told her that she could be prosecuted under the state's public nuisance laws and handed her a copy of the law that he had printed out.

Doughnut Lady then spoke to the warden for the first time since he had entered her home.

"You deserve a budget cut," she told him.

After he left, Doughnut Lady was angry and upset by what felt like both an intrusion and an accusation from distant strangers. She called Chief Poitras, but he told her there was nothing he could do.

Doughnut Lady was particularly stung by the apparent double standard applied to Grafton and to the state's elite.

"You should talk to these people in Hanover. I mean, it's terrible what's going on there," she says. "They didn't threaten anybody with public nuisance over there. I wonder why."

Doughnut Lady's lawyer was the one who convinced her to stop feeding the bears. When she called him, he told her that the legality of bear-feeding was a gray area, but he appealed to her better nature.

"You know, how would I feel if someone got hurt," she says.

Though falling down among wild bears did not frighten Doughnut Lady, the invisible threat of criminal prosecution held her in check. The Free Town era was at an end; law and order had begun to encroach. And so, the following morning, she stayed in, trying to find something to take her mind off the hungry bears waiting outside for her.

"It was, like, a lousy day," she says.

The feeling was terrible. She didn't even look outside where, presumably, the bears lingered hopefully for a while, then went on to knock over barbecue grills and garbage cans in the neighborhood.

"So," she says. Little traces of tears appear in the creases around her eyes. "That was it."

"It made you sad?" I ask Doughnut Lady. The answer is clearly a resounding yes, but I hope she will say something to help me convey the depths of her sorrow.

"Yeah," says Doughnut Lady.

She says it again.

"Yeah."

She says it twice more.

"Yeah. Yeah."

As I leave, I start making small talk to lighten the mood. She escorts me to the door. "I heard that since I stopped feeding them, they're grabbing garbage everywhere. But they don't come here," she says, a bit wistfully.

She stands on her front stoop, still subdued as I make my way to my car. Knowing that the people of Grafton have a special sensitivity to home invasions, I tell Doughnut Lady that, if she was told someone had been skulking around her residence earlier that morning, she needn't worry—it was just me.

Her tone brightens a bit. She doesn't worry about home invasions, she says.

"We'd get out the guns," she calls cheerily, waving.

11
A JEOPARDOUS JOURNEY

It is with me as I used to think it would be with the poor uneasy white bear I saw at the show. I thought he must have got
so stupid with the habit of turning backwards and forwards in
that narrow space that he would keep doing it if they set him
free. One gets a bad habit of being unhappy.

—George Eliot, *The Mill on the Floss*, 1860

Though her life had taken a dark turn, Jessica Soule still loved Grafton.
When she hired someone to drive her to the doctor's office, she never
tired of the woods and streams that rolled past her truck window, of the passing ghosts of her life with the Unification Church.

"I should be glad I made it this far," she said. "But the reality is that nobody wants to die. Everybody wants to live more."

One day Soule rolled her wheelchair out onto the front porch, did a
quick bear check, then went down the ramp, past the mailbox, and on out
to the truck in her driveway. Ordinarily, when she came out here, a helper
would give her an assist into the truck's high cab, but this time, she hadn't
told anyone what she was doing.

"Unless you're in the mood to jump in front of buses, you want to keep
living," she said. "And I'm way beyond jumping in front of buses."

Soule got the driver's side door open and then reached up to grip the
steering wheel for support. She hauled herself out of the chair, up into the
cab, and maneuvered herself safely into position. Her heart pounded, though
she couldn't blame it on the exertion.

"I was scared to death," she said.

Soule was on the precipice of a decision. She had looked into her future in Grafton and foreseen a rapid decline into death. But if she moved away, she would be leaving behind her meager network of remaining friends and family members, the people who helped her run errands and visit the doctor. If she was going to make it somewhere else, she wanted to be capable of driving.

She twisted the key in the ignition, and the pickup rumbled into life, the motor vibrating like a nervous thoroughbred, ready to run.

Soule's right leg was too weak to hold the brake down, so she couldn't even shift into gear safely. She grabbed the steering wheel again and scooched toward the center of the cab. With her left leg, which was stronger, she pinned the brake down with all her force before shifting into drive. Holding her breath, she eased off the brake and the truck lurched forward, down the driveway and up Wild Meadow Road, the same path she'd driven all those years ago to get to the church summer camp.

For the first time in years, Soule felt the flush of independence.

I can still drive, she thought as she pulled back into her driveway. *I can go places.*

When she got home, she began making calls, asking people whether they could provide a good home for her cats.

When Soule left Wild Meadow Road for the last time, she wasn't driving herself. She'd hired a woman to go with her, and they headed out, Route 4 up to I-89, south on I-91, and then west, out of New Hampshire.

As Grafton receded farther and farther into the distance behind her, she felt surges of anxiety, but she kept going. West, out of New England, west, across the endless Great Plains, and beyond.

A determined driver could cover nine hundred miles a day, but Soule found that traveling took a toll on her; she and her driver made less than half that time. They stopped for meals and at inexpensive hotels. In all, it took them six days to cover 2,700 miles; when she arrived at her new home, a house in Arizona previously owned by her brother, she was exhausted.

Soule's helper got her items into the house and then caught a plane back to New Hampshire the next day. As soon as Soule was alone, a hush settled over the strange new home. The silence was brought into sharp relief by the unnaturally bright sunlight that seemed to probe at her from every window.

For the next day or two, Soule busied herself with the details of unpacking from boxes into her new kitchen, her new bedroom. She hadn't brought much, so it didn't take long, but she fussed over the details, trying to take pleasure from the arrangement of dishes in the cabinets or knickknacks on the shelf. Sometimes she used the walker to hoist herself out of her wheelchair, so she could reach higher. But always, it was inside.

Soule had put thousands of miles between herself and the wilds of Grafton, but it turned out that wilderness was as much a state of mind as a geography. As long as she stayed isolated, an unbidden wilderness could spring up around her. As the days passed, a thin, barely visible layer of dust began to accumulate on the top surface of her plated front doorknob, atomized pieces of Arizona soil and long-burned meteorites, soft bits of wool and synthetic fibers from her clothing and blankets.

Soule ignored it. Whatever lay on the other side of the door was bright and intimidating. In here, she had her items, all laid out just as she liked.

Look! she exulted to herself. *The wheelchair rolls right into the bathroom!*

Time passed. The days were restful, but the nights occasionally brought seizures, paralyzing her body. She had fluid in her ear from an ear infection; sometimes she would wake up to find the world spinning in a vertiginous whirlwind.

Those were the moments when she thought of the thousands of miles between herself and her Grafton friends. Even when the walls of her bedroom slowly resumed their stationary places, she would be unable to go back to sleep, dark tendrils of worry crawling endlessly from one end of her brain to the other.

Had she made a terrible mistake?

In Grafton, neighbors were distant presences through thick buffers of woodland; here, where her house was hemmed in by others, she felt naked. When she peered through the window, she saw people in the streets, so many people, walking back and forth for unknown purposes. They were all strangers. Soule told herself that she would go outside when she felt a little better. She hadn't yet fully recuperated from her trip.

The layer of dust on her doorknob thickened infinitesimally as it added minuscule pieces of pollen from strange plants whose names Soule did not know, tiny bits of her own dead skin and hair intermingling with pieces of the home's former occupants, pinpoint-sized arachnids that fed on the skin, and feces from those arachnids. A whole chaotic ecosystem in miniature rose up on her doorknob.

One afternoon about a week after Soule came to Arizona, that little wilderness was thrown into turmoil. Even as fresh motes of lint and spiderweb descended from the sky, a vibration swept through, knocking hundreds of particles off the doorknob to ride the whisper-gentle air currents of Soule's living room.

More vibrations followed, pulse after pulse setting pieces of dust adrift. Soule heard the vibrations—they were the sound of civilization, the bass line of a song that was coming right through the walls and windows of her new home.

She wheeled herself to the window and peeked out through the shades. Outside, she saw people standing along the street in little groups, chatting and drinking from small plastic cups. It was a block party.

Soule steeled herself, gripped the doorknob, and, without realizing it, obliterated in that instant the tiny wilderness that had been growing in her home. When she opened her door, sunlight flooded in. She wheeled herself tentatively to the sidewalk, trying to hide her wariness with a smile.

Though she knew her primary concern should be the people in front of her, she couldn't help but notice the sky above. In Grafton, she'd enjoyed watching white cotton sliding across the crystalline background, but it was always just a little slice of air, bounded by the contours of New England's wrinkled, tree-whiskered face.

"Here, they get all depressed if there's any kind of clouds in the sky," she said. "The sunset was all red. The big blue sky, from one end to the other."

Before she knew it, somebody had pressed a plastic cup into her hand, and she was talking to a family from across the street. Next, she was talking to everyone.

"They know me," she told me afterward. "They'll look out for me because of my age. I feel like I'm adding positivity."

Someone told her where the nearest Walmart supercenter was, so she could do her grocery shopping. In the coming days, she hired someone to go with her, and they went in together. Soule rode a motorized cart, directing the shopping.

When the ear infection passed, Soule found that, with her balance restored, her legs felt stronger than they had in Grafton. The next time she used the walker to stand up, she took a few shaky experimental steps. She hadn't been able to do that for six or seven years.

She parked the wheelchair next to her bed and began using the walker to get around in her house. She spent long hours sitting on her back porch, marveling at the lack of New England bugs.

After the long, cold chill of Grafton, where one miserable winter had bled into the next, her body drank in the heat and dryness of the blazing hot afternoons. The angry screaming of her joints settled down to sullen mutters.

The porch allowed her a glimpse of the Superstitions, a mountain range that, like the bear, has been imprinted with the culture of the primates who live in its shadow. To the Apaches, who once used the Superstitions as a stronghold against European interlopers, the mountain range was a gateway to the underworld. To incoming white settlers, it was the site of the Lost Dutchman's Gold Mine, featured in a get-rich-quick legend that has led to the death of many seekers.

To Soule, who spent hours looking up at the rocky outcrops, the mountain range was the source of the cool breezes that ran down its slopes and tickled her neck, bearing tidings of a brighter future, where before there had seemed none.

"I believe in spiritual healing," she said. "And that you can turn things around with your mind-set. As long as you're breathing, there's a chance you can change yourself and the world around you."

The next time Soule and her helper went to Walmart, she left her wheelchair behind. A few times after that, she left the helper behind too.

In Phoenix, Soule has risen again. She walks into her backyard under her own power and looks upon the red rock and boundless blue sky, taking one miraculous step after another, knowing she is free.

12

THE FREEDOMS FORGOTTEN

The bear, wolf, lynx, wildcat, deer, beaver, and marten, have disappeared; the otter is rarely if ever seen here at present; and the mink is less common than formerly.

—Henry David Thoreau, *Excursions*, 1863

As I wrapped up my time in Grafton, I could see that the wheel would still turn, bringing players and conflicts that, though new, would run along the same fault lines as in generations past. Human-wildlife conflicts will continue to happen. Parasites will continue to drive the action. People wrapped in different realities will try to bend each other into compliance.

As the Free Town Project gave way to the Free State Project, the signs were everywhere. In 2017, eighteen miles from the spot where Tracey Colburn was attacked, a bobcat jumped onto the back of an eighty-year-old woman who was tending the roses in her garden, mauling her. The following year, another bobcat attacked two women in the nearby town of Hartford, Vermont. In both cases, the bobcats were being controlled by rabies parasites.

Doughnut Lady told me that she thought it would be legal to plant sunflowers, and blueberries, and other things bears like to eat. And sometimes bears eat plants before they have a chance to sprout.

"I could just put them on the ground," said Doughnut Lady. "And they're planted."

Tracey Colburn still froze her food scraps, to prevent bears from smelling them. And she considered buying a gun. Not because of bears, she said. Because of Grafton.

"Everybody else has got one," she told me. "I feel like I'm the only one."

When Hurricane the llama took ill, Dianne Burrington stitched together a harness and hooked it up to a tractor bucket, so that she could keep him on his legs, but it didn't help. The vet told her it was brainworm, a parasite that can make its host walk in circles, go blind, or lose its fear of humans. Hurricane's replacement, Eddie, wasn't a very good guard llama, she said. He wouldn't even stand in the rain.

Despite many calls for amity in the wake of John Connell's death, the libertarians and the town continued to fight over the tax bill associated with the Peaceful Assembly Church. They eventually crafted an agreement that offered tax forgiveness, on the condition that the libertarians seal the building envelope, so that it would not be degraded by the elements. Three years later, a structural engineer declared that the church was in danger of collapsing, and the parties resumed their legal battle.

And the New Hampshire Fish and Game Department concluded that there were too many bears in the Grafton area. In 2015, they set a goal to reduce the population by 34 percent from 2013 levels. It could take ten years to achieve that goal.

Babiarz told me that he was not sure how much longer Grafton's fire department can last, relying as it does on a shrinking group of volunteers to massage a few more months of service out of each vehicle and piece of equipment. If there's a fire during the day, when the volunteers are off working their day jobs (in towns with day jobs to offer), the community largely relies on mutual aid from other towns. Until it arrives, Babiarz said, "I can fight it by myself and basically put the fire in check."

The last time I saw him, he stepped out of his cluttered office in the fire station and told me why he helped start the Free Town Project in the first place.

"My goal was to hold what we have and not lose any more ground," he said. "I've seen the trends. More and more regulations, until you can't do anything on your own property. And if people come in demanding more services, Grafton would no longer be an affordable place to live."

But the Free Town Project was over. Babiarz said that the long-term effects of the social experiment will be ephemeral—"a blip on the radar"—like a June snowstorm melting away in the sunshine.

I have no doubt that Grafton will make news again, in some wild, unpredictable way. The soil there may be rocky, but it's fertile ground for dreams, and humans will always be drawn to places where they can slip off the radar of communal oversight and nurture their own private worlds.

That was the very quality that Babiarz believed was overlooked in every discussion of the Free Town. The combative libertarian colonizers didn't get it. The overly regulatory state government didn't get it. And the myopic media certainly didn't get it.

"They don't recognize," he said, "that the town was already free."

THE FIREFIGHTER AND THE BEAR

We talk of deviations from natural life, as if artificial life were not also natural. The smoothest curled courtier in the boudoirs of a palace has an animal nature, rude and aboriginal as a white bear, omnipotent to its own ends.

—Ralph Waldo Emerson, *Nature*, 1836

It was the summer of 2016.

The fire chief's tall, lean form could be seen moving among his outbuildings with hammers in his hand and nails in his teeth, reinforcing the chicken coop as he tried to match wits with the determined bear that always seemed to be watching. Though government control was seeping into every sphere of society, in Grafton at least, chicken-threatening bears were still the domain of the landowner.

"It is an affirmed right," Babiarz said. "If some private organization wants to save the bears, they have to convince me not to shoot them. I have my guns. I have my bullets. That's my solution."

After their tense standoff with the AR-15, Babiarz and the bear began a cycle of coop-destruction and coop-reinforcement in which the shed was slowly rebuilt from its humble beginnings into an ever-sturdier chicken fortress.

At the same time, Babiarz waged a campaign of pain-based bear deterrence.

He loaded an electric fence with strips of bacon to zap the bear on the inside of its mouth. He installed booby traps, though he was limited by the prospect of lawsuits from trespassers who might bumble into his coop.

"There's nothing explosive, a big boomerang coming out and chopping you, or anything like that," he said, in the tone of a man who has made certain compromises. "But if you step through that window, there's going to be pain."

Outside the coop, twenty gleaming tips rose skyward from the soil. Babiarz had buried boards in the dirt, with nails sticking out to puncture the soles of the bear's feet. One board had screws instead of nails, to do more damage. It had claw marks on it, and one of the screws was broken off.

"Yep, it went right through, but you know what? Obviously, I injured it. There was blood pouring," the fire chief said. "There was nice red all over."

In September, while trying to build its winter reserves of fat, the bear finally got too reckless. Babiarz caught it red-pawed, sitting on its rump like a kid at a campfire, feasting.

Just sitting right here! Babiarz thought. *Right here, munching on chicken.*

The chicken belonged to Babiarz. He fled from the bear, sprinted down the slope, and banged through the door of his schoolhouse home. Inside, short on breath but long on adrenaline, the man grabbed a Ruger .44 Magnum from his closet.

He had his gun. He ran back outside, joined in his skin by the ghosts of primeval hunters. His pupils shrank in the sunlight. The bear was walking uphill, toward the refuge of the tree line.

Babiarz charged toward the forest's wild embrace. In his guts, a thousand thousand bacteria sang their secret songs. His gun was in his hand. His homestead was at his back, and he was meting out justice. He had his gun.

His fingertip hooked the cool metal of the trigger and the Magnum startled awake in his hand. A thunderclap of noise tore through the cochlea of his inner ears, breaking untold numbers of tiny hairs, changing his sound perceptions.

The shot went wide. The bear, sensing danger, continued upslope, faster now.

The man crossed the feather-strewn ground. Synapses rippled frenetic electrical patterns throughout his brain's hidden spaces. Here, the land was wild and tamable; here, absent of paper pushers and tax collectors, he was law.

His breath came fast. Oxygen surged through his muscles. He could get off one more shot, maybe two, before the bear disappeared across the tree line. Finger on trigger, he rushed up the slope, the slope that was once a farmer's field, once a schoolchild's playground, once a bear's foraging ground, once a fire's fuel. Chemicals flooded his brain.

The primate aimed once more. He had his gun. He had his gun. He fired. Free at last.

A NOTION OF A NATION

Master Murray, was about 11 when I came; a fine, stout, healthy boy, frank, and good-natured in the main, and might have been a decent lad, had he been properly educated, but now, he was as rough as a young bear, boisterous, unruly, unprincipled, untaught, unteachable.

—Anne Brontë, *Agnes Grey*, 1847

And then what happened?

After the hardcover edition of this book was published in September 2020, it was easily the question I was asked the most.

One simple answer involves Grafton's church, left covered in soot and debris by the 2016 fire. Soon after, a local nonprofit called Mascoma Valley Preservation began raising funds to restore the church to its former glory. In 2020, the group auctioned off a signed copy of *A Libertarian Walks into a Bear* and also applied for a tax-supported economic development grant.

The book netted them $28; the grant, $315,000. I'm glad I helped.

But this answer leaves questioners unsatisfied. People want to know what happened in a broader sense. What happened to the bizarre and quirky Free Town movement as its members brought their ideas to the rest of the state? Did all those energetic libertarian activists succeed in their bid to bend New Hampshire to their free will–loving will? What are Grafton's human and ursine populations like today?

And then what happened?

In short, a lot. A lot has happened. And none of it suggests, particularly, that the cascade of absurdity sparked by America's first Free Town is likely to subside anytime soon.

For one thing, there's been another bear attack, this one in Canaan (the town next door). On a sweltering night in June 2020, a man was removing an air conditioner from his truck when he felt the bear's claws penetrating the skin of his back. Thankfully, when he shouted and shoved at the bear, it ran off into the night.

Though the attack demonstrated the continued effect of Grafton's laissez-bear attitude toward local bear management, it was pretty small potatoes in a landscape of bizarre bear tales that continued to roll, tidally, across the world, each one held up as a curiosity to delight the public. In the summer of 2020 alone, I read about bears wandering into and out of grocery stores, a bear overdosing on cocaine, a Canadian novel that centered on the sexual relationship between a woman and a bear, a bear punched by a drunken visitor at a Polish zoo, a bear found swimming in a lake with its head stuck in a giant container of Cheez-its, a bear castrated by the Italian government for escaping from its enclosure and eating donkeys. There was a bear illegally tagged with a pro-Trump MAGA sticker, a bear corpse starting a grass fire after being electrocuted by a power line, a bear breaking into a pizza delivery vehicle, bears vying for champion-level portliness during a government-sponsored "Fat Bear Week," bears tearing the doors off of rental storage units, an elderly bear treated for arthritis with stem cell therapy, a wild bear fed cookies from an idiot's mouth, and a 22,000-year-old cave bear unearthed by melting permafrost.

These stories, and thousands more like them, taught me something.

A bear is what a bear is. But also, a bear is whatever humans say it is.

To a human, a bear might be a comic bumbler, a horror-movie villain, or a noble savage; often, the bear is an emotional crutch, existing largely to reassure the hunter of his own strength, or the environmental activist of their own morality. And when people project their cultural biases onto a bear or a bear population, they invariably cause unintentional changes to the actual animals. Sometimes, as in Grafton, those changes boomerang back onto the people who indulged the most reckless expressions of their own anthropomorphic tendencies.

All of which is to say, the bears are not the only ones commanding headlines.

New Hampshire's libertarian community is still swollen with hot dreams that fester like untreated wounds; activists continue to weep ideas into the light of day, ideas that simultaneously fascinate and repel the public.

One of those ideas in particular seems to be gathering steam lately.

On a warm Sunday evening in June 2016, a baker's dozen of libertarians, mostly men, gathered in front of the Norris Cotton Federal Building in Manchester. They wore T-shirts, khakis, a kilt, and degrees of facial hair that ranged from a Selleck-adjacent mustache to an unkempt, Vikingesque beard.

Though they were political extremists, they seemed nice enough. The anarchist held a sign that politely let people know he was an anarchist. "Ask me anything!" the sign continued, unprompted. "Have a nice day ☺."

One of the rare clean-shaven faces in attendance belonged to Dave Ridley, a former Free Towner. Ridley, fifty-four, wore a white sweatband neatly dividing his bald pate from a case of "resting studious face," which was enhanced by his heavy eyebrows, black-rimmed glasses, and sonorous voice.

It was time for a new cause, a project bigger than the Free Town, bigger even than the Free State. Ridley had organized this event to kick-start an effort to form the world's first Free Nation. His proposed road map to this new utopia ran through New Hampshire's peaceful secession from the United States.

Just 238 years after Grafton's first ill-fated effort to secede from the United States, Ridley and his allies wanted New Hampshire to declare its independence, cut ties with the federal government, and make its own decisions about things like currency (including cryptocurrency), interstate highways, racial segregation, and the sale of heroin.

"Secession is like surgery," Ridley would later say. "It's scary. It's not something you just want to do for no particular reason. But it's sometimes necessary, like surgery is."

Ridley is a fixture in the state's libertarian circles. In the mid-2000s, he proposed two pieces of state legislation: the first was on gun rights, and the other would have made it easier for a manicurist to get a license. (The idea of outlaw manicurists has long been a source of libertarian amusement.) In 2006, as a political stunt, he showed up at a local IRS office with an anti-tax sign and refused to answer the questions of the staff there. Three weeks later, Homeland Security officers showed up at his door, sparking a six-month court process during which he was eventually arrested. He refused to pay a fine for illegally distributing handbills and ultimately served four days in jail for contempt of court.

The idea of secession was controversial within libertarian circles—the more polished members of the state Libertarian Party worried that it was just the sort of outlandish idea that would keep libertarians on the outer fringes of the halls of power. To appease people like Ridley, they sometimes staked out a milquetoast middle—seceding might be too extreme, but nurturing a credible threat of secession could gain concessions from the federal government on a whole host of freedom-related issues.

But the resounding success of the Manchester protest put renewed pressure on the state's libertarian leaders to embrace New Hampshire independence. Media outlets, their interest primed by Britain's vote to exit the European Union, reported widely on Ridley's Manchester gathering. Encouraged, he began working to advance the cause with a handful of others, including Russell Kanning (one of the Free Towners who was roasting hot dogs over the fire that brought out John Babiarz) and Ian Freeman (the Keene libertarian whose extreme positions about age limits for consensual sex got him disavowed by the Free State Project).

Acutely aware that New Hampshire was the first colony to declare independence in 1776, Ridley and his allies attempted to walk in the long-eroded footsteps of those founding fathers. They handed out flyers at independence festivals. Against a backdrop of exposed brick walls lined with sofas and laptop-friendly work desks, they gave rowdy speeches at The Shell, an underground liberty clubhouse in an old mill on the Salmon Falls River in Rollinsford. They pulled off more, and larger, secessionist demonstrations, including one in Portsmouth that drew supporters from around the state. In Manchester, in a small plaza dominated by a UPS store and a Mr. Mac's Mac and Cheese Restaurant, there was renewed activity in a small office for the Foundation for New Hampshire Independence, led by Carla Gericke.

It took only a few months before, in November 2016, their efforts bore fruit.

The Libertarian Party of New Hampshire broke with the national Libertarian Party by formally adding a secession plank to its official platform, a move that gave the idea both credibility and staying power within the libertarian community. Placed after clauses that identified tax as theft and sex work as an expression of human rights, the state platform now asserted that "the people of New Hampshire have the sole and exclusive right to govern themselves as sovereign, free, and independent individuals."

The idea was now officially mainstream—within the fringe.

It was a start.

THIS MIGHT BE a good time to answer another component of the "and then what happened" question. What happened in Grafton?

I thought that, as the influence of the Free Town Project faded, the town's civic-minded residents might reassert control and embark on a campaign of community investment that would make up for the ground that had been lost over the past sixteen or so years.

That was not to be.

Though the guard has changed, Grafton has remained a place where tax dollars are treated with roughly the same level of affection as root canals, Wells Fargo banking executives, and Nigerian princes with business opportunities.

In early 2020, town leaders met to craft an annual operating budget to bring before voters in the spring. Far from opening the spending floodgates, the forces of fiscal conservatism successfully argued that the $1.2 million budget could be reduced even further. They cut it by just a hair, $7,000, from the previous year.

In early 2021, town leaders heard a report that the ramshackle town office was having a drainage problem and that parts of the floor needed to be repaired or replaced. During the same meeting, they also expressed alarm that the Grafton Christmas tree had increased the town electricity bill by $30. After considering the use of a timer to leave the tree in darkness during off hours, they proposed a budget that would cut another $25,000 from municipal spending.

When voters convened to consider the budget, they also had another choice before them: in between posting circumcision horror stories on his Facebook feed, Richard "Dick Angel" Angell had filed as a candidate to serve as a town official.

Voters approved the emaciated budget, but rejected Dick Angel. They also rejected a ballot measure that would have allowed the library to set aside money toward a new building, the latest in a long line of defeats for the library's decades-long efforts to plan for a new facility.

And so, the argument in Grafton continues. Some people continue to believe that keeping taxes low will bring more people into the town.

State official estimates show that demographers expect the 2020 census to show a slight population decline.

AND THEN WHAT happened?

With secession established as a formal goal, libertarians continued to run for public office and continued to push New Hampshire toward waters that were, depending on one's perspective, either enticingly uncharted or inhospitable to reasonable people.

In 2018, Ian Freeman ran for the New Hampshire Senate on a platform of voluntary taxes and total legalization of drugs. That year he also served as campaign manager for a Venn-diagram–busting anarchist Satanist libertarian named Aria DiMezzo, whose flaming pink hair and tats drew somewhat less attention than her campaign slogan: "Aria DiMezzo For SherrifFuck the Police."

Neither Freeman nor DiMezzo were elected.

But a fellow Free Stater, Keith Ammon, served a term in the New Hampshire statehouse before introducing the "Jetsons Bill." When it became law in 2019, New Hampshire became the first state in the union to approve flying cars (or, more accurately, small airplanes that can be easily converted, *Transformers*-style, into a road-friendly iteration, sort of an aeronautical duck-boat). They require no state inspection.

In early 2019, Free Town founder Bob Hull passed away at the age of fifty-three, with John Babiarz and a few other close friends standing by his bedside. His statehouse seat was won by Lex Berezhny, the crypto-friendly protocol developer who also served in Grafton's volunteer fire department. Berezhny and fellow firefighter Tom Ploszaj (who finally won his own legislative seat) joined Tony Lekas and various other Free Staters as legislators.

Vermin Supreme, the candidate known for wearing a boot on his head, lost the Libertarian Party nomination for president of the United States to Jo Jorgensen, a professor of psychology at Clemson University. When Supreme's friend Spike Cohen was selected as Jorgenson's vice presidential nominee, it was widely seen as an olive branch to fans of Supreme's time-travel-and-unicorn-themed platform. Jorgensen's biggest media splash came serendipitously, when she was bitten by a bat and preemptively treated for possible rabies.

None of these developments did much for the secessionist movement.

Then 2020, a year that would live in infamy, dawned upon an unsuspecting planet.

That spring, Dave Ridley drove up to the closed entrance of a state park trailhead, rolled down his car window, and began speaking to a state park worker.

"I'm audio taping," Ridley said, with some authority. "What's going on here?"

Ridley, a former cameraman for a local television station, is best known among libertarians as an independent practitioner of what he calls "Gonzo journalism," which his work probably isn't, or "guerrilla journalism," which it might be.

In this particular video, he had targeted a worker with broad shoulders, a broad accent, an expansive belly, and the placid calm of one who has made complete peace with a mission of manning a solitary sawhorse on a lonely dirt road.

"It's been closed for the past eight weeks," the worker said. "We had about 150 vehicles down here that we couldn't get emergency vehicles through a couple weeks ago, and the governor told us to shut it down."

"Okay," said Ridley. "So how does keeping people from exercising help reduce—"

The man, anticipating the premise, cut Ridley off. He explained that the park was not keeping people from exercising.

"You go to 128 Moulton Road, that's the main park, you can go in there."

After some more back-and-forth, Ridley got a bit more personal.

"Will you be returning some of your salary to taxpayers," he asked, "now that you're allowed to work?"

"Sir," said the worker, with a blend of satisfaction and dignity, "all state parks are self-funded. Taxpayers don't pay for this."

"Now that you're allowed to work," Ridley continued, undeterred, "and taxpayers are not, in many cases?"

The worker opened his mouth.

"This is a—," he said, and stopped. Hadn't he just addressed this? "This is self-funded—"

Ridley, warming to his work, interrupted.

"Well, one of the reasons they want to be here is because your government has partially stopped them from working."

"Well," said the worker, "there's nothing I can do about that, sir."

"You can quit," Ridley said. He raised his voice, repeating, "You can quit!"

The worker indicated that he had bills to pay.

"Well, so do we," Ridley chastised him. "And your government's not allowing us to work."

The worker took this comment at face value. As far as he knew, Ridley had actually been fired because of the government's pandemic regulations.

"Sir," he said kindly, "if you look at the want ads, there's plenty of people out there still hiring. I know that for a fact."

During the entire exchange, everything about Ridley's tone was confrontational. But suddenly it was as if a switch had been flipped.

"Now, despite my anger, I do appreciate you answering my questions. Not every bureaucrat does." Ridley offered a hearty, if somewhat forced, laugh to demonstrate his humanity. "All right," he told the worker. "Be safe!" Then he drove away.

Ridley considered the whole encounter a success. He gave it top billing as a "featured" video on his YouTube channel, where over nine months it garnered 1,163 views, including my own.

Ridley's channel is full of footage of similar conflicts with librarians, census workers, cops, prison guards, local officials, politicians, town clerks, tax assessors, and college staffers. Often, Ridley's approach leads to him being asked (or forced) to leave.

It was often lonely work. But as the pandemic's death toll began to mount, Ridley's approach to the government response began to catch on.

———

AND THEN WHAT *happened?*

In America, the COVID-19 pandemic brought an avalanche of pressure from the government and the public health community to reduce the chance of transmission of the coronavirus. Every individual was pushed to maintain six feet of personal space, limit indoor gatherings, and wear a mask in public.

This flexing of governmental muscle created a common enemy that allowed Republicans and libertarians to bond at unprecedented levels. That was nowhere more apparent than in New Hampshire, where the anti-mask sentiment was, like a boor's flatulence, both loud and proud.

The stage was set. Over three short acts, a uniquely American tragedy unfolded in the legislative statehouse.

Act 1 took place on November 20. Having just won control of the state legislature, a group of Republicans asserted their commitment to freedom by gathering indoors, mostly maskless, at a ski resort. One of them, a realtor named Dick Hinch, lauded Republicans who refused to wear masks as patriots and the "freedom group." Admiringly, they asked Hinch to be their leader. He accepted.

Act 2 took place on December 1. Hinch, facing fire from Democrats and the press, admitted that "a very small number" of Republicans who had attended the ski resort gathering had come down with COVID-19. The following day Hinch was formally voted in as House Speaker by the full legislature.

Act 3 took place on December 9. Having led the House for barely more than a week, Hinch died of COVID-19. Five days later, the federal government released the first shipment of a coronavirus vaccine to the public.

The irony of the drama would have been comic if it wasn't so sad.

Though New Hampshire's statehouse provided an unusually neat example of a person dying over a principled stand against masking, variations on the same dynamic were happening all across the country. That very November a team led by Yale researcher Anton Gollwitzer used publicly available data to demonstrate that people in deep-red counties were catching and dying of COVID-19 at higher rates than other Americans, even when accounting for other factors.

With the mask debate adding life-and-death urgency to partisanship, observers, including political journalist Tom Elias, drew on historical examples to make the case that the pandemic was creating a state of instability that opened the door to secession.

And indeed, New Hampshire's secessionists were delighted to learn that the issue of sovereignty was at long last finding a place in the hearts of millions of Americans. Polls in September 2020 and March 2021 found that between 30 and 40 percent of Americans favored secession, up sharply from the 24 percent a Reuters poll had found six years earlier.

These and many other signs of secessionism convinced me that I needed to learn more about New Hampshire's local movement. I began to reach out to secessionists, seeking an interview.

I wound up approaching Dave Ridley.

———

AND THEN WHAT *happened?*

Via email, Ridley instantly agreed to talk to me, though there were certain conditions and logistical considerations. The condition was that he be allowed to record the conversation. The logistical consideration had to do with his schedule.

His email responses often came at odd hours of the night, and he seemed to be mostly available in the evening. This piqued my curiosity. Was he working a night shift?

When we eventually connected, I asked him about it. The answer was simple, Ridley explained. Our schedules were out of sync because I was on a 24-hour cycle. He was on a 24.25-hour cycle.

Every day, Ridley stays up fifteen minutes later, elongating his work (or leisure) time compared to the rest of us. (About every three months he has to recalibrate by skipping a day on the calendar, going directly from, say, June 3 to June 5.) This practice means there are times when he is nocturnal, and I had happened to catch him during the night-owl phase of that cycle. There were practical downsides, he conceded, but they were manageable.

"It wouldn't be very consistent with having a corporate job. So I just cut my expenses and don't have a corporate job."

Ridley and I spoke with the implicit understanding that we came from different political perspectives. I gathered that he considered the risk of being ridiculed an acceptable cost for a chance to bring attention to the cause. Over the course of a few conversations by phone and email, he was unfailingly open, straightforward, and friendly.

He does not believe that New Hampshire's libertarian-inspired secession movement is on the precipice of success. It may be more accurate to say that it's on the precipice of not being laughed out of the room. Ridley and his allies are holding the vision together with spit, baling wire, and letters to the editor.

"Right now," he told me, "the secession ingredients are not there. They will be there later, probably, if and when the Biden administration overplays its hand. Or if all the federal spending results in hyperinflation—that would be another trigger."

But Ridley made a compelling argument that secession is not an outlandish, or even particularly unrealistic, idea. In his view, it's more like same-sex marriage, a long-held libertarian position that moved from fringe to reality in less than thirty years. He also compared the matter to the Slovenian independence movement.

"In Slovenia, there was no one talking about it in 1988," Ridley said. "Three years later, they were independent."

Ridley likes to point to international examples as proof that secession is possible. Years ago, he traveled to Europe and witnessed firsthand the independence drives in Slovenia, Bosnia, and Croatia. Estonia and Catalonia are good examples, he said, because they won independence with limited violence.

They all had one thing in common, Ridley said: abusive governments.

Ridley seems to really feel the weight of an estimated 200,000 pages of federal law—a dense and incomprehensible thicket that is nevertheless all the basis needed for one to be arrested.

"For me, it's the fear we have to live under in the United States," he said. "The fear that the IRS will come for you for a minor mistake they think is a big deal. That the SWAT team will come through your door."

I ventured that, in a government-lite world, the more odious master would be corporations, unchecked by adequate regulation.

He allowed that the state government in New Hampshire "is a little bit less evil than Google." But Washington, DC, he said, is worse than the two put together.

Other secessionists often make a fiscal argument to persuade traditional anti-tax conservatives. The Foundation for New Hampshire Independence claims on its website, without citation, that New Hampshire gets back only about 70 cents for each dollar it pays the federal government in taxes.

But that assertion conflicts with the conclusions of the Rockefeller Institute of Government, which studies such things. It reports that, while there have been recent years in which New Hampshire paid more into the federal coffers than it received, on balance it benefited by $1.2 billion between 2015 and 2019.

Ridley doesn't particularly rely on the argument that New Hampshire is losing money to the feds. Even if the state is profiting by the relationship, he says, it's at the expense of taxpayers somewhere else. This leaves unanswered the question of whether those somewhere-else-dwelling taxpayers want New Hampshire to secede on their behalf.

The unease that libertarian activists feel living under the American government came into sharp relief when Ridley sent me an email about Ian Freeman.

When Freeman was running for the state Senate in 2018, he told the local newspaper that government enforcement inevitably escalates into force. First, he said, "it'll be a threatening letter. And if you don't listen to the threatening letter, eventually, men with guns will probably show up at your door, and they will do something to you."

And indeed, in March 2021, men with guns showed up at Freeman's door and did something to him.

In this case, the men with guns were FBI agents, and the something they did was arrest him. He and five other New Hampshire libertarians (including Satanist anarchist Aria DiMezzo) were charged with allegedly laundering money in a scheme that involved cryptocurrency and the misrepresentation of revenue as charitable donations to a religious organization. Prosecutors have not publicly named the religious organization, but Freeman was active in the John Connell–inspired Shire Free Church, with its foam-sword fights and rituals of pie.

For Ridley, the next obvious step for secession is to introduce a bill into the state legislature that would receive, if not full-throated support, at least the sort of consideration that could advance the argument. Ridley says he's run up against a self-imposed ethical constraint to taking this step.

"This is probably my Achilles' heel, my unwillingness to do it the way everyone else does," he said.

Ridley has estimated the cost of legislative consideration to be about $2,000 in taxpayer funds. Because he is opposed to taxes on principle, he won't introduce a secession bill without paying for the costs of its consideration. And as a guy who is living on the sort of budget that supports a 24.25-hour lifestyle, he does not expect to front the cash himself.

At some point, he hopes, a donor will step forward and pony up the $2,000 price tag.

Until then, he will wait.

And then what happens... is anyone's guess.

ACKNOWLEDGMENTS

ACKNOWLEDGMENTS ARE AN opportunity to rectify the chief structural problem of a book: namely, that credit is misleadingly assigned to a single "author" when (as is also true for the theory of evolution and several major wars) credit is more rightly dispersed among a host of quiet toilers. My incomplete list of those who deserve hearty thanks starts with editor Athena Bryan, who fired me out of the starting gate, and editor Ben Adams, who dragged me over the finish line; both provided endless wisdom, kindness, and support. Gratitude also to other members of the PublicAffairs team, including Cindy, Melissa R., Melissa V., Amy, Chris, and Clive. Major thanks are due to the people of Grafton who were kind enough to allow me to document how their lives were affected by bears, the Free Town Project, or both—that includes Tom Ploszaj, Tim Bowen, Tracey Colburn, "Beretta," Rosalie Babiarz, Russell Poitras, Onshin, Ellen Kraus, Adam Franz, Annie, Cheryl Senter, Steve Darrow, John Redman, Dave Thurber, Fred Duefield, "Doughnut Lady," Dianne Burrington, and especially John Babiarz, Jessica Soule, Deb Clough, and the Grafton Public Library regulars. And though I never met him, Grafton historian Ken Cushing's meticulously researched writings about Grafton's past were critical to the historical chapters. I also received invaluable insight and advice from bear experts Ben Kilham and Andrew Timmins, human expert Mary Flanagan, editor Seyward Darby and the *Atavist* magazine support staff, agent Ross Harris, friends Martin Frank and Sam Eaton, the *Valley News* staff, and writers Mike Finkel, Lisa Rogak, Don Hough, and Rob Wolfe. Thanks, too, to the support and input of family members, including Jennifer Vincent, John Hetling, Marc Hetling, and Marjorie Hetling. And, of course, my wife Kimberly, whose faith in me never wavered.

I also thank the bears, who, during several wild encounters, have not eaten me.

Yet.

BIBLIOGRAPHY

Anderson, Dave, and Andrew Parrella. "Something Wild: Why Coyotes Seem to Be Everywhere." *New Hampshire Public Radio*, February 23, 2018. www.nhpr.org/post/something-wild-why-coyotes-seem-be-everywhere-2#stream/0.

Appleton's Annual Cyclopaedia and Register of Important Events of the Year 1893, vol. 18 (new series) and vol. 33 (whole series). New York: D. Appleton and Company, 1894.

Asch, Joseph. "What to Do About the Bears?" *Dartblog*, June 5, 2018. www.dartblog.com/data/2018/06/013865.php.

Asch, Joseph. "Please Don't Kill Mink." *Change.org* petition started by Joe Asch. www.change.org/p/please-don-t-kill-mink (accessed October 14, 2019).

Associated Press. "Vermont Probes Man with 70 Goats in House." *World-Wide Religious News*, March 29, 2004. https://wwrn.org/articles/4769/.

Associated Press. "Townspeople Oppose Libertarian Settlement." *Sun Journal*, June 20, 2004. www.sunjournal.com/2004/06/20/townspeople-oppose-libertarian-settlement/.

Associated Press. "Corinth Goat Farmer Goes on Hunger Strike." *Barre Montpelier Times Argus*, June 26, 2004. www.timesargus.com/news/corinth-goat-farmer-goes-on-hunger-strike/article_d89ac735-1077-5d5d-9cfc-671274e9dd0c.html.

Associated Press. "Plea Bargain Gets Goats Back to Vt. Man." *Boston Globe*, December 12, 2004. http://archive.boston.com/news/local/articles/2004/12/12/plea_bargain_gets_goats_back_to_vt_man/?camp=pm.

Associated Press. "Man Facing Animal Cruelty Charges for Alleged Mistreatment of Goats." *Free Republic*, March 24, 2005. http://freerepublic.com/focus/f-chat/1369865/posts.

Associated Press. "10,000-Year-Old Camel Bones Found in Arizona." *NBC News*, April 30, 2007. www.nbcnews.com/id/18397911/ns/technology_and_science-science/t/-year-old-camel-bones-found-arizona/#.XZ3SAmYpDIU.

Associated Press. "NH Officials Searching for Bear in Attack." *NBC5*, June 18, 2012. www.mynbc5.com/article/nh-officials-searching-for-bear-in-attack/3303765.

Associated Press. "Property Owner Kills 3 Cubs Going After Honey." *Concord Monitor*, September 20, 2018. www.concordmonitor.com/Property-owner-kills-3-cubs-going-after-honey-20324388.

Associated Press. "Bobcat That Attacked 3 Had Rabies." *Associated Press*, December 13, 2018. www.apnews.com/ff0be739bc234bcdb9c2c9a167291058.

Ayoob, Massad. "38 Super." *Guns Magazine*, March 2001.

Babiarz, John. "About Me." *John Babiarz: Libertarian Leader*. www.johnbabiarz .com/john-babiarz-about (accessed September 27, 2019).

Baillie, Jonathan, Ulf Gärdenfors, Brian Groombridge, George Rabb, and A. J. Stattersfield, eds. *1996 IUCN Red List of Threatened Animals*. Gland, Switzerland, and Cambridge, UK: International Union for Conservation of Nature, 1996.

Banks, Louis. *White Slaves; or, the Oppression of the Worthy Poor*. Boston: Lee and Shepard, 1893.

Barrick, Daniel. "Libertarians Set Sights on Grafton, NH." *Concord Monitor*, June 12, 2004.

Barrick, Daniel. "Libertarian Head Hosts Benson." *Concord Monitor*, August 12, 2004.

Barrick, Daniel. "Protestors Hurl Invective at FEMA." *Concord Monitor*, September 22, 2005.

Barringer, Bernie. "Everything You Ever Wanted to Know About Bear Eyesight." *Outdoor Hub*, April 4, 2015. www.outdoorhub.com/stories/2015/04/01 /everything-ever-wanted-know-bear-eyesight/.

Batchellor, Albert Stillman, ed. *Town Charters, Including Grants of Territory Within the Present Limits of New Hampshire, Made by the Government of Massachusetts, vol. 25, Grafton Regrant, 1769*. Concord, NH: Edward N. Pearson, 1895.

Baylor University. "Americans Are Happier in States That Spend More on Libraries, Parks, and Highways." *EurekAlert*, January 7, 2019. www.eurekalert .org/pub_releases/2019-01/bu-aah010219.php.

Bears in Mind. "The Evolution of Bear Species." www.bearsinmind.org/Page/ The-evolution-of-bear-species (accessed October 9, 2019).

BearSmart Durango. "About Black Bears: Hibernation and Cubs." http:// bearsmartdurango.org/black-bears/hibernation/ (accessed October 12, 2019).

Beer, Jeff. "Carter Got His Wendy's Nuggs and a Twitter World Record." *Fast Company*, May 9, 2017. www.fastcompany.com/40419538/carter-got -his-wendys-nuggs-and-a-twitter-world-record.

Belknap, Jeremy. *The History of New Hampshire*, vol. 3, 2nd ed. Boston: Bradford and Read, 1813.

Bigfoot Field Researchers Organization. "Grafton County, New Hampshire" (multiple reports). www.bfro.net/GDB/show_county_reports.asp?state =nh&county=Grafton (accessed October 6, 2019).

Biographical Publishing Company. *Book of Biographies, Grafton County*. Buffalo, NY: Biographical Publishing Company, 1897.

Blake, Mariah. "Unification Church Profile: The Fall of the House of Moon." *The New Republic*, November 12, 2013. https://newrepublic.com/article/115512 /unification-church-profile-fall-house-moon.

Blumenthal, Ralph. "1 Cafe, 1 Gas Station, 2 Roads: America's Emptiest County." *New York Times*, February 25, 2006. www.nytimes.com/2006/02/25 /us/1-cafe-1-gas-station-2-roads-americas-emptiest-county.html.

Boothroyd, John C. "*Toxoplasma gondii*: 25 Years and 25 Major Advances for the Field." *International Journal of Parasitology* 39, no. 8 (July 1, 2009). www.ncbi .nlm.nih.gov/pmc/articles/PMC2895946/.

Broder, John. "Silos Loom as Death Traps on American Farms." *New York Times*, October 29, 2012.

Brontë, Emily. *Wuthering Heights*. London, New York: Penguin Books, 2003.

Bryner, Jeanna. "Spider Phobia Cured with 2-Hour Therapy." *LiveScience*, May 21, 2012. www.livescience.com/20468-spider-phobia-cured-therapy.html.

Budds, Diana. "This Failed Utopia from the 1970s Sparked an International Dispute." *Curbed*, July 12, 2019. www.curbed.com/2019/7/12/20690898 /republic-of-minerva-south-pacific-michael-oliver.

Buncombe, Andrew. "Hunters Outraged by Video of Poachers Killing Hibernating Bear and Cubs, Says Prosecutor." *Independent*, March 29, 2019. www .independent.co.uk/news/world/americas/bear-video-hibernating-poachers -kill-cubs-andrew-owen-renner-trial-prosecutor-a8846591.html.

Camerato, Tim. "Engineer: Historic Grafton Church a Safety Hazard." *Valley News*, March 10, 2019. www.vnews.com/Grafton-Meetinghouse-Report-2400 7258.

Canaan, New Hampshire. "Business Directory." www.canaannh.org/directories /business-dir.html (accessed October 7, 2019).

Carmon Community Funeral Homes. "Lloyd Danforth Obituary." August 2012. www.carmonfuneralhome.com/obituary/Lloyd-Robert-Danforth /Grafton-NH/1101254 (accessed October 14, 2019).

Carroll, Lewis. *Sylvie and Bruno*. London: Macmillan and Company, 1890; Project Gutenberg, 1996. www.gutenberg.org/files/48630/48630-h/48630-h .htm.

Carryl, Guy Wetmore. "The Confiding Peasant and the Maladroit Bear." In *Fables for the Frivolous*. New York: Harper & Brothers, 1898; Project Gutenberg, 2009. www.gutenberg.org/ebooks/6438.

Cassidy, Maggie. "Grafton Church Founder Identified as Fire Victim." *Valley News*, January 14, 2016. www.vnews.com/Archives/2016/01 /GraftonFireFolo-mec-vn-011416.

Catholic Culture. "Catholic Dictionary." www.catholicculture.org/culture /library/dictionary/index.cfm?id=34640 (accessed October 10, 2019).

Centers for Disease Control and Prevention. "Parasites: Toxoplasmosis: Epidemiology and Risk Factors." Updated September 4, 2018. www.cdc.gov/parasites /toxoplasmosis/epi.html (accessed October 9, 2019).

Cereno, Benito. "Mysteries of the Superstition Mountains." *Grunge*. www.grunge .com/80931/mysteries-superstition-mountains/ (accessed October 14, 2019).

Chase, Stacey. "Goat 'Sanctuary' Triggers Some Concern." *Barre Montpelier Times Argus*, December 14, 2001. www.goatworld.com/archives/5000-5999/5790 .shtml.

Cherico, Courtney. "4 Famous Organizations You Might Not Know Are Nonprofits." *Guidestar Blog*, October 13, 2016. https://trust.guidestar.org /four-famous-organizations-you-might-not-know-are-nonprofits.

Child, Hamilton, ed. *Gazetteer of Grafton County, NH, 1709—1886.* Syracuse, NY: Syracuse Journal Company, 1886. https://archive.org/stream/gazetteer ofgraft00chil/gazetteerofgraft00chil_djvu.txt.

Chow, Lorraine. "Alaska Poachers Sentenced for Killing Mother Bear and 'Shrieking' Cubs." *EcoWatch*, January 25, 2019. www.ecowatch.com/alaska -bear-poachers-2627094092.html.

Coles, Barbara. "Zach Harvey the Man Behind the Bitcoin ATM." *NH Magazine*, February 11, 2015. www.nhmagazine.com/zach-harvey-the-man -behind-the-bitcoin-atm/.

Community Lutheran Church. "Mascoma Valley Thanksgiving Ingathering 2019." http://clcenfield.org/thanksgiving-ingathering (accessed October 12, 2019).

Condon, Tim. "Finding the Free Town in the Free State." *Free State Project*, February 18, 2004. https://web.archive.org/web/20040627234936/http:// freetownproject.com/Finding_the_Free_Town.html (accessed October 18, 2019).

Condon, Tim. "The Magnificent Small-Government Activists of Grafton, New Hampshire." *GraniteGrok*, February 14, 2013. http:// granitegrok.com/blog/2013/02/the-magnificent-small-government -activists-of-grafton-new-hampshire.

Condon, Tim. "Tim Condon." *GraniteGrok*. https://granitegrok.com/author /tim (accessed September 29, 2019).

Council of State Governments. "The Book of the States 2017." http:// knowledgecenter.csg.org/kc/category/content-type/bos-2017 (accessed October 10, 2019).

Crouch, Jake. "Northeast Joins Drought, Spring 2012." *NOAA: Climate. gov*, May 11, 2012. www.climate.gov/news-features/videos/northeast-joins -drought-spring-2012.

Cuddemi, Jordan. "One Missing in Grafton Fire." *Valley News*, January 12, 2016. www.vnews.com/Archives/2016/01/Graftonfire-jc-vn-011316.

Cuddemi, Jordan. "Officials: Wild Boar Struck and Killed on Interstate." *Valley News*, June 21, 2017. www.vnews.com/Wild-Boar-Killed-on -Interstate-89-Lebanon-NH.

Cuddemi, Jordan. "Cornish Police Shoot Bear That Attacked Chickens." *Valley News*, June 6, 2018. www.vnews.com/Police-shoot-bear-in -Cornish-NH-18006432.

Cushing, Kenneth R. *Isinglass, Timber, and Wool: A History of the Town of Grafton, New Hampshire, 1761—1992.* Lebanon, NH: Hanover Printing Company, 1992.

Dartmouth Geisel School of Medicine. "Gene Targeting Discovery in Model Parasite Opens Door for Vaccines and Drugs." April 13, 2009. https://geiselmed .dartmouth.edu/news/2009/04/13_bzik.shtml.

Darwin, Charles. *The Descent of Man and Selection in Relation to Sex*, vol. 1, 2nd ed. London: John Murray, 1871; Project Gutenberg, 1999. www.gutenberg.org /ebooks/2300.

Davis, Helen, and Alton Harestad. "Cannibalism by Black Bears in the Nimpkish Valley, British Columbia." *Northwest Science*, no. 70 (1996): 88–92.

Davis, Mark. "Man Pleads Guilty to Grafton Murders." *Valley News*, January 9, 2013. www.vnews.com/Archives/2013/01/GraftonMurderPlea-mcd-vn -010913.

Dawson, Jacob. "Data Sheds Light on Bears Killed by NH Fish and Game." *Concord Monitor*, July 22, 2018. www.concordmonitor.com/Fish -and-Game-data-sheds-light-on-bear-euthanization-18894334.

Death Penalty Information Center. "State by State." https://deathpenalty info.org/state-and-federal-info/state-by-state (accessed September 29, 2019).

Dickens, Charles. *Barnaby Rudge*. Philadelphia: T. B. Peterson, 1841; Internet Archive, 2008. https://archive.org/details/barnabyrudge00dickrich /page/4.

Dickens, Charles. *The Mudfog Papers: and Other Sketches*. London: Richard Bentley & Son, 1837–1838; Project Gutenberg, 2015. www.gutenberg.org /files/912/912-h/912-h.htm.

Dickens, Charles. "Tom Tiddler's Ground." Reprinted in *Christmas Stories*, ed. David Price. London: Chapman and Hall, 1894; Project Gutenberg, 2005. www.gutenberg.org/ebooks/1413.

Dillon, Raquel Maria. "Town Doesn't Welcome Libertarians." *New Hampshire Public Radio*, June 21, 2004. www.npr.org/templates/story/story.php ?storyId=1967764.

Discovering Lewis & Clark. "Grizzlies in the Journals: 28 Jun 1805: A Frolick?" (Meriwether Lewis journal entry). http://www.lewis-clark.org/article/467 (accessed October 20, 2019).

Doherty, Brian. "New Hampshire Now Has Third Sitting Libertarian Party Legislator." *Reason*, June 29, 2017. https://reason.com/2017/06/29 /new-hampshire-now-has-third-sitting-libe/.

Doyle, Arthur Conan. *The Lost World*. London, 1912; Project Gutenberg, 2008. www.gutenberg.org/ebooks/139.

Dubey, Jitender P. "The History of Toxoplasma gondii—The First 100 Years." *Journal of Eukaryotic Parasitology* 55, no. 6 (November/December 2008). www .ncbi.nlm.nih.gov/pubmed/19120791.

Dubey, J. P., and Chunlei Su. "Population Biology of *Toxoplasma gondii*: What's Out and Where Did They Come From." *Memórias do Instituto do Oswaldo Cruz* 104, no. 2 (March 2009). www.scielo.br/scielo .php?script=sci_arttext&pid=S0074-02762009000200011.

Dublin Penny Journal. "The Black Bear." *Dublin Penny Journal* 4, no. 197 (April 9, 1836): 324–25.

Duffort, Lola. "80-Year-Old Woman Fights off Rabid Bobcat." *Valley News*, June 27, 2017. www.vnews.com/A-bobcat-attacks-in-Sunapee-10950944.

Duffy, A. R., T. M. Beckie, L. A. Brenne, J. W. Beckstead, A. Seyfang, T. T. Postolache, and M. W. Groer. "Relationship Between Toxoplasma gondii and Mood Disturbance in Women Veterans." Military Medicine 180, no. 6 (June 2015). www.ncbi.nlm.nih.gov/pubmed/26032378.

Duffy, John J., Samuel B. Hand, and Ralph H. Orth, eds. The Vermont Encyclopedia. Lebanon, NH: University Press of New England, 2003.

Early Detection & Distribution Mapping System (EDDMaps). "Status of Invasive [New Hampshire]." Data project of the University of Georgia Center for Invasive Species and Ecosystem Health. www.eddmaps.org/tools/statereport .cfm?id=us_nh (accessed October 9, 2019).

Economic & Labor Market Information Bureau, New Hampshire Employment Security. "Community Profiles: Grafton, NH." May 11, 2016. www.nhes .nh.gov/elmi/products/cp/profiles-htm/grafton.htm (accessed October 1, 2019).

Edge TV. "Robert Sapolsky Interview: Toxoplasmosis." YouTube, posted December 13, 2012. www.youtube.com/watch?v=m3x3TMdkGdQ.

Eliot, George. The Mill on the Floss. London: William Blackwell, 1860; Project Gutenberg, 2004. www.gutenberg.org/ebooks/6688.

Emerson, Ralph Waldo. Nature. Boston: Thurston, Torry and Company, 1849; Project Gutenberg, 2009. www.gutenberg.org/ebooks/29433.

Federal Election Commission. "Federal Elections 88: Election Results for the US President, the US Senate, and the US House of Representatives." Washington, DC: June 1989. https://transition.fec.gov/pubrec/fe1988 /federalelections88.pdf.

Find A Grave. Memorial page for Chloe Barney Barney. Find A Grave Memorial 124527960, created February 2, 2014, by Lorie Greenwood. www .findagrave.com/memorial/124527960/chloe-barney (accessed September 22, 2019).

Finke, Roger, and Rodney Stark. The Churching of America, 1776–1990. New Brunswick, NJ: Rutgers University Press, 1992.

Fish, Isaac Stone. "The Strange Life of Reverend Sun Myung Moon." Foreign Policy, September 4, 2012. https://foreignpolicy.com/2012/09/04 /the-strange-life-of-reverend-sun-myung-moon/.

Flavin, Patrick. "State Government Public Goods Spending and Citizens' Quality of Life." Social Science Research 78 (February 2019): 28–40. https:// cpb-us-w2.wpmucdn.com/blogs.baylor.edu/dist/2/1297/files/2010/09/Public _goods_SWB_SSR-1y6ql2s.pdf.

Flegr, Jaroslav, and Radim Kuba. "The Relation of Toxoplasma Infection and Sexual Attraction to Fear, Danger, Pain, and Submissiveness." Evolutionary Psychology 14, no. 3 (August 1, 2016). https://journals.sagepub.com /doi/10.1177/1474704916659746.

Florida Fish and Wildlife Conservation Commission. "Black Bear Behavior." https://myfwc.com/wildlifehabitats/wildlife/bear/facts/behavior/ (accessed October 1, 2019).

FMTV. "John Connell on FMTV at PorcFest 2007." YouTube, posted July 1, 2007. www.youtube.com/watch?v=ZYmP9ZRs-qg.

Freeman, Ian. "Chris Cantwell Has Become What He Once Hated—A Total Statist." *Free Keene*, January 17, 2019. https://freekeene.com/2019/01/17/chris-cantwell-has-become-what-he-once-hated-a-total-statist/.

Free State Project. "Free State Project Successful." *YouTube*, posted February 3, 2016. www.youtube.com/watch?v=C07Hj6_nM-s.

Free State Project. "The New Hampshire Advantage: Liberty Lives in New Hampshire." www.fsp.org/nh/#qol (accessed October 14, 2019).

GameWardenEDU.org. "How to Become a Fish and Game Warden in Maine." www.gamewardenedu.org/maine/ (accessed October 9, 2019).

Gannett, Henry. *The Origin of Certain Place Names in the United States*, 2nd ed. Washington, DC: US Government Printing Office, 1905.

Gleason, Dan. "The Legend of the Lost Dutchman Mine." *Cowboys & Indians*, January 1, 2018. www.cowboysindians.com/2018/01/the-legend-of-the-lost-dutchman-mine/.

Globe and Mail. "Even Dead, Huge Bear Inspires Awe," *Globe and Mail*, September 7, 2001. www.theglobeandmail.com/news/national/even-dead-huge-bear-inspires-awe/article4152575/.

Grafton Board of Selectmen. "Meeting Minutes, 2010." Town Archives, Grafton, NH.

Grafton Board of Selectmen. "Grafton Selectmen Deny PAC Tax Exemption" (June 30, 2014). *YouTube*, posted July 11, 2014. www.youtube.com/watch?v=zSDCUKKfmqo.

Grafton Board of Selectmen. "Grafton Public Meeting Re: Peaceful Assembly" (January 24, 2016). *YouTube*, posted January 25, 2016. www.youtube.com/watch?v=e9DCTXSrY4Q&feature=youtu.be&fbclid=IwAR0MDS45JrUP87yxyn5KULze8YPyv6xl6hDSTzRff8PurAv4k_5GE5P8BO4.

Grafton Board of Selectmen. "Minutes, September 4, 2018." Town Archives, Grafton, NH.

Grafton Ledger. "Town News." *Grafton Ledger*, October 1999. Archived at the Grafton Public Library.

Grafton, New Hampshire, municipal government. *Annual Reports of the Town of Grafton, NH, 1939, 1942–1948, 1990–1993, 2000–2019*. Bristol, NH: R. W. Musgrove, 1939–2019.

Greene, Britta. "Mink, the Famous Hanover Bear, Has Returned to the Upper Valley." *New Hampshire Public Radio*, April 12, 2019. www.nhpr.org/post/mink-famous-hanover-bear-has-returned-upper-valley#stream/0.

Gregg, John. "In Grafton, Burn Pile Becomes Protest for Libertarian Activist." *Valley News*, May 26, 2010. www.vnews.com/05262010/05262010.htm.

Griffin, Simon Goodell. *The History of Keene, New Hampshire*. Keene: Sentinel Printing Company, 1904, 317–18.

Gross, Ludwik. "How Charles Nicolle of the Pasteur Institute Discovered That Epidemic Typhus Is Transmitted by Lice: Reminiscences from My Years at the Pasteur Institute in Paris." *Proceedings of the National Academy of Science USA* 93, no. 20 (October 1996). www.ncbi.nlm.nih.gov/pmc/articles/PMC38186/?page=1.

Grossmith Pat. "Routine Stop Leads to Arrest of Armed Man in Body Armor." *New Hampshire Union Leader*, October 10, 2008.

Haddadin, Jim. "New Hampshire Has Most Machine Guns per Capita in the Country." *Fosters News*, January 20, 2013.

Hammond, Isaac W. *Town Papers: Documents Relating to Towns in New Hampshire, Gilmanton to Ipswich*, vol. 12. Concord, NH: Parsons B. Cogswell, 1883.

Hanaford, Mary E. Neal. *Meredith, NH Annals and Genealogies*. Concord, NH: Rumford Press, 1932.

Harai, Yuval Noah. *Sapiens: A Brief History of Humankind*. New York: Harper Perennial, 2015.

Harding, Adam. "Grafton Woman Attacked by Bear: Bear Attracted by Smell of Pot Roast." *WMUR*, June 17, 2012. www.wmur.com/article/grafton-woman-attacked-by-bear-1/5174477.

Harte, Bret. *The Luck of Roaring Camp and Other Tales*. New York: Dodd, Mead, 1961.

Hawthorne, Nathaniel. *Twice Told Tales*. Philadelphia: David McKay, Publisher, 1889; Project Gutenberg, 2004. www.gutenberg.org/ebooks/13707.

Hawthorne, Nathaniel. 2007. *The Snow-Image and Other Twice-Told Tales*. New York: Hurst & Co., 1912.

HearCast. "Facets: How State, Local, and Private Worked Together to Keep a Bear Family Safe." https://herecast.us/954782 (accessed October 14, 2019).

HearCast. "Spotlight on Our Sponsors: SAVES, Mike Barskey." https://herecast.us/795962 (accessed October 6, 2019).

Heinrich, Bernd. *The Trees in My Forest*. New York: Cliff Street Books, 1997.

Henneberger, Melinda. "Seeking Converts, Controversially." *New York Times*, December 30, 1992. www.nytimes.com/1992/12/30/nyregion/seeking-converts-controversially.html.

Herald. "Orange County Court Cases." *Herald* (Vermont), February 8, 2018. www.ourherald.com/articles/orange-county-court-cases-27/.

Hershberger, Andy, and Ray Brewer. "Bear Seriously Hurts Woman, 71, in Her Groton Home." *WMUR*, July 9, 2018. www.wmur.com/article/woman-71-seriously-hurt-in-encounter-with-bear-in-groton-home/22214964.

Historical Society of Cheshire County. "Monadnock Moments No. 27: Eleazer Wilcox and the Bear." https://hsccnh.org/2017/03/24/monadnock-moments-no-27-eleazer-wilcox-bear/ (accessed September 22, 2019).

Hongoltz-Hetling, Matt. "After Serving, Handicapped Vets Suffer in Silence." *Valley News*, February 5, 2017.

Hongoltz-Hetling, Matt. "A Life: Harold Edward 'Duffy' Duefield III 'Always Wanted to Have Fun.'" *Valley News*, April 2, 2017. www.vnews.com/Harold-Duffy-Duefield-A-Life-Grafton-9016810.

Hongoltz-Hetling, Matt. "Area Bears Are Becoming Bolder; Trackers Say Some Residents Still Aren't Eliminating Food Sources." *Valley News*, June 15, 2018. www.vnews.com/Hanover-bears-multiplying-18183655.

Howard, R. H., and Henry E. Crocker. *A History of New England*, vol. 2, *Maine, New Hampshire, Vermont*. Boston: Crocker & Co. Publishers, 1881.

Humane Society of the United States. "They'll Never Be Able to Link It to Us." *YouTube*, posted March 27, 2019. www.youtube.com/watch?v=i7SoGMv 4eMg.

Illinois State Museum. "Explore the Ice Age Midwest: Helmeted muskox, *Bootherium bombifrons*." http://iceage.museum.state.il.us/mammals /helmeted-muskox (accessed October 9, 2019).

Introvigne, Massimo. *The Unification Church: Studies in Contemporary Religion*. Salt Lake City: Signature Books, 2000.

Iyer, Ravi, Spassena Koleva, Jesse Graham, Peter Ditto, and Jonathan Haidt. "Understanding Libertarian Morality: The Psychological Dispositions of Self-Identified Libertarians." *PLOS/ONE* 7, no. 8 (2012): e42366. https://doi .org/10.1371/journal.pone.0042366.

Jack News. "Three Front-Runners Emerge for the 2020 Libertarian Party Presidential Nomination." *Jack News*, August 21, 2017. www.thejacknews.com /politics/survey-poll-results/three-front-runners-emerge-for-the-2020 -libertarian-party-presidential-nomination/ (not secure).

Jacobson, Louis. "Budget Proposal Would Cut EPA by 31% in One Year." *Politifact*, March 29, 2017. www.politifact.com/truth-o-meter/promises/trumpometer /promise/1436/dramatically-scale-back-epa/.

Jarvis, Kyle. "Group Aims to Counter Free Keene." *Keene Sentinel*, March 30, 2014. www.sentinelsource.com/news/local/group-aims-to-counter-free-keene /article_26147f56-8fbf-5b06-8755-7aaec554bc2b.html.

Jones, Tim. "Police: Convicted NH Felon Found with Uzi, Assortment of Knives." *NECN*, October 6, 2017. www.necn.com/news/new-england/Police -Convicted-NH-Felon-Found-With-Uzi-Assortment-of-Knives-449770063 .html.

Joyce, James. *Ulysses*. London: Bodley Head, 1969.

Kanning, Kat. "A Big Deal over a Small Fire." *New Hampshire Free Press*, June 2010. https://web.archive.org/web/20100703055658/http://newhampshire freepress.com/node/634.

Keller, Richard C. *Colonial Madness: Psychiatry in French North Africa*. Chicago: University of Chicago Press, 2008.

Kilham, Benjamin. *In the Company of Bears: What Black Bears Have Taught Me About Intelligence and Intuition*. White River Junction, VT: Chelsea Green Publishing, 2014.

Kilham, Benjamin. *Among the Bears: Raising Orphan Cubs in the Wild*. Self-published, 2015.

Kim, Hyung-eun. "Business Engine of a Global Faith." *Joongang Daily*, April 11, 2010. www.tparents.org/Moon-Talks/KookJinMoon/KookJinMoon-100411 .htm.

Kipling, Rudyard. *Kipling: A Selection of His Stories and Poems*. Garden City, NY: Doubleday & Company, 1956.

Koziol, John. "Driver Shot During April Road Rage on Route 4 Had It Coming, Defense Will Argue." *New Hampshire Union Leader*, May 29, 2019. www .unionleader.com/news/crime/driver-shot-during-april-road-rage-on-route -had-it/article_b9bbfdad-246b-57da-8127-349077ac4918.html.

Koziol, John. "Prosecutors Cite History of Road Rage in Man Charged in Shooting." *New Hampshire Union Leader*, June 16, 2019. www.unionleader.com /news/crime/prosecutors-cite-history-of-road-rage-in-man-charged-in/article _44c8f6bd-7a38-52b6-9962-020f7c458fc1.html.

Kronenwetter, Mary T. "Corbin's 'Animal Garden.'" *Eastman Living*, Fall 2011. https:// web.archive.org/web/20150312212809/http://eastmanliving.com/2011/11 /corbin%E2%80%99s-%E2%80%9Canimal-garden%E2%80%9D.

Kumar, Vikas, Fritjof Lammers, Tobias Bidon, Markus Pfenninger, Lydia Kolter, Maria A. Nilsson, and Axel Janke. "The Evolutionary History of Bears Is Characterized by Gene Flow Across Species." *Scientific Reports* 7 (October 2017). www.nature.com/articles/srep46487.

LaFollette, Hugh, ed. *The International Encyclopedia of Ethics*. Hoboken, NJ: Wiley-Blackwell Company, 2013.

Lake Winnipesaukee Historical Society. "Bear Island: An Early History." Reprinted from *Bear Island Reflections* (2nd ed., Bear Island Conservation Association, 2000). www.lwhs.us/islands/bear/bearislandearlyhistory.htm (accessed September 22, 2019).

Lane Memorial Library. "History of the Hampton Fire Department." January 10, 1984. www.hampton.lib.nh.us/hampton/history/firedept/fire3.htm (accessed October 7, 2019).

Lawrence, Brandon. "Resident Puts Property Rights Above All." *Monadnock Ledger-Transcript*, March 15, 2013. www.ledgertranscript.com/Archives /2013/02/anJohnRedman-ml-030513.

Lawrence Edward Pendarvis v. State of Florida, no. 2D98-216, decided February 18, 2000. https://caselaw.findlaw.com/fl-district-court-of-appeal/1065979 .html.

Layne, J. R., Jr. "Freeze Tolerance and Cryoprotectant Mobilization in the Gray Treefrog (*Hyla versicolor*)." *Journal of Experimental Zoology* 283, no. 3 (February 1999): 221–25.

LBRY. "The Team." https://lbry.com/team (accessed October 14, 2019).

Leubsdorf, Ben. "Open Assembly." *Concord Monitor*, August 9, 2010. www .concordmonitor.com/Archive/2010/08/999788122-999788122-1008 -CM?page=0,0.

Libertarian National Committee, Inc. "About the Libertarian Party." www.lp.org /about/ (accessed September 27, 2019).

Libertarian National Committee, Inc. "Issues." www.lp.org/issues/ (accessed September 27, 2019).

Libertarian Party. "Statewide Libertarian Vote Totals That Will Give LP Ballot Access." November 5, 2012. www.lp.org/blogs-staff-statewide-libertarian-vote -totals-that-will-give-lp-ballot-access/ (accessed October 8, 2019).

Lincoln, Abraham. "The Bear Hunt," *Poetry Foundation*. www.poetryfoundation. org/poems/45901/the-bear-hunt (accessed September 22, 2019).

Lippman, John. "Mine Could Be Yours: Ruggles for Sale." *Valley News*, June 17, 2016. www.vnews.com/Grafton-Attraction-on-the-Market-2811479.

Little, William. *The History of Weare, New Hampshire 1735–1888*. Lowell, MA: S. W. Huse & Co., 1888.

London, Jack. *The Iron Heel*. New York: George Platt Brett Sr., 1908; Project Gutenberg, 2006. www.gutenberg.org/ebooks/1164.

Longfellow, Henry Wadsworth. *The Song of Hiawatha*. Boston: Ticknor and Fields, 1855; Project Gutenberg, 2007. www.gutenberg.org/ebooks/19.

Longfellow, Henry Wadsworth. *The Complete Poetical Works of Henry Wadsworth Longfellow*. London, 1852; Project Gutenberg, 2004. www.gutenberg.org /files/1365/1365-h/1365-h.htm#link2H_4_0368.

Lorrey, Mike. "About." www.f6s.com/mikelorrey (accessed October 3, 2019).

Lowell, Amy. "The Travelling Bear." In *Some Imagist Poets: An Anthology*, ed. Richard Aldington Boston, 1915; Project Gutenberg, 2009. www.gutenberg .org/ebooks/30276.

Macaulay, Thomas Babington. *The History of England from the Accession of James II*, 5 vols., vol. 1. Philadelphia: Porter and Coates, 1890.

Maher, Savannah. "Groton Woman Recovering After Bear Attack in Her Home." *New Hampshire Public Radio*, July 18, 2018. www.nhpr.org/post /groton-woman-recovering-after-bear-attack-her-home#stream/0.

Maupassant, Guy de. *Selection from the Writings of Guy de Maupassant*, vol. 7. Akron: Saint Dunstan, 1903; Charlottesville: University of Virginia Press, 2009.

McDuffee, Franklin. *History of the Town of Rochester, New Hampshire, from 1722 to 1890*, vol. 1. Manchester, NH: John B. Clarke Co., 1892.

McMaster, John Bach. *A Brief History of the United States*. American Book Company, 1883; Project Gutenberg, 2004. www.gutenberg.org/ebooks /6896.

McNish, Kevin. "Free Town Project Falls Flat." *Vanderbilt Torch*, September 20, 2004. https://web.archive.org/web/20041225111822/http://www.vutorch.org /blog/archives/000051.html (accessed September 29, 2019).

Melville, Herman. *Moby-Dick: Or, the Whale*. New York: Harper & Brothers, 1851; Project Gutenberg, 2008. www.gutenberg.org/ebooks/2701.

Milius, Susan. "Bears That Eat 'Junk Food' May Hibernate Less and Age Faster." *Science News*, March 4, 2019.

Miller, Joshua Rhett. "Body of Man Who Hunted Legendary 'Lost Dutchman's' Gold Mine Believed Found in Arizona Mountains." *Fox News*, November 29, 2012. www.foxnews.com/us/body-of-man-who-hunted-legendary-lost -dutchmans-gold-mine-believed-found-in-arizona-mountains.

Mink The Bear (@mink_the_bear). "I'm home bitches!" Twitter post, May 18, 2019. https://twitter.com/mink_the_bear/status/1129729903073681410.

Mistral, Pixeleen. "BNT Claims $500,000 USD in Damages—Hopes to Join Class Action Lawsuit." *Alphaville Herald*, April 23, 2010. http:// alphavilleherald.com/2010/04/bnt-claims-500000-usd-in-damages-hopes -to-join-class-action-lawsuit.html.

Morissette, Naomi, and James W. Ajioka. "The Early Years of Toxoplasma Research: What's Past Is Prologue." *International Journal for Parasitology* 39, no. 8 (July 1, 2009). www.ncbi.nlm.nih.gov/pmc/articles/PMC2727930/.

Muir, John. *My First Summer in the Sierra*. Boston: Houghton Mifflin Company, 1911; Project Gutenberg, 2010. www.gutenberg.org/ebooks/32540.

Musgrove, Richard W. *History of the Town of Bristol, Grafton County, New Hampshire,* vol. 2, *Genealogies.* Bristol, NH: Author, 1904.

National Archives. "From Thomas Jefferson to Zebulon Pike, 6 November 1807." *Founders Online.* https://founders.archives.gov/documents/Jefferson/99-01-02-6721 (accessed October 20, 2019).

National Oceanic and Atmospheric Administration, National Centers for Environmental Information. "Climate at a Glance: Statewide Time Series." www.ncdc.noaa.gov/cag/statewide/time-series.

New Hampshire Department of Justice. "Kelly A. Ayotte: Methamphetamine Labs in Grafton County." Press release. January 17, 2006. http://doj.nh.gov/publications/nreleases/011706methamphetamine.html (no longer available).

New Hampshire Department of Revenue Administration, Municipal Services Division. "Tax Rates 2010." December 22, 2010. www.revenue.nh.gov/mun-prop/municipal/documents/2010-local.pdf.

New Hampshire Department of Revenue Administration. "Completed Public Tax Rates 2018." www.revenue.nh.gov/mun-prop/municipal/documents/18-tax-rates.pdf (accessed October 14, 2019).

New Hampshire Department of Revenue Administration. "Proposed Budget: Canaan." 2019 MS-737. www.canaannh.org/town_meetings_and_voting/ms737-2019.pdf.

New Hampshire Department of Revenue Administration. "Proposed Budget: Enfield." 2019 MS-737. www.enfield.nh.us/sites/enfieldnh/files/uploads/2019_proposed_budget.pdf.

New Hampshire Department of Revenue Administration. "Proposed Budget: Grafton." 2019 MS-737. Available upon request from Grafton, NH, town office.

New Hampshire Fish and Game Department. "2017 New Hampshire Wildlife Harvest Summary." https://wildlife.state.nh.us/hunting/documents/2017-harvest-summary.pdf (accessed October 10, 2019).

New Hampshire Fish and Game Department. "Bear Harvest (2018)." https://wildlife.state.nh.us/hunting/bear-harvest.html (accessed October 9, 2019).

New Hampshire Fish and Game Department. "Eastern Coyote (*Canis latrans var.*)." www.wildlife.state.nh.us/wildlife/profiles/coyote.html (accessed October 6, 2019).

New Hampshire Fish and Game Department. "New Hampshire Fish and Game Through the Years." https://wildlife.state.nh.us/150/timeline.html (accessed October 9, 2019).

New Hampshire Fish and Game Department. "Something's Bruin in New Hampshire: Learn to Live with Bears." https://wildlife.state.nh.us/wildlife/bears/index.html (accessed October 9, 2019).

New Hampshire Office of the Legislative Budget Assistant. "State of New Hampshire Fish and Game Department: Performance Audit Report." January 2008. www.vision.ca.gov/docs/NH_Fish_and_Game_Audit.pdf (accessed October 1, 2019).

New Hampshire Office of Strategic Initiatives. "Age, Race and Gender Estimates." www.nh.gov/osi/data-center/age-race-gender.htm (accessed October 1, 2019).

New Hampshire Secretary of State. "2000 General Election Results: Governor." https://sos.nh.gov/2000GovGen.aspx?id=3167.

New Hampshire Secretary of State. "2002 General Election Results: Governor." https://sos.nh.gov/2002GovGen.aspx.

New Hampshire Secretary of State. "2010 General Election Results: Governor." https://sos.nh.gov/2010GovGen.aspx?id=321.

New Hampshire Supreme Court. *Jeremy Olson & a. v. Town of Grafton*, no. 2015-0264, argued January 7, 2016, opinion issued February 12, 2016. https://law .justia.com/cases/new-hampshire/supreme-court/2016/2015-026.html.

New Hampshire Supreme Court. *John J. Babiarz v. Town of Grafton*, no. 2006-542, submitted May 23, 2007, opinion issued July 20, 2007. www.courts.state .nh.us/supreme/opinions/2007/barbi108.pdf.

New York State Department of Environmental Conservation. "Brain Worm." www.dec.ny.gov/animals/72211.html (accessed October 14, 2019).

Normandeau, Glenn. "My Turn: The Facts About Bear Hunting in New Hampshire." *Concord Monitor*, October 23, 2016. www.concordmonitor.com /The-story-of-NH-bear-hunting-5516328.

North American Bear Center. "Do Black Bears Hibernate?" https://bear.org /do-black-bears-hibernate/ (accessed October 1, 2019).

Nosowitz, Dan. "The 2012 Heat Wave 'Almost Like Science Fiction.'" *Popular Science*, March 23, 2012. www.popsci.com/science/article/2012-03 /2012-heat-wave-almost-science-fiction-mind-boggling/.

O'Donnell Funeral and Cremation Service. "Obituary: John J. Connell." http:// hosting-6738.tributes.com/obituary/show/John-J.-Connell-103197519 (accessed October 6, 2019).

Olson, Jeremy. "The Résumé of Jeremy J. Olson." Updated May 13, 2016. www .jeremyjolson.com/sites/default/files/resume.pdf (accessed October 10, 2019).

Olson, Jeremy. "Who Is J'raxis 270145?" www.jraxis.com/about (accessed October 10, 2019).

Orff, Eric. "NH Fish and Game Enters the Computer Era." https://wildlife.state .nh.us/150/documents/nhfg-first-pc.pdf (accessed October 9, 2019).

Osborne, Samuel. "Mind-Altering Parasite Spread by Cats Would Give Humans More Courage and Overcome 'Fear of Failure,' Research Suggests." *Independent*, July 25, 2018. www.independent.co.uk/news/science/parasite-cat -faeces-mind-alter-humans-courage-fear-failure-toxoplasma-gondii-a8463436 .html.

Pelis, Kim. *Charles Nicolle Pasteur's Imperial Missionary: Typhus and Tunisia*. Rochester, NY: Rochester University Press, 2006.

Philips, Matt. "Free State Project Statement Regarding Ian Freeman and Free Talk Live." *Free State Project*, March 17, 2016. www.fsp.org /free-state-project-statement-regarding-ian-freeman-and-free-talk-live/.

Pierson, Sandi. *Bricks, Books, and Barnyards: The History of Slab City School-house, Grafton, New Hampshire*. Self-published, 2009. Archived at the Grafton Public Library.

Plottner, Sean. "Ursa Major: Please Don't Feed the Bears." *Dartmouth Alumni Magazine*, September/October 2019. https://dartmouthalumnimagazine.com /articles/ursa-major.

Poli, Domenic. "Man Shot, Killed in Walpole Had Long Criminal History." *Brattleboro Reformer*, April 2, 2013. www.reformer.com/stories /man-shot-killed-in-walpole-had-long-criminal-history,385830.

Purdue University Grain Quality Laboratory. "Frequently Asked Questions About Flowing Grain Entrapment, Grain Rescue and Strategies, and Grain Entrapment Prevention Measures." Updated April 2011. https://extension .entm.purdue.edu/grainlab/content/pdf/QuestionFlowingGrainEntrap .pdf.

Quimby, Taylor. "You Asked, We Answered: What Is the Free State Project?" *New Hampshire Public Radio*, April 12, 2018. www.nhpr.org/post /you-asked-we-answered-what-free-state-project#stream/0.

Rand, Ayn. *Atlas Shrugged*. New York: New American Library, 2018.

Randlett, David. "New Building for Millbrook Christian Fellowships Draws Attention to God's Hand in Nature." *The Foresee: News from the Conservative Congregational Christian Conference*, April 2012. www.ccccusa.com/wp -content/uploads/2017/09/FORESEE-April-2012.pdf.

Redman, John. *Cops Being Cops* (blog). http://cops-being-cops.blogspot.com/ (accessed October 12, 2019).

Redman, John. "Peaceful Assembly Church Fire." Seventeen-part video series posted on *YouTube*, January 13, 2016. www.youtube.com/user/Knowaymr /videos.

Reid, Nick. "Liberty Activists in High Court Cases Say Their Newly Created Religions Afford Them Tax Exemptions." *Concord Monitor*, July 29, 2015. www .concordmonitor.com/Archive/2015/07/COTS-cm-072815.

Ricker Funeral Homes & Crematory. "Robert Peter Hull of Grafton, New Hampshire (1965–2019): Obituary." www.rickerfuneralhome.com/obituary/robert -hull (accessed September 29, 2019).

Roach, John. "Black Bears Adapting to City Living, Study Says." *National Geographic*, November 26, 2003. www.nationalgeographic.com/animals/2003/11 /black-bears-adapt-cities-animals/.

Robert P. Hull & a. v. Grafton County & a., no. 2009-527, opinion issued October 19, 2010. www.courtlistener.com/opinion/2549900/hull-v-grafton-county/.

Roche, B. J. "Grafton's Messy Liberation." *Boston Globe*, June 20, 2004.

Rodolico, Jack. "Libertarians Move in to Make a Small NH Town Even Smaller." *National Public Radio*, March 9, 2014. www.npr.org/2014/03/09/288069880 /libertarians-move-in-to-make-a-small-n-h-town-even-smaller.

Rogers, James. "Exiled Doughnut-Loving Bear Travels Thousands of Miles to Return Home." *Fox News*, May 22, 2019. www.foxnews.com/science /doughnut-loving-bear-returns-home.

Romero, Simon. "Deep in Brazil's Amazon, Exploring the Ruins of Ford's Fantasyland." *New York Times*, February 20, 2017. www.nytimes.com/2017/02/20/world/americas/deep-in-brazils-amazon-exploring-the-ruins-of-fords-fantasyland.html.

Ryan, Katie Beth. "'Not the Government's Church': Grafton Pastor Refuses to File with State for Tax-Exempt Status." *Valley News*, June 20, 2011.

Sandberg, Louise. "Cookeville: Goat Farm No Longer." *Journal Opinion*, July 1, 2009. http://jop.stparchive.com/Archive/JOP/JOP07012009p010.php.

San Diego Zoo Global Library. "Extinct Teratorn (Family Teratornithidae) Fact Sheet: Summary." https://ielc.libguides.com/sdzg/factsheets/extinctteratorn (accessed October 9, 2019).

Schaff-Herzog Encyclopedia. "Banks, Louis Albert." In *New Schaff-Herzog Encyclopedia of Religious Knowledge*, vol. 1, *Aachen—Basilians*, ed. Samuel Macauley Jackson. Grand Rapids, MI, 1908; Christian Classics Ethereal Library, 2005. www.ccel.org/ccel/schaff/encyc01.html?term=Banks,%20Louis%20Albert.

Schoonover, Kelley. "Vermont Man Loses Custody of Goats After Trail of Death in Multiple States." *Associated Press*, March 16, 2005.

Seton, Ernest Thompson. *The Biography of a Grizzly*. New York: Century Co., 1900; Project Gutenberg, 2008. www.gutenberg.org/ebooks/25023.

Settle, Mary Lee. *Learning to Fly: A Writer's Memoir*. New York: W. W. Norton & Company, 2007.

Shakespeare, William. *Henry VI, Part 3*. Project Gutenberg, 2000. www.gutenberg.org/ebooks/2256.

Shakespeare, William. *The Winter's Tale*. Project Gutenberg, 2000. www.gutenberg.org/ebooks/2248.

Shire Society. "History." https://shiresociety.com/history/ (accessed October 14, 2019).

Sinclair, Upton. *The Jungle*. New York: Doubleday, Page, 1906; Project Gutenberg, 2006. www.gutenberg.org/ebooks/140.

Sisinyak, Nancy, Alaska Department of Fish and Game. "The Biggest Bear . . . Ever." *Alaska Fish & Wildlife News*, August 2006. www.adfg.alaska.gov/index.cfm?adfg=wildlifenews.view_article&articles_id=232.

Settle, Mary Lee. *Learning to Fly: A Writer's Memoir*. New York: W. W. Norton & Company, 2007.

Single Action Shooting Society. "SASS: A Brief History." www.sassnet.com/About-What-is-SASS-001A.php (accessed October 1, 2019).

Smith, Elias, ed. "New England Gleanings." *Herald of Gospel Liberty* 101 (1909): 24. https://play.google.com/store/books/details?id=dGTMen35RDkC&rdid=book-dGTMen35RDkC&rdot=1.

Smithsonian's National Zoo & Conservation Biology Institute. "Panamanian Golden Frog." https://nationalzoo.si.edu/animals/panamanian-golden-frog (accessed October 1, 2019).

Snyder, Gary. "Smokey the Bear Sutra." In *Sacred-Texts*. www.sacred-texts.com/bud/bear.htm (accessed October 7, 2019).

Sorens, Jason. "The Early Years of the Free State Project." *Free State Project*. www
.fsp.org/history/ (accessed October 14, 2019).

State of New Hampshire v. Sharon Ankrom, 2009-0202–5 and 2011-0744.

Stearns, Ezra S., William F. Whitcher, and Edward Everett Parker. *Genealogical and Family History of the State of New Hampshire: A Record of the Achievements of Her People in the Making of a Commonwealth and the Founding of a Nation*. New York: Lewis Publishing Company, 1908.

Stevenson, Robert Louis. *Treasure Island*. New York: C. Scribner's Sons, 1911.

Stiffman, Eden. "Dozens of 'Hate Groups' Have Charity Status, *Chronicle* Study Finds." *Chronicle of Philanthropy*, December 22, 2016. www.philanthropy.com /article/Dozens-of-Hate-Groups-/238748.

Stone, Abbey. "15 Things You Might Not Know About New Hampshire." *Mental Floss*, October 6, 2014. http://mentalfloss.com/article/58977/15 -things-you-might-not-know-about-new-hampshire.

Studer, Nina Salouâ. *The Hidden Patients: North African Women in French Colonial Psychiatry*, vol. 8. Cologne: Böhlau Verlag Köln Weimar, 2015.

Tennyson, Alfred. *Becket and Other Plays*. London, 1884; Project Gutenberg, 2003. www.gutenberg.org/ebooks/9162.

Thoreau, Henry David. *Excursions*. Boston: Ticknor and Fields, 1863; Project Gutenberg, 2003. www.gutenberg.org/ebooks/9846.

Thoreau, Henry David. *The Writings of Henry D. Thoreau*. Princeton, NJ: Princeton University Press, 1972.

Timmins, Andrew A., New Hampshire Fish and Game Department. "Grafton 10 year." Report compiled for the author, 2017.

Timmins, Andrew A., New Hampshire Fish and Game Department. "New Hampshire Black Bear Assessment 2015." November 2014.

Timmins, Andrew. "Documented Bear Complaints in New Hampshire, 1995–2014." *New Hampshire Wildlife Journal*, July/August 2015. www.wildlife.state .nh.us/pubs/documents/samples/somethings-bruin-july-aug-2015.pdf.

Torres, Paola Vega. "GM1-gangliosidosis in an American Black Bear." *Molecular Genetics and Metabolism* 93, no. 2 (February 2008).

Tuohy, Dan. "Free State 'Porcupines' Fight Prickly Reception." *Eagle Tribune*, June 27, 2004.

Twain, Mark. *Following the Equator: A Journey Around the World*. Hartford, CT: American Publishing Co., 1897; Project Gutenberg, 2006. www.gutenberg .org/ebooks/2895.

Twain, Mark. *Mark Twain's Letters*, 2 vols., vol. 1. New York: Harper & Brothers, 1917.

Underwood, Katherine. "71-Year-Old NH Woman Mauled by Bear: 'He Just Let Me Have It.'" *NBC Boston*, August 17, 2018. www.nbcboston.com/news /local/71-Year-Old-Groton-NH-Woman-Mauled-by-Bear-He-Just-Let-Me -Have-It-491150861.html.

Underwood, Katherine, and Marc Fortierc. "'Shocked': Daughter Reacts After Woman Attacked by Bear in Her Groton, New Hampshire Home." *NBC Boston*, July 18, 2018. www.nbcboston.com/news/local/Wheelchair-Bound

-Woman-Attacked-by-Bear-in-Her-Groton-New-Hampshire-Home-488406101
.html.

Underwood, Lamar, ed. *Man Eaters: True Tales of Animals Stalking, Mauling, Kill-ing, and Eating Human Prey.* Guilford, CT: Lyons Press, 2000.

US Department of Agriculture. "Agriculture—New Hampshire." 1929–1935. http://usda.mannlib.cornell.edu/usda/AgCensusImages/1935/01/02/1514 /Table-01.pdf (accessed October 7, 2019).

US Department of Agriculture. "Table 1: County Summary Highlights: 1992." http://usda.mannlib.cornell.edu/usda/AgCensusImages/1992/01/29/1570 /Table-01.pdf (accessed October 7, 2019).

US Environmental Protection Agency. "The Origins of EPA." www.epa.gov /history/origins-epa (accessed October 9, 2019).

US Fish & Wildlife Services. "Midwest Region Endangered Species: Extinct Spe-cies." Updated May 29, 2919. www.fws.gov/midwest/endangered/lists/extinct .html (accessed October 9, 2019).

Vermin Supreme. "Vermin Supreme for President." Facebook page. www .facebook.com/VerminSupreme/posts/vermin-supreme-libertarian -candidate-for-president/1074191295951621/ (accessed October 14, 2019).

Vermont Fish & Wildlife Department. "2017 Vermont Black Bear Harvest Re-port." https://vtfishandwildlife.com/sites/fishandwildlife/files/documents /Learn%20More/Library/REPORTS%20AND%20DOCUMENTS /HUNTING/HARVEST%20REPORTS/bear/2017-Black-Bear-Harvest -Report.pdf (accessed September 29, 2019).

Volk, Oleg. "Tony Lekas." United States Concealed Carry Association. www .usconcealedcarry.com/blog/tony-lekas/ (accessed September 29, 2019).

Wade, Peter. "White Supremacist Cantwell Promises Revenge over Con-viction of Charlottesville Killer." *Rolling Stone*, December 9, 2018. www .rollingstone.com/politics/politics-news/chris-cantwell-charlottesville -reaction-766695/.

Wagner, Scott W. "The Taurus Judge: .45 Colt/.410 Shotshell Defender." United States Concealed Carry Association. www.usconcealedcarry.com/blog /taurus-judge-45-colt-410-shotshell-defender/ (accessed October 1, 2019).

Walker, Bill, and Ivy Walker. "License Need to Exercise Fundamental Right." *The High Road*, October 21, 2008. www.thehighroad.org/index.php?threads /license-need-to-exercise-fundamental-right.401274/ (accessed October 3, 2019).

Wallace, Gordon D., Leslie Marshall, and Mac Marshall. "Cats, Rats, and Toxoplasmosis on a Small Pacific Island." *American Journal of Epidemiol-ogy* 95, no. 5 (May 1972). https://academic.oup.com/aje/article-abstract/95 /5/475/215953?redirectedFrom=PDF.

Wallace, William Allen. *The History of Canaan, New Hampshire.* Concord, NH: Rumford Press, 1910.

Weiss, Louis M., and Jitender P. Dubey. "Toxoplasmosis: A History of Clinical Observations." *International Journal of Parasitology* 39, no. 8 (July 1, 2009). www.ncbi.nlm.nih.gov/pmc/articles/PMC2704023/.

Western Abenaki Dictionary. "Western Abenaki Moons." http://westernabenaki
.com/dictionary/moons.php (accessed September 22, 2019).

Westra, H., and Nanne van der Zijpp. "Braght, Tieleman Jansz van (1625–1664)." *Global Anabaptist Mennonite Encyclopedia Online*, 1953. https://gameo.org /index.php?title=Braght,_Tieleman_Jansz_van_(1625-1664)&oldid=141505 (accessed October 13, 2019).

Wheeler, Scott. "Slipperyskin—Bear, Bigfoot, or Indian?" *Vermonter.com.* https://vermonter.com/slipperyskin-bear-bigfoot-or-indian/.

Wilbur, James Benjamin. *Ira Allen Founder of Vermont 1751–1814.* Boston: Houghton Mifflin Company, 1928.

Williams, Dan. "Letter: Mink the Bear Isn't the Problem." *Concord Monitor*, May 25, 2019. www.concordmonitor.com/Mink-the-bear-25710064.

WMUR-TV. "Officials Say One Man Dead After Grafton Church Fire." *YouTube*, posted January 12, 2016. www.youtube.com/watch?v=pH_ktKkt6ZM (accessed October 13, 2019).

WMUR-TV. "Person Killed in Fire at Grafton Church." *YouTube*, posted January 12, 2016. www.youtube.com/watch?v=VnMrkdX81-U (accessed October 13, 2019).

WMUR-TV. "Investigation of Fatal Grafton Fire Continues." *YouTube*, posted January 13, 2016. www.youtube.com/watch?v=50yxZDhse4I (accessed October 13, 2019).

WMUR-TV. "Officials Investigate Fatal Grafton Fire." *YouTube*, posted January 13, 2016. www.youtube.com/watch?v=w6kCu73fvZs (accessed October 13, 2019).

WMUR-TV. "Woman Mauled by Bear in Groton Home." *YouTube*, posted July 17, 2018. www.youtube.com/watch?v=bKT0XIva4lQ.

WNDS-TV. "New Hampshire Gubernatorial Debate." Moderated by Alicia Preston. *C-SPAN*, October 2, 2000. www.c-span.org/video/?159588-1 /hampshire-gubernatorial-debate.

Wooley v. Maynard, 430 U.S. at 705 (1977).

Zimmer, Josh. "Island Sale on eBay to Benefit Libertarians." *Chicago Tribune*, July 31, 2005. www.chicagotribune.com/news/ct-xpm-2005-07-31-0507310383 -story.html.

MATTHEW HONGOLTZ-HETLING is a freelance journalist specializing in narrative features and investigative reporting. He has been named a finalist for the Pulitzer Prize, won a George Polk Award, and was voted Journalist of the Year by the Maine Press Association, among numerous other honors. His work has appeared in *Foreign Policy*, *USA Today*, *Popular Science*, *Atavist*, the Associated Press, and elsewhere and has been reprinted by the Pulitzer Center on Crisis Reporting. He lives in Vermont.

PublicAffairs is a publishing house founded in 1997. It is a tribute to the standards, values, and flair of three persons who have served as mentors to countless reporters, writers, editors, and book people of all kinds, including me.

I. F. Stone, proprietor of *I. F. Stone's Weekly*, combined a commitment to the First Amendment with entrepreneurial zeal and reporting skill and became one of the great independent journalists in American history. At the age of eighty, Izzy published *The Trial of Socrates*, which was a national bestseller. He wrote the book after he taught himself ancient Greek.

Benjamin C. Bradlee was for nearly thirty years the charismatic editorial leader of *The Washington Post*. It was Ben who gave the *Post* the range and courage to pursue such historic issues as Watergate. He supported his reporters with a tenacity that made them fearless and it is no accident that so many became authors of influential, best-selling books.

Robert L. Bernstein, the chief executive of Random House for more than a quarter century, guided one of the nation's premier publishing houses. Bob was personally responsible for many books of political dissent and argument that challenged tyranny around the globe. He is also the founder and longtime chair of Human Rights Watch, one of the most respected human rights organizations in the world.

•   •   •

For fifty years, the banner of Public Affairs Press was carried by its owner Morris B. Schnapper, who published Gandhi, Nasser, Toynbee, Truman, and about 1,500 other authors. In 1983, Schnapper was described by *The Washington Post* as "a redoubtable gadfly." His legacy will endure in the books to come.

Peter Osnos, *Founder*